TROLLEY WARS

Also by Judi Bevan

The Rise and Fall of Marks & Spencer
(Winner of WHSmith Business Book Award 2002)

for June Jay, who loved to shop

TROLLEY WARS

The Battle of the Supermarkets

JUDI BEVAN

P

PROFILE BOOKS

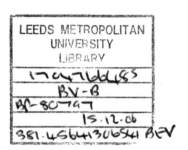
First published in Great Britain in 2005 by
Profile Books Ltd
58A Hatton Garden
London EC1N 8LX
www.profilebooks.com

1 3 5 7 9 10 8 6 4 2

Typeset in Minion by MacGuru Ltd
info@macguru.org.uk

Printed and bound in Great Britain by
Clays, Bungay, Suffolk

A CIP catalogue record for this book is available from the British Library.

ISBN 1 86197 661 5

CONTENTS

A DISPATCH FROM THE FRONT

I like supermarkets. They have liberated women like me from the slavery of daily shopping. If I am focused, I can buy a week's provisions in ninety minutes, freeing up time to help my daughter with her homework, earn my living or read a good book in the bath. Increasingly often I order my shopping online and have it delivered.

Supermarkets have brought the world to my doorstep. But they do not just provide an astonishing choice of fresh and pre-prepared food, they have also give me freedom to choose the kind of meals I make.

Should I wish to spend several hours cooking a special three-course dinner for friends, I can find everything I need, including the wine, in my local Sainsbury, Tesco or Waitrose. If I decide on an Italian meal, there are porcini mushrooms, fresh basil and mozzarella cheese. Should another cuisine take my fancy then herbs, spices, sauces and vegetables from every continent are seconds away from my trolley.

If, on the other hand, I am dog-tired and just want to get a tasty nutritious family meal on the table as soon as possible, I can buy a ready-made lasagne, curry or macaroni cheese, a bag of mixed leaves and some fresh-fruit salad and be serving it within ten minutes of arriving home. I can choose high fat or low fat, desserts made with sugar or aspartame, fresh vegetables or frozen.

If I crave the therapy of chopping up carrots or topping and tailing beans, carrots and beans abound. If I would rather file my nails, I can toss a bag of carrot batons or trimmed beans into my trolley and pay for someone else's labour.

My mother had no such choices. My memories of shopping with her in the 1950s are of intense tedium as she queued at three or four drab little shops to buy what she needed that day. In winter those open to the elements were bitterly cold. Only Sainsbury, with the drama of the bacon slicer, the noise of butter being slapped into shape by big wooden paddles and the smell of cheese as the wire cut through it, fills me with fond nostalgia. For the rest, the quality was far from assured, the choice was pitiful, the shop-keepers were not especially friendly and the prices, protected by resale price maintenance, were high relative to our income. In 1950, a third of household income went on food – today it is a sixth.

The shops in the outer London suburb where I grew up opened from 9 a.m. to 5 p.m. Monday to Saturday, although the butcher and fishmonger closed on Mondays and everything shut at lunchtime on Thursdays. Thanks to the intense and largely unregulated competition between British super-markets, I can shop whenever the mood takes me, unlike shoppers across the Channel.

The nimble response of British supermarkets to consumer demand has left their American counterparts standing over the past two decades. British customers have driven the demand for convenience foods, longer hours, international dishes, organic produce, fair-trade items, informative labelling of ingredients, non-food items and value for money.

I do not mourn the dreary shops of my youth, although I admire the good butchers and speciality shops that, for those who can afford it, provide something the supermarkets do not.

For the majority of people, however, household and food shopping remains a repetitious chore, which is why they refuse to travel longer than fifteen minutes to do it. Few people could claim that flogging round their crowded local Sainsbury, Tesco or Asda on a Saturday morning fills their hearts with joy, although I, for one, do so prefer it to what went before.

But the British supermarket is not an overnight phenomenon. It has evolved as a result of protracted, ongoing and often ruthless conflict between the big chains. Beneath the seductive camouflage of smiling here-to-help faces, celebrity endorsement, generous offers, slick slogans and the mantra of 'healthy competition', the fight to win the hearts and wallets of the British shopper continues unabated. Each time we pass through the portals of a major supermarket, we enter one of the world's largest battle zones – the front line of the Trolley Wars.

ACKNOWLEDGEMENTS

My warmest thanks to all those who have given their valuable time to help with this book. These include many executives inside the supermarket groups, former directors, suppliers, advisers, retail consultants, analysts and commentators. You know who you are.

I would also like to thank Andrew Franklin, Stephen Brough and Penny Daniel at Profile Books for their patience and professionalism, my copy editor Trevor Horwood for his encouragement and my husband John for his unwavering support and help during what has been a personally harrowing time.

THE TOP BRASS

Tesco

Sir John (Jack) Cohen, founder, chairman, life president; d. 1979

Sir Leslie Porter, managing director 1972–3; chairman 1973–85; president 1985–90

Hyman Kreitman, chairman 1968–73; d. 2001

Dorothy (Daisy) Hyams, assistant bookkeeper 1930–41; chief buyer 1941–82; d. 1996

Ian MacLaurin, Lord MacLaurin of Knebworth, managing director 1973–85; chairman 1985–97

David Malpas, director 1979; managing director 1983–97

Sir Terry Leahy, joined 1979; marketing director 1992–7; chief executive 1997–

Sir John Gardiner, non-executive chairman 1997–2004

David Reid, director 1985–2004; chairman 2004–

Sainsbury

Alan Sainsbury, Lord Sainsbury of Drury Lane, chairman 1956–67; d. 1998

Sir Robert Sainsbury, chairman 1967–9; d. 2000

John Sainsbury, Lord Sainsbury of Preston Candover, chairman and chief executive 1969–92

David Sainsbury, Lord Sainsbury of Turville, chairman 1992–8

Sir Tim Sainsbury, property director 1956–83; MP for Hove 1983–95; non-executive director 1995–2000

The Right Honourable Simon Sainsbury, finance director 1959–69; deputy chairman 1969–

Sir Peter Davis, assistant managing director 1979–86; chief executive 2000–2004

Sir George Bull, chairman 1998–2003
Peter Levene, Lord Levene of Portsoken, senior non-executive director
    2001–2004; chairman of Lloyd's of London 2002–

Asda
Tony de Nunzio, chief operating officer 2000–
Archie Norman MP, chief executive 1991–6; chairman 1996–9
Allan Leighton, marketing director 1992–6; chief executive 1996–2000
George Davies, creator and managing director of George at Asda 1989–2001
Sir Patrick Gillam, non-executive chairman 1991–6
Sir Godfrey Messervy, interim chairman 1990–91

Safeway (formerly Argyll Group)
David Webster, finance director 1977–97; chairman 1997–2004
James Gulliver, chairman 1978–88; d. 1996
Sir Alistair Grant, chairman 1988–97; d. 2001
Carlos Criado-Perez, chief executive 1999–2004

Wm Morrison
Sir Kenneth Morrison, chairman 1950–
Marie Melnyk, joined 1975; director 1997; joint managing director 2002–
Robert Stott, joined 1973; buying director 1997; joint managing director
    2002–

Quartermasters
Chris Haskins, Lord Haskins, chairman of Northern Foods 1986–2002
Sir Gulam Noon, chairman of Noon Products 1989–
Sir Harry Solomon, chairman of Hillsdown Holdings 1987–93
Sir John Nott, chairman of Hillsdown Holdings 1993–9

Neutral Powers
Sir Martin Jacomb, former chairman of Prudential, Pos Tel, Barclays de
    Zoete Wedd
James Blyth, Lord Blyth of Rowington, chief executive of Boots 1987–97;
    chairman 1997–9
Margaret Thatcher, Baroness Thatcher of Kesteven, British prime minister
    1979–90

Paul Hamlyn, Lord Hamlyn of Edgeworth; d. 2001

Sir Richard Greenbury, chief executive of Marks & Spencer 1988–98 and chairman 1991–9

Stanley Kalms, Lord Kalms of Edgware, founder of Dixons Group and chairman 1972–2002

Sir Geoffrey Mulcahy, chairman of F. W. Woolworth 1984–95; chief executive of Kingfisher 1994–2002

Sir Martin Sorrell, chief executive of WPP plc 1986–

Sir Derek Morris, chairman of the Competition Commission 1998–2004

Sir Geoffrey Owen, editor of the *Financial Times* 1981–90; professor and fellow of the London School of Economics 1991–

Dr Philip Beresford, wealth watchdog and compiler of the *Sunday Times* Rich List 1989–

LIST OF ILLUSTRATIONS

We would like to thank the following individuals and organisations for the use of their photographs.

The Sainsbury Archive for photographs 3, 4, 5, 6, 7, 8, 12 and 31; Sainsbury Press Office for 9, 11 and 21. Tesco Press Office for 1, 18 and 19 and Dame Shirley Porter for 6, 13, 14 and 15. Photograph 32 was taken by John Jay. Morrison Press Office supplied 2 and 24. David Webster provided 25 and 26, Archie Norman 27, Allan Leighton 10 and Asda Press Office 28.

CHAPTER ONE

BATTLE LINES

'Rather than comparing war to art, we could more accurately compare it to commerce, which is also a conflict of interests and activities.'

Karl von Clausewitz

On 15 November 2002 David Webster, the chairman of Safeway, then Britain's number three grocer, stepped into his dark blue Mercedes outside his Hertfordshire home, which during the Second World War had been the temporary residence of Charles de Gaulle. Webster had been delayed by the late arrival of his companion on the journey – Robert Swannell, a Citigroup investment banker and a key adviser to Safeway. Swannell had lost his way and apologetically settled into the back seat alongside Webster as the driver headed north. Their destination was Nuthurst Grange, a luxurious country-house hotel nestling in seven acres of rolling parkland just off the M42 in Warwickshire. They had no intention of being spotted by any City associates or fellow businessmen.

In another chauffeur-driven Mercedes, driving south to meet them from Bradford in Yorkshire, sat Sir Ken Morrison, the gruff, tough septuagenarian founder and chairman of William Morrison, a smaller but highly profit-able supermarket chain with stores mainly confined to the north-east of England. Morrison had suggested the discreet venue about halfway between their respective headquarters, but his suggestion must have amused Webster as Nuthurst Grange had a century before been the home of his great grand-father.

Nigel Turner, an urbane banker at the Dutch-owned ABN Amro, also drove to Nuthurst Grange that day to advise Morrison on financial technicalities and on the all-important matter of price. The two sides had the same goal: to merge their companies in a way mutually advantageous to both sets of shareholders.

Anyone spotting them being ushered into a private room for lunch might have imagined that Safeway, with its 494 stores, was courting Morrison, which owned only 119 outlets. They would have been wrong.

Within a few hours the four men thrashed out the broad outlines of a deal that would radically change the dynamics of Britain's supermarket industry. The two chains would merge, but the smaller Morrison would launch a recommended takeover for Safeway – at the time the UK's largest supermarket group after Tesco and Sainsbury. A marriage of the third and fifth players – one predominant in the south of England, the other in the north – would create a formidable new force. Working on the details took a few weeks over a busy Christmas, but then on 9 January 2003 Ken Morrison launched his £2.9 billion bid for Safeway on an unsuspecting stock market. It was the opening salvo of a new campaign in the decades-old conflict between Britain's big grocers.

Britain's supermarkets are at war. Competition between the big four – Tesco, Asda, Sainsbury and Morrison – has never been more ferocious in the battle to capture the customer's loyalty.

The past five years have been the most tumultuous since the first supermarket was opened in Britain in 1950. The bid by Wal-Mart, the world's biggest retailer, for Asda in 1999 and the feeding frenzy that followed Morrison's bid for Safeway have radically changed the dynamics of food retailing in Britain and have prompted two lengthy Competition Commission reports. In the stores, the rise of non-food sales has helped those groups that possess plentiful retail footage to leap ahead of those that do not. Scrambling for yet more locations, the supermarkets, constrained on the edges of town by planning permission, have expanded by opening smaller shops in town and city centres and in new locations such as petrol-station forecourts. They have also been buying up convenience chains.

During 2004 price-cutting campaigns came in convoy, as espionage and counter-espionage became the order of the day. Spies routinely pushed trolleys along the aisles of rivals, searching for any flaws they could find and any new ideas they could copy. Competitors flung mud at each other with increasing abandon over claims of low prices, with Tesco, the 800-pound gorilla of the sector, becoming the favourite target of the other three.

Take, for example, a headline on 19 September of that year in the *Sunday Times*, 'Revealed: the secret of Tesco's phoney price war', above a story written by Richard Fletcher telling of unnamed 'rivals' claiming that while a Tesco advertising campaign trumpeted £30 million of price cuts covering 460 items, the company had also increased prices of 150 high-volume product lines, more than paying for the reductions. Tesco countered that many of the increases were seasonal.

Tesco was not the only target. The beleaguered Sainsbury was also attacked for attempting to manipulate public perception. When Justin King, a sprightly fortysomething, left Marks & Spencer to take the reins at Sainsbury in March 2004 and launched a price-cutting campaign, rival spin doctors also complained of manipulation. His alleged sin had been to target his price cuts on the thirty-three products used by the *Grocer* magazine to calculate which supermarket was the cheapest each week. Ironically, such tricks were well known to his former colleagues at Asda, which headed the *Grocer*'s cheapness league table for seven years up to 2004.

Supermarket groups are at war not only with each other. Hostilities have also broken out with other retailers such as WHSmith, Boots, Dixons and Marks & Spencer, which increasingly see look-alikes of their products appearing on supermarket shelves. And many suppliers feel they are fighting an endless battle of attrition with their biggest customers.

At the same time, supermarkets are under attack from pressure groups and media commentators. Their huge financial success – the big four made profits of £3.5bn in 2004 – has prompted a ferocious backlash against their size. Market dominance – as aspired to globally by the American giant Wal-Mart, the Microsoft of food retailing – strikes fear into the hearts of competitors, suppliers and consumer lobby groups alike. In the UK, Tesco now has a staggering 29 per cent of the British grocery market (including non-food), giving it a lead of more than 12 percentage points over its three nearest rivals, each with between 16 and 17 per cent. But all the big four – and to a lesser extent Somerfield and Iceland – stand accused of bullying suppliers, putting independent shops out of business and laying waste to historic urban centres.

Tesco, the biggest, has tried to project an 'ordinary' image – adopting the modern business mantra of 'thinking global but acting local'. Thinking global has resulted in Tesco having more space abroad than at home and being market leader in six of the twelve countries in which it operates. Acting local means, among other things, that in Shanghai, Tesco, through a joint venture, sells live toads for the cooking pot. Toad porridge is a popular dish.

In Britain Tesco's apparent omnipresence has made it a favourite 'enemy of the people' among the anti-capitalists. In September 2004 the actress Vanessa Redgrave, described by the *Evening Standard* as 'probably the most famous Trotskyite' in the world, led a campaign to prevent a new Tesco in Hammersmith, West London, from even reaching the planning stage. The cause was taken up by the novelist Celia Brayfield and other columnists. But in the business and investment world, Tesco is much admired. Terry Leahy, Tesco's stony-faced chief executive since 1997, was named European Businessman of the Year by *Fortune* magazine and at home won the *Sunday Telegraph*'s National Business Awards Business Leader of the Year in both 2003 and 2004.

Few industry sectors are as politically sensitive as food retailing. This should not be a surprise – we are, after all, what we eat. From the moment an enraged shopper threw a shopping basket at Alan Sainsbury in 1950 at the opening of the first Sainsbury self-service store in Croydon, supermarkets have been controversial. Led by entrepreneurs who responded nimbly to the immense social and economic changes that followed the Second World War, they have turned into monuments to modern capitalism – fêted for their convenience by some yet reviled by others as bullies of small suppliers and destroyers of provincial high streets.

Most consumers welcomed supermarkets when they first arrived. They provided a liberating alternative to queuing separately at the butcher, the baker, the greengrocer, the fishmonger and the ironmonger. And they seemed wonderfully modern in those monochrome days of the 1950s. Many people, however, now resent what they see as their dependence on these purveyors of all anyone could possibly want and feel they are less in control of what they eat than they used to be.

In the past decade supermarkets have found themselves at the heart of an ideological battle concerning how and in what condition the food we eat arrives on our plates. Will it poison us? Have others less fortunate had to suffer to produce it? Is the labelling honest? Is the food wholesome? Does its journey to the shop pollute the environment? Do ours? Barely a day passes without an inflammatory headline in a newspaper highlighting the possible hidden dangers in supermarket food. 'Cancer hazard in packed salad', screamed a headline in the *Daily Mail* in September 2004. The following February, hundreds of millions of pounds of ready-meals and other items were pulled off the shelves because they contained Sudan 1, a carcinogenic dye.

Governments are intimately involved in the food wars as the regulators of the rules of engagement. They are asked to make judgements on many questions. Do supermarkets abuse their power? Have they become effective monopolies? Is everyone involved in food production getting a fair share of the cake? Are supermarkets charging too much? Is the way we buy our food producing social and health problems that will cost the taxpayer money? Are out-of-town stores killing our towns and villages?

Having brought increasingly cheap and convenient shopping to the masses, supermarket bosses might have expected to be hailed as the champions of the consumer. They have, however, been cast by their critics as the whipping boys for many of society's ills. The sheer scale of their operations and the power they are seen to have over their suppliers have created a climate of suspicion. The press loves an underdog and complaints by less efficient suppliers, most of them in the commoditised fresh-produce sector where it is hard to gain advantage against competitors, provide good copy.

Supermarkets come under attack in the media from four distinct lobby groups: the 'foodies', the 'health police', the 'greens' and the 'anti-capitalists'. The first three groups flourish in the articulate middle classes and both overlap and clash with each other. The foodies demand that food tastes better while the health lobby wants reductions in sugar, salt and fat – all of which add flavour. Foodies call for meat that is properly hung and cheese naturally ripened while the health police say all food should be microbiologically safe. Foodies overlap with the organic lobby in claiming that some organic products taste better, but at the same time clash with pro-organic vegetarians and health watchers.

The authorities have been drawn into this ideological battleground and the issues have been debated several times over the years by the Competition Commission, the government watchdog on commercial fair play, and before it the Monopolies and Mergers Commission. The Competition

Commission's two reports in 2000 and 2003 investigated whether supermarkets were giving customers – and just as important – their suppliers a fair deal. The first, entitled 'Supermarkets: a report on the supply of groceries from multiple stores in the United Kingdom', was launched in response to an Office of Fair Trading report that coincided with the *Sunday Times* 'Rip-Off Britain' campaign. The *Sunday Times* accused supermarkets of charging more than their counterparts in continental Europe and asked if they could be colluding on price. The rest of the media joined in the campaign with gusto.

Public opinion often lags reality and some sections of the media and the government itself were behind the times. The truly cosy days of the high-spending, high-margin 1980s, when supermarket bosses met regularly to exchange views, had gone. They vanished in the early 1990s with the arrival of European discounting marauders such as Aldi, Lidl and Netto, which had far more impact on supermarket pricing policy than any government commission ever could.

In the event the inspectors found that food prices had actually fallen by 9.4 per cent in real terms from 1989 to 1998. True, prices were still 12–16 per cent higher than those in France and Germany, but most of that differential was due, it was said, to the strength of sterling against the Continental European currency at the end of the 1990s.

Nevertheless, profit margins in Britain were higher than elsewhere and the press wanted to know why. The report, suitably lengthy and detailed, pointed out that land and building costs are higher in the UK than elsewhere – and cleared the supermarkets of anti-competitive pricing practices. The inspectors did, however, identify fifty-two unwelcome, although not illegal, ways in which they put pressure on their suppliers. They also identified a 'complex monopoly situation' among the big players, whose buying strength made it difficult for smaller suppliers to compete. The Office of Fair Trading drew up a code of practice enabling aggrieved suppliers to complain to the OFT but life went on much as before, with Tesco and Asda gaining ground and Sainsbury and Safeway losing it.

Although the big grocers emerged relatively unscathed from the 2000 competition inquiry, they recognised the need to respond to criticism by the media and various interest groups. Allan Leighton, one of the duo responsible for turning round the Asda chain in the early 1990s and more recently chairman of the Royal Mail, describes the challenges the industry faces as the three Rs – not 'reading, 'riting and 'rithmetic,' but 'reputation, regulation and resupply'.

Reputation is crucial, he says, because constant criticism undermines staff morale and ultimately harms sales and profits. Regulation is the knock-on effect of a damaged reputation, as the supermarkets found out in the Rip-Off Britain campaign, and government constraints inhibit growth. In Leighton's view, the only way Wal-Mart will be stopped from opening 300 stores a year across America is if it is regulated in the same way as Microsoft has been in recent years.

The third preoccupation is resupply because the one thing that sends customers running to a rival is finding a bare shelf where a staple or favourite product should be. Customers hate being unable to complete their shopping list, as Sainsbury discovered to its cost when profits plummeted in the second half of 2004. This means that in their various ways the major supermarket groups nurture and invest in their favoured suppliers even though it is a harsh regime and feelings run high. For example, an 'own-brand' supplier to Sainsbury will be actively discouraged from supplying Tesco and vice versa – although possibly 'allowed' to supply Waitrose or one of the smaller groups.

The bigger a supermarket group grows, the bigger the headache of resupply becomes. 'Good suppliers that can supply consistently in volume are very difficult to find,' says Leighton. 'At Asda, we spent a lot of time building relationships with suppliers that would encourage and enable them to keep on supplying.' To survive, the supermarket managers strive to cater for as broad a range of customers as possible and that means being quick to respond to consumer demands. Organic food now accounts for 3 per cent of the overall supermarket spend – although that figure is much higher at Sainsbury and Waitrose. There are various ranges of 'healthy eating' products with lower fat, sugar and salt content, although some may not be as beneficial as they appear at first glance. Prepared food is labelled with a list of ingredients, the number of calories contained and a breakdown of fats, sugars and carbohydrates. In response to pressure groups, customers and the market, all of the big supermarket groups now sell 'fair trade' products such as coffee and bananas. One recent Waitrose advertising campaign trumpeting its 'fair' purchasing policies pictured a Caribbean beach in the shape of a banana while another announced that it had moved to selling only fair trade coffee.

This book charts the battles of the big beasts of the supermarket jungle. Between them Tesco, Asda, Sainsbury and Morrison made profits of about £3.5bn on sales of more than £75bn in 2004. In the UK alone they employ more than 500,000 people directly and many more indirectly among suppliers, where their patronage has created many fortunes. More than sixty people in the *Sunday Times* Rich List owe their wealth to food and drink manufacturing for the big supermarket groups. Two examples are Alan Wiseman of Robert Wiseman Dairies, whose wealth in 2004 was estimated at £108m million, and the Warburton bread family, who at that time were reckoned to be worth £230m. The increasing concentration of custom towards the bigger suppliers makes for a 'winner takes all' culture that has forced some smaller suppliers, particularly small farmers, out of business.

This book also tells the story of how these big beasts were born, how they grew and how they shape up today. It tells of their different histories and their distinct cultures and seeks to answer the key questions about their successes and failures. How, for example, did Tesco, which started in 1920 with one market stall in London's East End, come to challenge and overtake the aristocratic Sainsbury, which began life in 1869 as a Victorian dairy shop run by newlyweds?

Like rock'n'roll, hamburgers and jeans, supermarkets began in America. Clarence Saunders, a flamboyant innovator, came up with the idea that shoppers should serve themselves and he opened the world's first self-service store in 1916. It was an idea that would revolutionise the entire grocery industry. He called his group Piggly Wiggly because he believed the name would intrigue people. He was right, although, like so many revolutionary ideas, it did not find instant favour among the chattering classes of the era. Many people at the time predicted that this new kind of store would fail. The first Piggly Wiggly opened on 6 September 1916 at 79 Jefferson Street, Memphis, to mixed reviews: 'Operating under the unusual name Piggly Wiggly, it was unlike any other grocery store of that time', declared one report; 'Shopping baskets, open shelves, no clerks to shop for the customer – unheard of!' gasped another.

Customers, however, soon grew to like self-service shopping, enabling

Saunders to issue franchises to hundreds of grocery retailers for the operation of look-alike stores. Within a few years Piggly Wiggly was so successful that Saunders was able to float the company on the New York Stock Exchange, becoming the Jeff Bezos of his generation and making his company the Amazon of Wall Street in the early 1920s. Although he lost control of the corporation by gradually diluting his stake, Piggly Wiggly continued to prosper as franchiser for hundreds of independently owned grocery stores for many years until bigger groups such as King Kullen, founded by Michael J. Cullen in 1931, overtook it. Trolleys were invented in 1937.

The self-service revolution did not hit the UK until after two world wars. By the time Alan Sainsbury and Jack Cohen, Tesco's founder, decided to visit the United States just after the Second World War as part of a government-sponsored initiative to educate British businessmen about the latest trends on the other side of the Atlantic, American supermarkets were thriving.

Both men returned from their travels fired with enthusiasm – they had seen the future and were sure it would work back home. Cohen's first attempts to emulate the American model involved simply turning his shop counters back-to-front and piling them with produce. That was his classic seat-of-the-pants style. He even appears to have bowdlerised the King Kullen slogan 'Pile it high, sell it low' became 'Pile it high, sell it cheap.' Sainsbury adopted the self-service approach in a more rigorous way, using its well-established Croydon store as a prototype. Within a decade, most of the old-style Sainsbury shops, with their different counters for bacon, cheese and bread, had become memories of a past when nobody complained if they shut on Saturday afternoons and did not open again until Tuesday.

Many others followed Sainsbury and Tesco into the supermarket business – the Co-operative movement, Fine Fare, International Stores, Allied Foods and Gateway were just some who enjoyed what Geoffrey Owen, the former editor of the *Financial Times*, called 'the golden age for UK food retailing' in a paper for the London Business School.

'Thanks in part to the deregulatory zeal of the Thatcher government, planning requirements for out-of-town developments were eased, leading to a rapid growth in the number of superstores and, to a lesser extent, hypermarkets,' he wrote. 'This coincided with changes in logistics and distribution.'

Electronic point-of-sale (EPOS) scanning systems allowed automatic reordering and were linked into the computer systems of the suppliers. As a result the bigger, better-off groups that could afford the new technology began to pull away from the smaller players, taking over activities such as distribution, packaging and product development from the suppliers, and by the beginning of the 1990s Sainsbury, Tesco, Asda and Safeway had emerged as the premier-league players by a comfortable margin. Like medieval knights on horseback, they prepared to battle to the death.

When supermarkets first arrived in post-war Britain, they were a novelty – part shopping, part entertainment. Throughout the 1950s and 1960s the opening of a big supermarket was an excuse for a party – and party they did. Film stars and comedians were shipped in to cut the ceremonial opening ribbons to the sound of brass bands and the bursting of balloons. At Tesco, the chimpanzees used by PG Tips to advertise tea made regular appearances and on one occasion a manager arranged for a 'Lone Ranger' to arrive on horseback to open a store – but the horse ran amok.

It was not long before this new form of shopping made an impact on popular culture. In the film *Billy Liar*, the young anti-hero played by Tom Courtenay, attempts to attach himself to the fictional famous comedian who opens the local supermarket to much razzmatazz, plucking out from the crowd Courtenay's co-star, Julie Christie.

A decade and a half later, supermarkets were no longer a novelty but were part of the social fabric. They had become a necessity for most people, and for the next twenty years they captured an ever-growing proportion of people's non-discretionary spending – on food and other necessities. In the 1990s they began to go after the discretionary spending markets for goods such as clothing, stationery and electrical items and started to explore less tangible product areas such as insurance, financial services and banking.

Today, British supermarkets deliver a diversity and quality of products undreamed of in the 1970s. The influence of 'abroad' has been enormous. Twenty years ago Parmesan cheese, porcini mushrooms, chapatti flour, Greek yoghurt and marinated artichokes were the preserve of specialist delicatessens. But the combination of cheap travel and pioneering food writers such as Elizabeth David and her followers created a popular demand for a host of delicacies from around the world.

Yet the amount the British spend on food as a proportion of household income has dropped from a third in 1950 to a sixth today. This is due partly to a rise in real incomes, but is also a result of the growth of supermarkets, their increased buying power and the competition between them. Super-markets, say their supporters, represent a triumph for free markets, each group competing with all its might to outgun the others to the benefit of customers, shareholders and staff.

How did this happen in just half a century? Three main factors have enabled the growth of what one clergyman dubbed 'these temples of Mammon'. The first is sheer convenience. The second is the compact nature of the British Isles, which allows chilled food to be delivered overnight to stores serving 50 million people. The third was the liberalisation of grocery prices. Indeed, the Trolley Wars would never have broken out without the abolition of resale price maintenance in 1964, a reform that unshackled Britain's retailers to compete freely with each other. Until then, manufac-turers had controlled the price of their goods by setting a 'resale price', so a jar of Nescafé would cost the same in the corner shop as in the supermarket. Resale price maintenance was great for the manufacturers, who could dictate the prices retailers charged for their goods, but not so great for consumers or aggressive retailers such as Jack Cohen. It went against all his trading instincts and he approached Edward Heath, then trade minister, who saw an opportunity to further his political ambitions by smashing RPM.

Backed by the Institute of Economic Affairs, a free-market think tank that in 1960 had published an influential pamphlet by Basil Yarney entitled 'Resale Price Maintenance and Shoppers' Choice', Heath set about pushing a bill to abolish it through Parliament. It brought him prominence, although the backlash of sentiment generated by small shopkeepers who saw their livelihoods disappearing helped lose the 1964 election for the Conservatives, whose support had already been weakened by the unpopularity their new leader Alec Douglas Home.

Heath's Act opened the gates to true competition and without it super-markets could never have been able to use their buying power to deliver lower prices in their stores. Once it was enshrined in law, supermarket managements took on the primary producers – growers and farmers – as well as the big-brand manufacturers who had until then called the shots.

Today the customer is king. Regular listeners to *The Archers*, the BBC's long-running everyday story of country folk, will know just how schizophrenic Britain's farming community feels about supermarkets. In 2004, for instance, the young Tom Archer was attempting to break into a national chain with his range of specialist sausages while David and Ruth Archer were engaged in anguished debates about whether they should break ranks with their milk-selling cooperative and sell direct, making more profit in the process but ceasing to show social and economic solidarity with their neighbours.

On one front the supermarkets fought the manufacturers by demanding volume discounts. On another, their chosen weapons were 'own-label' or 'private-label' goods. Retailers such as Marks & Spencer and Sainsbury realised that they could sell own-label products cheaper than those of well-known brands. But who would make these own-brand products? The big manufacturers threatened to withhold supplies of their 'must have' brands if supermarkets sold own-label products. But consumers who trusted Marks & Spencer and Sainsbury snapped up own-label goods in many categories. Where the manufacturers of well-known brands refused to make supermarket-label products, new suppliers were found such as Northern Foods, Hillsdown Holdings and Noon Products, all of whom leapt at the chance to make private-label sandwiches, chilled ready-meals and desserts. The results were significant. With Marks & Spencer and Sainsbury concentrating on high quality in these areas, 'own label' established credibility and a market penetration undreamed of in the rest of Europe or the United States.

By the 1990s the supermarkets called the shots and even brand giants such as Mars, Heinz, Coca-Cola, Kellogg's, Procter & Gamble and Unilever saw their power over the consumer weakened as they battled for shelf space. In response they have honed back their product ranges to those brands where they are number one or two in the market. In autumn 2004, both Unilever and Colgate-Palmolive brought gloom to the branded consumer products sector by delivering profit warnings on the same day. It seemed consumers were increasingly happy to save money by buying an own-label version of a product, as long as it came up to scratch.

Even after fifty years of innovation, the most powerful force that drives the market onwards and upwards remains convenience – not just the desire of shoppers to trade mundane tasks for something more fulfilling, but convenience in its broadest sense.

Despite initial resistance from those post-war ladies who enjoyed personal service, customers soon saw the virtues of self-service and were prepared to exchange a little physical labour for the benefits of one-stop-shopping and lower prices. Once the majority of families owned a car and a freezer, the once-a-week shop could become a reality, freeing women in particular from the daily drudge of food shopping. For many, the weekly shop has become a family outing and Saturday mornings are the time when working parents have a chance to reacquaint themselves with their children by way of a trip to the supermarket.

The big beasts of the supermarket jungle wage their battles in an ever-changing market dictated by fashion, product innovation and technology. Although one in ten new products fail, customers have embraced many innovations that make their lives easier – frozen food, chilled ready-meals, vegetables peeled and chopped ready for the pot. When Premier Foods took Branston Pickle out of a jar and put it in a squeezy bottle, moving it, in its own words 'from the back of the cupboard to the front of the fridge', sales shot up. Customers, it seems, had become too lazy to unscrew a jar and use a spoon – or forage in the cupboard.

Convenience became the Holy Grail as the British turned into a nation of snackers and lazy eaters, too indolent to peel a full-size orange and cope with the pips. Health and convenience appeared to go hand-in-hand in the closing decade of the twentieth century. Between 1990 and 2000, sales of yoghurt and fromage frais rose by 45 per cent. Sales of bananas soared by 65 per cent and seedless-grape sales rocketed by 75 per cent as consumers trended towards 'instant' fresh food at the expense of, for example, oranges – down 33 per cent over the same period.

In recent years a new trend has emerged, with the big grocers attempting to move beyond the once-a-week shop to capture those top-up midweek sales that traditionally went to local convenience stores rather than out-of-town or edge-of-town emporiums. They have opened smaller stores such as Sainsbury Local, Tesco Metro and Tesco Express with the aim of attracting the custom of workers and commuters. Some of the expansion has been organic, but since 2000 Tesco and Sainsbury have taken control of more than 1,500 convenience shops through buying independent chains, bringing comfortable retirement to many small-business owners whose children had their sights set higher than on running a small grocery outlet. Those small traders who remain are inevitably facing a tougher future as the buying power of the giants is deployed against them.

Despite the opposition supermarkets face from small traders fearing greater competition, food lobbyists, suppliers who resent the brutal buying tactics of supermarkets and those who object to Sunday trading and Britain's ever-more consumerist society, some 30 million customers continue to flock through their doors each week, pouring money into their tills. Tesco alone took £1 out of every £8 spent on all shopping in 2004 and in total the British buy about three-quarters of all shop-sold fresh food and groceries in super-markets – although such purchases account for less than half of the total spend on food as a result of the growth in eating out. The big four chains have 3,300 stores totalling about 70 million square feet in the UK. A standard Tesco, Asda or Sainsbury superstore sells up to 40,000 different product lines – a line is a distinct category of a product – while a Tesco Extra hypermarket sells 50,000.

British supermarkets rank among the best in the world. Not only are they financially successful, they constantly innovate and produce new products. In the past decade they have proved themselves more attuned than their US counterparts to customer trends such as the demand for chilled convenience food and for organic produce. They open early and close late six days a week, with opening hours on Sundays limited only by legislation, and they offer a range of products that would have amazed people thirty years ago: fresh fruit and vegetables from around the world whatever the season, from the mundane to the exotic, fresh meat and fish as well as the ready-meals and processed dishes that have caused such controversy among food and health commentators. They have also moved aggressively into toiletries, medicines, newspapers and magazines while Tesco and Asda also offer a large range of clothing, homewares and electrical goods.

Some way below the big four, Somerfield, with a 5.4 per cent market share, has shown that by reinventing itself under new management it is still possible at the lower end of the market to attract new customers and make reasonable returns for shareholders. Up at the quality end, Marks & Spencer, which styles itself as a specialist food retailer rather than a full-service super-market, has about 3 per cent of the grocery market.

Waitrose had 4 per cent of the market in 2004 and was growing rapidly. Favoured by many of the well-heeled professionals who used to frequent Sainsbury, Waitrose is set on boosting its market share and has bought nineteen Safeway stores from Morrison, a move that extended it north out of its south-east heartlands. It is also developing new sites. John Sainsbury's former 'bag carrier', Steven Esom, who heads Waitrose, believes he can capture 7 per cent of the market although his ambitions may be held back by the chain's conservative owner, the John Lewis Partnership.

Taken together, supermarkets contribute around 3 per cent of gross domestic product (GDP). According to Taylor Nelson Sofres, a market research firm, the four big players account for three-quarters of the grocery market, which includes some non-food – the catch-all term that embraces clothes, homewares, electrical goods, books and stationery.

One reason for this success is that retailers have adapted to the change from the highly stratified class system of post-war Britain when few married women worked to an increasingly classless and ethnically mixed society in which a woman can rise to become prime minister.

Twenty years ago supermarkets had a clear idea of the market segment at which they were aiming and stuck mostly to a particular social class. Tesco served the urban working classes – the socio-economic C2s and Ds – while the middle classes, the As, Bs and C1s, shopped at Sainsbury. But in the past few years the market has become more homogeneous as the big four, led aggressively by Tesco, have attempted to cater for anyone from any social group likely to walk into the store. A large Tesco effectively contains three different supermarkets. Customers on a tight budget can concentrate on Value lines in the blue and white striped 'prison uniform' packaging – a range of products where prices fell by a third in the decade to 2004, according to Tesco. The mainstream Tesco own-label items offer relatively good value and cover the widest range of goods, while Tesco Finest – a high-quality range of ready-meals, cakes, biscuits and wines – competes with the ready-meal offerings of Marks & Spencer and Waitrose.

This 'something-for-everyone' message was nicely highlighted by Tesco's late-2004 TV advertising campaign, which openly compared the price and quality of similar products from its Finest and Value ranges, effectively telling the consumer, 'The choice is yours'.

In addition to this attempt to appeal across the social classes, Tesco's chief executive Terry Leahy and his colleagues also try to capture their 'share of purse' wherever the customer might be. Thus the company now has four distinct store formats from Tesco Extra, which opens twenty-four hours a day, graduating through standard-size stores down to Tesco Metro on the high street and in office complexes and the tiny Tesco Express shops carved out of former convenience shops or tucked into petrol stations.

This approach was summed up by Allan Leighton when he nicknamed Tesco 'Martini' because it fulfilled the promise of the Martini advertisement – 'any time, any place, anywhere'. Tesco is the embodiment of what many like to think of as Britain's modern classless society where a peer might find himself behind a plumber at the checkout. In short, Tesco targets everybody's money, an ambition of which Justin King was well aware when he stepped into the hot seat at Sainsbury, a company that appeared to take a more snobbish approach to its customers. Thus, when he made his first presentation to Sainsbury's shareholders he bemoaned the fact that, under the previous management's more stratified approach, the cheapest orange juice had been available at only a quarter of the company's stores. 'There is no reason why better-off customers should be prevented from buying it. It is good value and it has no bits in it, which means children like it,' said the father of two with feeling.

Of course, Britain is not quite a classless society yet. The proportion of manual labourers may have dropped from 36 per cent of the population in 1987 to 12 per cent today, leaving more than half of UK citizens describing themselves as being middle class, but a quarter of households include adults who are claiming means-tested state benefits. Even among the broad swathes of middle England, people like to define their social status by the shops from which they buy their food. Verdict, the retail consultancy, found that 47 per cent of Waitrose customers in 2004 came from the A and B social groups, followed by Sainsbury with 34 per cent, Marks & Spencer with 22 per cent, Tesco 21 per cent and Safeway 17 per cent. At the bottom of the market 50 per cent of the people who shopped at Somerfield were blue collar Ds or Es while 72 per cent of shoppers at discounter Netto were in this category.

One reason for this tribal behaviour is habit. Most shoppers enjoy the familiar feel of the same store each week. Ed Garner, the commercial director at Taylor Nelson Sofres, believes that people in the UK are still judged socially by where they shop. He has dubbed this phenomenon the 'olive index'. In other words, the higher up the social scale you are, the more varieties of olives you demand. 'In Waitrose, there is a whole fixture selling olives,' says Garner. 'In Kwik Save, the most you would find is some olives in a jar.'

Garner has identified a peculiarity of the British food market compared with other countries. The food writer Jonathan Meades makes a similar point. 'If you take a labourer in Marseilles and a CEO in Marseilles, they will eat approximately the same food,' he says. 'In this country there is no link between what a guy who is working in a building site in Southampton eats and the guy who runs that site – they eat completely different things.'

Another research house, Experian, has identified no fewer than 61 sub-groups of shoppers and has come up with labels such as White Van Culture or Golden Empty Nesters to help supermarkets identify their customers.

In the face of social changes, supermarket bosses have striven to differentiate their chains in the ferocious competition for the hearts and minds of customers, even though regional differences have tended to dissolve under the influence of modern mass communications. In Yorkshire, Ken Morrison developed a 'market street' concept in which counter service for fresh fish, meat and pies was emphasised. The fresh fish – and it really was fresh so near the North Sea – had pride of place in the front of the stores and the staff on the counter knew how to skin and fillet their wares. Safeway put in pizza ovens, Sainsbury specialised in esoteric products such as truffle butter and palm hearts. Tesco and Asda went for wide-open aisles with the emphasis on price, price and price.

There is, however, a growing trend among customers towards pragmatism and away from loyalty. Repertoire shopping is the new game in retail according to Waitrose's Steven Esom. In the *Financial Times* in 2004 Richard Tomkins explained the phenomenon this way: 'The schmucks are getting cleverer all the time. In the US the consumer who shops at Wal-Mart in the morning and Neiman Marcus in the afternoon – saving money at the discount store to spend it at the luxury retailer – has already become a cliché.'

Well-heeled travellers will save money on a no-frills airline service on a short trip to Venice, but might splash out on the five-star Cipriani hotel once they arrive. When it comes to clothes shopping, women of varied income groups and ages mix cheap and cheerful from Top Shop or Miss Selfridge with Prada or Gucci. All but the richest people furnishing a home will endure the misery of queuing for the basics at Ikea for the outstanding value, but trot off to John Lewis to buy decent china for the dining table.

In food, repertoire shopping may mean going to Tesco or Asda for the weekly shop but picking up deli items from Waitrose or specialist shops and ready-made desserts from Marks & Spencer. Foodies may get everything at a supermarket apart from the meat or fish, preferring to buy those at their local butcher or fishmonger (if one exists) or at one of the growing number of farmers' markets. Organic devotees may patronise Planet Organic or order 'boxes' from farmers to be delivered to the door.

Location, however, is often the deciding factor. Though customers may tell a market researcher they prefer a particular chain, the vast majority will rarely drive for longer than fifteen minutes to go food shopping and tend to shop at the supermarket nearest to them. More than any other, it will be a Tesco simply because it won the race for space in the recession of the early 1990s when Ian MacLaurin and his team, alone among the supermarket groups, carried on buying large edge-of-town sites despite the government's intensifying assault on out-of-town shopping. By 2004 Tesco had more than double the number of Sainsbury stores.

The battle for supremacy among the big grocers started to hot up in the 1990s and competition became so fierce that the profits and the investment performance of the third and fourth players – Safeway and Asda – began to suffer, making them vulnerable to takeover. Scale – that prerequisite of buying power – became the buzzword. The chains that could extract the lowest prices and the highest promotional payments from their suppliers to pass on to their customers surged ahead. In these conditions, bidding wars broke out.

Two takeover bids proved to be defining moments in recent supermarket history. The first came in December 1999 when Wal-Mart pounced unexpectedly on Asda with a knock-out cash bid. The surprise appearance of the legendary American company sent shock waves through the food industry. Wal-Mart gazumped Kingfisher, whose agreed bid with Asda was within seven days of closing. The bid stunned the stock market and left in ruins the so nearly completed plans of Kingfisher's chairman, Geoff Mulcahy, to merge his company with Asda.

The arrival of the rapacious American group in Britain sent a surge of adrenaline rushing into the boardrooms of the three main competitors, galvanising them into action as never before, triggering the start of a new era in the Trolley Wars.

At Tesco, Terry Leahy was on stage addressing his troops during a morale-boosting trip to outposts in the Far East when David Reid, then the international director, gave him a note telling him what had happened. When his speech was over Leahy, dubbed the Pete Sampras of the supermarket business, sent a simple email message to his top managers: 'Be Tesco – Go faster.' He and Reid then got the first available flight back to London and convened an emergency board meeting at Tesco's Cheshunt headquarters. They decided that the best form of defence was attack. 'We decided to set the agenda for Wal-Mart, not the other way round,' said Leahy.

Yet Wal-Mart's arrival in Britain has not had the impact that many predicted. Its scary reputation in the US had retail observers predicting it would, through Asda, put the squeeze on British suppliers and carpet the British countryside with superstores. The reality is that it has taken a more softly, softly approach and has impressed suppliers by its efficiency in rolling out promotional deals to benefit both manufacturer and retailer. Five years on, one supplier even hailed Asda as 'the best date in town' for living up to its promises as a retailer. Expansion had been modest – not entirely through design – and much work had been done to improve goodwill in local communities. Ironically, Leahy and his team have, in the eyes of some, become the bad boys of the sector, facing accusations of squeezing suppliers ruthlessly and using their legendary property expertise, willingness to pay generous prices and mastery of Britain's planning laws to cover the country with their stores.

The second defining moment came in January 2003 when, after a series of clandestine meetings, a 71-year-old Yorkshireman decided it was time to change the dynamics of British food retailing.

When Sir Ken Morrison launched his bid for Safeway on an unsuspecting stock market, it came as a bombshell to City traders still bleary eyed from the Christmas festivities. Trading almost exclusively in the north of England, Morrison was ranked fifth in the supermarket hierarchy. The group was highly profitable and admired for efficiency, high quality and low prices but it was less than half the size of its target. Safeway and Morrison had kept the deal tight as a drum and the market was caught unawares. Even Peter Davis, then Sainsbury chief executive, and Asda's Tony de Nunzio, who had both been conducting sotto voce negations with Safeway's David Webster, declared themselves completely surprised. Safeway shares soared while those of the competition fell back, fearing increased competition. Respected for its efficient operation in the north, Morrison in possession of the 494 Safeway stores would pose a threat even to Tesco.

It proved a busy week for London's investment bankers, who had suffered a couple of lean years. Within the week every other big super-market group had thrown their hats in the ring. Sainsbury, Wal-Mart and Tesco all announced their intention to bid for Safeway if the Competition Commission allowed. The American private equity house Kohlberg Kravis Roberts and Philip Green, the aggressive owner of the Bhs clothing chain, also expressed interest, adding to the drama. Teams from more than a dozen investment banks including UBS, Goldman Sachs, Lazard Brothers and Merrill Lynch were drafted in to advise the bidders.

Most of the new bidders had plans to break up Safeway and share the spoils in different ways. But all the putative bids apart from Green's were placed firmly on ice as the Competition Commission once again trawled through the sector, giving a voice to anyone who wanted it from trade union officials and Boys' Clubs to rafts of suppliers, big and small.

The commission's verdict, which allowed Morrison to acquire Safeway but strictly limited the disposal of individual stores, made it clear that any future takeover reducing the big four down to the big three would be blocked. It spelt disaster for Sainsbury, where Davis saw the competition becoming ever more powerful while his hands were tied. At Tesco, on the other hand, the decision spurred the young lions to even greater triumphs. Tesco had been on the offensive since Wal-Mart's acquisition of Asda in 1999, storming ahead not just in Britain but in new territories such as Hungary, Poland, Thailand and Malaysia. Then in September 2004, after years of deliberation, Tesco made its first investment in China, buying a 50 per cent holding in Hymall, the owner of twenty-five hypermarkets in and around Shanghai. The move meant that for the first time, half of Tesco's selling space was overseas, although the UK remained the main profit generator.

In 2004 it seemed Tesco was winning the war so decisively that some began to argue that its dominance posed a threat to the public interest. From the time when Wal-Mart had bought Asda in 1999, Tesco's sales had risen by two-thirds to £33.5bn, almost double the £1.8bn generated by Sainsbury. Pre-tax profits for the year to February 2004 were £1.6bn, up 66 per cent on 1999 and two and a half times those of Sainsbury.

Tesco had 1,878 stores covering 23.3m square feet compared with Sains-bury's 828 stores totalling 15.5m square feet. Six months later, half-year results showed Tesco still gathering momentum, with sales 12 per cent higher and profits up by a quarter to £822m for the six months to August

2004, prompting analysts to predict profits of £2bn for the 2005 financial year. It was hard to believe that Tesco had overtaken Sainsbury only ten years before.

Market dominance, though pleasurable, has its price, as Wal-Mart, the world's biggest retailer by a mile, has discovered. As well as books such as *How Wal-Mart Is Destroying America* and numerous critical press articles, the giant has also had to fight a welter of court cases, mainly about employment practices. And Tesco, in the eyes of many, has become the nearest thing that Britain has to Wal-Mart.

According to the City's star retail analyst Dave McCarthy, Tesco owes its success to the ability of successive managements to adapt the company to ever-changing market conditions in a way that Sainsbury and Marks & Spencer have spectacularly failed to do in recent years. That ability, the product of astute decision making at the top, is a measure of the quality of its management over the last thirty years. The Tesco culture is long and strong and most of the directors on the board in 2004 had been at the company since their early twenties. They live and breathe the business, focusing on pushing sales ever upward, irrespective of new store openings. David Potts, the director of stores in 2004, says that the first question in his mind when he wakes each morning is: 'What were yesterday's like-for-like sales?' Senior executives rarely move to another company before retirement.

Unlike its rivals, which all suffered setbacks during the 1990s and early years of the new century resulting from poor leadership, Tesco has never had a weak leader since Sir Jack Cohen started the business. In the 1980s the partnership between Ian MacLaurin and David Malpas was comparable to that between Simon Marks and Israel Sieff, who together built up Marks & Spencer, and between James Hanson and Gordon White, who created the UK's most successful industrial conglomerate of the Thatcher era. In each case one partner was the thinker, the other the doer.

Tesco's leaders have since the 1960s made a few critical calls that have given the company leadership in the development of food retailing as we know it today. At the right time, Cohen took Tesco into Green Shield Stamps – those trading emblems of a bygone era that could be exchanged for small consumer goods such as toasters or cutlery. MacLaurin forced him to relinquish stamps when the public had become bored with them. Operation Checkout, with its focus on low prices and good value at a time of high inflation, gave the company an air of integrity and seriousness. Most important of all, the decision to buy out-of-town sites for stores like they were going out of style during the recession of the 1990s put Tesco streets ahead of the competition. In particular, the acquisition of the Scottish supermarket chain William Low gave the group the critical mass to overtake Sainsbury in 1995.

At Citigroup, McCarthy believes Tesco has been particularly adept at taking advantage of relaxations in the planning regulation PPG6, which had been put in place by John Gummer in the early 1990s. McCarthy reckons that Leahy has the scope to extend as many as 300 of his superstores into hypermarkets, bringing the total number of Tesco Extras to close to 400.

If Tesco was winning, Sainsbury, once Britain's premier food retailer, had got lost in the dust, struggling to come to terms with the legacy of a glorious past. According to Taylor Nelson Sofres, Asda had pushed Sainsbury into third place in the pecking order – although still number two in food only – while the newly enlarged Morrison was not far behind.

In October 2004, Sainsbury shocked shareholders by cutting its dividend for the first time in its 31-year history as a public company following its first ever half-year loss after writing off £550m, much of it from Peter Davis's spending programme on new systems and distribution.

Speculation soared about possible bidders following a noisy boardroom battle culminating in the ousting of Davis as chairman and the departure of most of his colleagues. The phone lines of the extended Sainsbury family, who between them own more than a third of the shares, sizzled as the siren voices of investment bankers acting for predators wooed them. Their short-term decision was to take the pain of a dividend cut and put their faith – at least for a few months – in the hands of Justin King, their new young, chief executive, but that did little to quell speculation about a takeover in the City of London and in the business pages of the national newspapers. In stark contrast, Tesco was marching on towards annual profits of £2bn. Headed by the stony-faced Terry Leahy, its boardroom had never looked stronger.

At retailing conferences, McCarthy, who once worked at Tesco, made it clear how misguided he thought the Sainsbury management were in not taking more radical action to protect their reputation, comparing his former employer to Wal-Mart and Sainsbury to Kmart. Kmart went bankrupt.

To the casual shopper in a big-four store there is little hint of the cultural chasms that lie between the companies that run them. Jack Cohen and Ken

Morrison both began life as street traders; Sainsbury grew from a single dairy shop; Asda was a retail experiment by Associated Dairies, which had originally been a farmers' co-operative; Safeway was assembled by three ambitious young entrepreneurs through numerous bids and deals. The histories and corporate cultures of these companies differ greatly and they still, perhaps surprisingly, reflect the ethos of their founders. The contrast between a Tesco supermarket and a Sainsbury of equal size may not be especially obvious, but the mindsets behind them are like night and day.

Jack Cohen was a trader by nature, building Tesco from a market stall on his hunches and love of a bargain. Today Tesco is the ultimate risk-taking meritocracy. It may have moved on from the days when Cohen would take a punt on a pot-luck consignment, but the culture is still to take calculated risks. The ethos remains 'Who dares, wins.'

Sainsbury began life as a tiny dairy shop run by John James Sainsbury and his wife – a Victorian couple with a passion for quality. Altogether more sedate than Tesco, Sainsbury became the aristocrat of the supermarkets. Five generations ruled Sainsbury before the family finally called for an outsider to be chief executive and for more than a century it was a family business where if somebody named Sainsbury asked people to jump, they asked: 'How high?' Success bred arrogance and pomposity.

Such cultural differences are evident in the companies' headquarters. In order to meet Tesco's chief executive, visitors from the capital have to trail through north-east London along the A13 to Cheshunt, a sleepy Hertfordshire commuter town. They drive past a tatty parade of shops just before the turning into a 1960s-style sprawling office complex. Parking nearby in a gloomy oversized car park does not lift the spirits. Once signed in by security staff, visitors wait in the dismal entrance hall with the lowest of low-pile carpet on the floor until their hosts or their secretaries come to greet them.

How different from Sainsbury's gleaming glass cylinder at Holborn Circus on the site of Robert Maxwell's former empire, where under Peter Davis's regime the vast, minimalist entrance hall gave way to a modern café with Italian coffee, croissants and no end of treats for visitors to nibble while waiting. Justin King swiftly axed the treats.

Travellers to Leeds soon spot the big green sign announcing Asda House at the company's headquarters a short walk from the station. Inside, the modern brick building all is light and bright with an air of bustle and mateyness. Friendly receptionists bid visitors to take a seat on the mezzanine level 'on one of our splendid blue settees'. There is no hiding place in the open-plan offices, which hum with energy.

Before its takeover by Morrison in January 2004, Safeway had the best of both worlds, at least for its directors. A small Mayfair flat gave them a perfect venue for discreet meetings with investment bankers and somewhere to lay their heads after a late function. The main headquarters in Hayes was factory-like and functional. Morrison's offices in Bradford, the former wool capital of England, are the smallest and least pretentious of all, although a new modern headquarters is under construction.

Their cultural colours are also on display in the way they entertain their suppliers and opinion formers such as politicians, civil servants and journalists. If Tesco directors want to entertain a supplier they invite him to play golf with professionals at a top club in an exotic location such as Valderrama in Spain, putting him up at a luxury hotel. Most of the directors are sports mad. Tim Mason, Tesco's marketing director, regularly takes part in triathlons; the stores director, David Potts, heads the Tesco football team while the Tesco Badgers compete regularly with the best golfers Unilever or other suppliers can provide.

At Asda, Allan Leighton and Archie Norman used to lead five-a-side football with suppliers' teams every week. Sainsbury's idea of corporate entertainment is an evening at the Royal Opera House, where both John Sainsbury, the chairman from 1969 to 1992, and the recently departed Peter Davis, sat on the board.

Differ though they may, the executives of these four companies share one characteristic – they are ferociously competitive, and have become more so in the past decade. Davis, who left Sainsbury in 1986 and returned in 2001 after heading Reed International and Prudential, recalled that the most striking change he found was the heightened competition. During his first career at Sainsbury he, Ian MacLaurin, then head of Tesco, James Gulliver of Safeway's precursor, Argyll Group, and Noel Stockdale at Asda would take the opportunity to chat at food-industry dinners and would discuss any problems – such as undue poaching of executives – over the telephone. At the time, such cosy relationships led to suggestions that they were fixing prices and running a cartel.

When Davis became Sainsbury chief executive fifteen years later, he found a far chillier climate prevailing. When he made courtesy calls to his counterparts at other companies they did not always call back. If there had ever been a conspiracy by the supermarket groups against the public to prop up prices it had dissolved – at least as far as Davis was concerned.

Davis discovered that only David Webster at Safeway was happy to chat – although even then it was only to tell him he was a fool for coming back into food retailing. It had become a case of each chief executive for himself. By the end of 2004 Webster had moved on to chair InterContinental Hotels, following Morrison's bid, and Davis was out on his ear, albeit with pay and pension contributions to July 2005 and a grudging £2.6m 'golden goodbye'.

As the 2005 results season approached, Terry Leahy and his triathletes at Tesco were way ahead of the other three management teams. Ken Morrison had suffered some indigestion as his company began to assimilate Safeway. Even Asda hit a trading slowdown. At Sainsbury, bid speculation mounted as Justin King laid out his plans for revitalising the company to investors against flat sales. His biggest enemy was time and he knew it.

Watching Tesco advance like a Roman army sweeping all before it, retail experts asked whether the Competition Commission's decision to prevent the big four from consolidating into the big three would prove to be best for the consumer and suppliers in the long run. Might Sainsbury be so weakened that it would be taken over or broken up? After spending fourteen months and several million pounds of taxpayers' money probing the sector and trying to decide how best to create a more level playing field, had the Commissioners got it wrong?

CHAPTER TWO

SAINSBURY'S OPENING SALVO

'Every great institution is the lengthened shadow of a single man.
His character determines the character of the organisation.'

Ralph Waldo Emerson

Queen Victoria had ruled Britain and its empire for thirty-two years when John James Sainsbury and his fiancée, Mary Ann Staples, opened a tiny dairy shop at 173 Drury Lane in London. The year was 1869. The British Empire was still expanding, William Gladstone was prime minister for the first time and the industrial revolution had brought people to the cities in unprecedented numbers; railways were opening up the farmlands at home and abroad, making imports and deliveries of fresh food to towns much easier. The worst of the Hogarthian poverty was over and Charles Dickens had already penned the last of his social novels, *Great Expectations*.

That first little shop of 'no more than 500 square feet' sold just butter, milk and eggs when it opened, later adding cheese. But the two young owners were unwittingly putting in place the foundations of what became Britain's premier food retailing dynasty.

Barely out of their teens, the young couple could have had no inkling they were founding a mighty empire when they married a few weeks after they began trading. John James's early ambitions stretched to just a handful of shops – one for each son. The concept of self-service was unimaginable in the Victorian era. Yet their little undertaking contained in embryonic form some of the key ingredients of the modern supermarket. It is where the story of modern food retailing begins.

Most successful businesses grow from one good idea. Jack Cohen brought the housewife outlandish bargains. John James and Mary Ann wanted their milk and butter to be of the highest quality. They wanted, quite simply, 'to have the best butter in London'. It may not sound revolutionary, but in 1869 it set their enterprise apart from the myriad other small food shops whose stalls cluttered the pavements of the day – and where hygiene was a vaguely understood concept.

Quality became a passion for Mary Ann, who ran the Drury Lane shop for the first three months while John James worked out his notice with his previous employer. Her father was a dairyman with half a dozen shops and he had taught her to be punctilious. 'It was Mrs Sainsbury who made the shop famous for the quality of its butter,' one of her first employees, Sarah Pullen, later recalled. 'She was always up very early in the morning and took great pride in the cleanliness of the shop.'

John James followed her lead. The signs he commissioned for the window of the Victorian frontage read 'Daily arrivals of pure rich butters' and 'Purveyor of high-class provisions'.

Unwittingly they were establishing the key elements of the Sainsbury brand, although they would not have understood the word in its modern sense, a brand that customers could rely upon for good quality at fair prices.

It was an idea in tune with the times. The *JS 100* – a history of Sainsbury published to celebrate the centenary in 1969 – painted a picture of a growing and increasingly affluent London. 'There were three million people living in London, the world's largest city and capital of a country with a foreign trade greater than the combined trades of the USA, France, Italy and Germany. Britain's people, for all the poverty that existed among them, had more money to spend than they had ever thought possible. The rich invested it, the middle class spent theirs on solid comfort and the workers made good a chronic need – they bought more food.'

By the middle of the nineteenth century living standards were on the rise and even the poorest urban families were beginning to demand food that was wholesome and fresh. Housing conditions had also begun to improve while underground sewers and sanitised water were reducing the incidence of epidemics. Such historical details underline the vast social changes that have taken place in the 135 years Sainsbury has been trading.

Sainsbury is the dowager of the big four supermarket groups. Not until fifty years after the Drury Lane shop opened did Jack Cohen, a young Jew from London's East End, disillusioned at finding no work available after fighting in the First World War, set up his first market stall in Hackney in 1919. He soon started selling tea with a Tesco label, but it was 1932 before Cohen registered Tesco as a company name. Still later, in 1950, Ken Morrison took over his father's market stall; Asda began trading in 1965 while Safeway's roots go back only to 1972.

Of the others, Marks & Spencer began life at the end of the nineteenth century, but the food retailing arm took off only in the 1960s under Marcus Sieff's chairmanship. Waite, Rose & Taylor, 'High-class grocers and provision merchants', started with one shop in Acton Hill in 1904. As it grew the name was changed to combine the surnames of two of the founders and in the mid 1930s the John Lewis Partnership, Britain's biggest workers' co-operative, bought the enterprise. The first Waitrose supermarket as such opened in Streatham in the early 1950s.

Four generations of Sainsburys and five family chairmen led the company to ever-greater glories until 1996 when, under the lacklustre leadership of David Sainsbury, profits fell for the first time since the Second World War. Sainsbury's share register was still dominated by a family holding of more than a third – which meant a very small group of people could decide its fate should a predator come prowling.

In 1969, to celebrate Sainsbury's centenary a magnificent banquet was held at the Savoy Hotel with a glittering guest list from business and politics. Around the stores and depots every staff member received a slice of birthday cake. And in the same year, as colour television arrived on BBC1 and the Rolling Stones sang 'Honky Tonk Woman', Princess Margaret visited the 100th Sainsbury supermarket – in Balham, south London.

By then Sainsbury had developed an unrivalled reputation for food quality, and had become a national institution – at least south of Birmingham. The brand that John James and Mary Ann had begun was now a magnet for the middle classes, who trusted the stores to give them good quality at reasonable prices. But it was only under the autocratic leadership of John

Sainsbury, the eldest of the fourth generation who took charge in that year, that the company rose to dominate food retailing in the UK.

John James and Mary Ann were married on 20 April 1869. He was 24 and she a mere 19, both brimming with energy and enthusiasm. But the retailing venture was no idle whim; both had plenty of experience in their chosen field. John James grew up near the Old Vic theatre in Short Street, Southwark, the son of a frame and ornament maker. As a boy he ran errands to the New Cut street market, just round the corner from his home, and when he was 14 he left school to work in a grocer's shop. Records show that his father also lived for a while in Peter Street, Soho, close to Berwick Street market.

From the grocer he joined an oil-and-colour merchant – a general store selling 'everything from chicory to gunpowder'. The owner was Henry Jeans and he found that John James soon displayed initiative beyond his years. There had been a spate of thefts of soap and when the miscreant was caught the case went to trial. John James was called as a witness and the defence asked how he could identify the goods – surely, all bars of soap looked the same. John James produced a pocket-knife and asked the magistrate to slice off the end of a bar. He found a matchstick which John James had embedded there. 'Young man,' said the magistrate, 'if you apply as much care and thought to your work as you have done in this case, you will go a long way.'

His father died when John James was 19, leaving him as the sole bread-winner for his mother and two sisters. It may have been his father's death that fired his ambition to have his own shop, but he did not decide to go it alone until he had nine years' experience in the retail trade.

Mary Ann had spent her childhood surrounded by milk and butter. Her father, Benjamin Staples, had built up a small chain of half-a-dozen dairy shops in which she helped out. When she met John James, she was working in a dairy shop owned by a family friend, Tom Haile.

When they met, both were working in Strutton Ground, Victoria. Perhaps John James visited Mary Ann's shop to buy milk, butter or eggs and stayed to chat. Or maybe she went into his emporium to stock up on candles or groceries. Either way, their courtship was swift and fuelled by an ambitious dream – that of setting up shop together. Family folklore has it that John James had saved £100 – an impressive sum in those days. It is also probable that Mary Ann's parents lent them money to help pay the rent of £128 a year and to equip the shop.

Despite rising standards, many milk sellers still kept cows in backyards close to sewage and it was common practice to dilute milk with water and add yellow colouring to make it look creamier. In her history of Sainsbury, *The Best Butter in the World*, Bridget Williams writes that the water pump was ironically known as 'the cow with the iron tail'. Although adulteration of food had been illegal since 1860, the law was still widely disregarded.

Discerning customers soon caught on. The Sainsbury's wares met their rising expectations. They liked the sweet-smelling shop and the taste of its unadulterated milk. It had become known as 'railway milk' since daily deliveries by train had started from the Home Counties and as far away as Somerset.

An early shop sign promising 'Quality perfect, prices lower' summed up what was to become a winning trading philosophy. The simple idea that quality had to be paramount meant that Sainsbury thrived while less scrupulous competitors came and went.

The business grew swiftly in a way that was rare at a time when most traders contented themselves with a couple of shops, or at most, like Mary Ann's parents, half a dozen branches. Food retailing was a family business and extended only as far as the family could staff it. Chain stores such as Lipton's and Maypole Dairies were still in their infancy and by 1875 such chains had only 108 shops between them.

Childbearing curtailed Mary Ann's role in the business, but not her influence. Their first child, a daughter, died at just seven months and Mary Ann was devastated when the doctor told her she should not risk another pregnancy. But unknown to her or her doctor, she was already pregnant and eight months later she gave birth to a son, John Benjamin. Defying doctor's orders, she went on to have ten more children – five girls and five boys.

John Benjamin, who would later take over as head of the business from his father, was born above the Drury Lane shop and trained for the job from the start. As a toddler he was put on a swing in the doorway between the shop and the warehouse to keep him entertained. As soon as he could talk, his mother made him a special apron and encouraged him to help.

Mary Ann's influence on quality continued to be felt in the business as it expanded. In 1873 they opened a second shop in Queen's Crescent in the more affluent Kentish Town. Within a few years they had three branches trading in Queen's Crescent known as Upper Sains, Middle Sains and Lower Sains as well as the original Drury Lane shop. Middle Sains featured a 'mechanical cow' into which customers could insert a copper and collect a jugful of milk by pulling a lever.

By modern standards the shops were tiny – less than 500 square feet with living accommodation above – but in an age without cars it made more sense to have three small branches than one bigger one. Stall-holders selling vegetables and fruit would set up directly in front of the shops.

In 1880 Mary Ann's parents were thinking of retirement and it seemed logical to keep their outlets in the family. So John James first took over one of their cheesemonger's shops run by his brother-in-law and then two Staples shops at Hoxton and King's Cross. Keeping it in the family had its advantages. Taking over a business when you were related to the former owners meant less hostility from rivals in what was an intensely competitive field.

Then as now, many held the view that in certain areas there were simply too many shops for the local population to support. In 1876 one such commentator, W. Glenny, wrote that in the East End of London 'the number of shopkeepers is greatly in excess of what is necessary for safe competition in the sale of food generally'.

If that sounds familiar, so too does the formation of an informal trade association, known as the 'pact', set up by a number of food retailers. The pact was formed mainly to enhance the buying power of the shops, which could cut a better deal with suppliers by acting as one. There was also an understanding that pact members should not open up too close to one another – although this caused a number of heated disputes.

Today the big four supermarket groups in Britain have quite enough, some say too much, buying power individually, but independent convenience stores such as Londis still band together in pact-style buying organisations.

Another similarity with modern times is that towards the end of the nineteenth century customers expected to be able to shop when they wanted. Saturday was payday for most people so Saturday nights were the busiest of the week and regular customers expected someone to be available to serve them on Sundays. They were difficult to ignore if you lived above the shop.

Even if the family home was elsewhere, it was traditional to have at least one member of staff living in.

The Victorians had their own 'Trolley Wars', although they were more like street fights than national confrontations. Competition was so fierce in those days that to ignore customers who called at inconvenient times might mean losing them to a rival a few doors along the street, and there were bigger players with national aspirations springing up at the time.

Of today's big chains, only the Co-op began before Sainsbury. In 1844, twenty-eight weavers in Lancashire set up the Rochdale Society of Equitable Pioneers and started a co-operative grocery shop. The concept mushroomed and by 1915, according to *The Grocers* by Andrew Seth and Geoffrey Randall (1999), Co-op stores 'probably accounted for almost 20 per cent of grocery and provision sales'.

In 1885, Home & Colonial opened its first shop and within five years had more than a hundred outlets throughout Britain. The International Tea Company had two hundred shops while Thomas Lipton, another tea trader, had one hundred branches. These multiples concentrated on supplying the working classes with a limited range of groceries at low prices.

The Sainsburys had a different approach. Displaying his innovative spirit and responding to Mary Ann's obsession with hygiene, John James started to spend far more on fitting out his shops than was deemed prudent at the time. The Croydon 'model' branch, which opened in 1882, was the first Sainsbury store outside London and it marked the beginning of a new era in other ways. John James, supported by Mary, decided to lavish money on the fittings and spent about £1,400. This equates to around £90,000 today – a relatively modest sum by modern standards but one that also undoubtedly reflects the cheapness of Victorian labour.

Sainsbury public relations folklore has it that the marble tops, mosaic floors and handsome tiles they used were all chosen in the name of hygiene. But although they banished mice and rats they also created a cool, pleasant atmosphere and made a statement that here was a high-quality establishment selling superior foods.

Croydon was expanding rapidly at the time. According to Bridget Williams, the Sainsbury archivist, it had no fewer than eleven railway stations and was served by four different railway companies, which operated 400 trains to and from London daily. John James chose a site opposite the important West Croydon station for his store and once it was fitted out to his liking – he hand picked the tiles himself – he ensured it was stocked with a range of produce far wider than in any other branch. An 1894 advertisement makes it sounds more like the food halls of Harrods or Fortnum & Mason than a grocery store serving the middle classes. 'The choicest butters of absolute purity, obtained direct from the farms of Brittany, Dorset and Aylesbury; new-laid eggs; Wiltshire and Irish bacon; York, Cumberland and Irish hams … and all descriptions of poultry and game in season.' The selection of cheeses advertised would not disgrace any modern-day Sainsbury. 'Stiltons, rich ripe and blue, Gorgonzolas of the finest quality, gold medal Gruyère, Canadian Cheddar and American Cheshire, Camembert, Neufchatel, Roquefort and Port du Salut.' In addition there was a wide range of poultry and game including grouse, pheasant, Egyptian quails, Bordeaux pigeons, jellinots and larks (by the dozen).

Importing food became much easier towards the end of the century as improvements in transport and technology helped slash the price of agricultural goods. Railways opened up vast tracts of North America, Argentina and Russia, where food could be produced far more cheaply than in Britain. Refrigerated ships could transport meat across the Atlantic. The banks of the Thames became lined with busy warehouses built to receive foreign produce.

Sainsbury's competitors doubted that the expense of fitting out the Croydon shop would pay off. They were confounded. The store proved so successful that John James swiftly opened several more branches in the town. One of these was a specialist pork butcher's shop, which was the first branch to sell Sainsbury's own sausages, made on the premises. They proved so popular that the shop was soon producing them for sale at other branches.

The Croydon shops were aimed deliberately at the rapidly growing middle classes, yet they undercut the specialist purveyors of luxury foods, rather as Marks & Spencer was soon to do with clothing. There are no profit figures available for these early stores but it is clear they generated more than enough cash to finance continued expansion.

The huge variety of produce on sale was due partly to the amount of imported food. Britain's free-trade policy meant there was little or no duty levied on imported produce while canning, processing and refrigeration enabled beef and lamb from America and products from Russia to be shipped relatively cheaply so they might adorn many a Victorian dining table. This was a world without the Common Agricultural Policy and where intensive animal husbandry in Britain had yet to arrive.

Up until 1886 Sainsbury, like most other food retailers, bought the bulk of its supplies from London wholesalers based on the south side of the Thames, but around this time John James realised he could do better buying direct from overseas producers. In an incident that became part of the Sainsbury folklore, he discovered that the importers who supplied him with Dutch butter had been storing it in ice caves with the aim of selling when the market price was high – even though storage affected the taste. Bridget Williams writes: 'He therefore appointed the Royal Buisman Dairy Exchange of Leeuwarden to act as his agents in the Friesland markets.' From then on deliveries of butter arrived direct at Sainsbury, where John James personally inspected every consignment. Every case, at his insistence, was stamped in Holland with the date of its production.

Towards the end of the century Sainsbury moved into food production thanks mainly to John James's third son, Frank. He had always wanted to be a farmer and resisted joining the family firm, but like his brothers before him he was steamrollered into the business. Young Frank acquired a reputation for a fiery temper, eccentricity and lax management. One evening his father paid a surprise visit to his store to discover him riding his bicycle inside the shop. There was a huge row and John James fired him.

Luckily for the headstrong Frank, Mary Ann suggested that he should be allowed to follow his calling and go to work on the farm of a family friend. The young man threw his heart and soul into his farm work to such an extent that before long John James bought his own farm in Suffolk and installed Frank as manager. Naturally the farm became a supplier to Sainsbury.

At the time most of the eggs sold to the urban public came from abroad – Austria, Italy, Holland and France all exported eggs to Britain. English eggs, although laid closer to the point of sale, were usually less fresh because farmers would delay sending them to market, preferring to sell them in batches. So Frank started supplying Sainsbury with fresh eggs from well-fed hens and they proved so popular that by 1912 he had established his own egg-collection scheme from a number of farms in East Anglia.

Before long Frank had branched out into pig farming, and once again set about innovating and improving. His 'pig-house' provided the meat for the sausages and cooked pork products that Sainsbury sold.

For two decades John James appeared to be content with providing premier-quality food to the middle classes while leaving Home & Colonial,

Lipton's and the International Tea Company to cater for the mass market. Nor did he and his wife have any ambition to build a national chain.

Competition, however, changed his mind. In 1890 Home & Colonial opened a shop in Queen's Crescent – effectively Sainsbury's back yard. The move came as a wake-up call to John James, who understood, as he had not before, that he had no alternative but to speed up growth. 'Otherwise,' he said, 'we shall be beaten in our position as buyers in the sources of production.' He saw all too clearly that Sainsbury needed weightier buying power – rather as Sainsbury and Safeway recently realised they needed more buying power against Tesco and Asda. Crucial to the growth he needed was a modern depot and he commissioned the building of a state-of-the-art affair in Stamford Street in Blackfriars to handle larger quantities of produce. It proved an historic decision. Until 2000, when the company moved to a gleaming glass structure at Holborn Circus, Stamford Street remained the nerve centre of the Sainsbury operation.

The effect in routine terms was dramatic – a trebling of branches to forty-eight in the ten years to 1900. Yet Sainsbury stuck to its quality roots with a range of food that was far more varied and sophisticated than the likes of Lipton's or Home & Colonial.

Despite the swift growth John James also took great care in his choice of sites. The benchmark for all the shops was the Croydon store. To pass muster, a site had to be a long rectangle with a central position in a parade flanked by shops on either side. He refused to countenance a corner site. Corner sites allowed more dust and dirt from the traffic into the store while a long shop with windows only at the front helped keep food cool in the summer. 'Corners,' said John James, 'are for banks.'

He decorated the stores with Sicilian marble counters, tiled walls and mosaic floors. The ceramic tiles and floors were produced specifically for Sainsbury by Minton Hollins and John James insisted that every shop was brightly lit. It was an enduring format that lasted more than half a century into the early 1950s when the first self-service stores began to appear. Even today the memories of those shops remain strong. 'I still remember the patterns of the tiles, the smells of bacon mingling with cheese, the thrill of watching the bacon slicer at work and the men slapping the butter into blocks,' said one customer recalling her childhood fifty years earlier.

At the time Sainsbury stood midway between the small independent retailers with between one and perhaps a dozen shops and the multiple retailers, which, intriguingly, attracted much the same kind of atavistic criticism that supermarket groups receive today. They were said to threaten the existence of the independents and according to *The Times* in 1902 'were nearly all conducted upon the same impersonal iron routine'. The chief objective of the company shops was merely 'to make profits for their shareholders, even at the expense of customer service'.

The reality was that there was room for lots of competitors. Between 1861 and 1911 the population of London more than doubled from 3,223,000 to 7,251,000 and increasing affluence meant those people had more money to spend on food.

John James aimed at providing competitive prices but a higher standard of quality and service than his rivals. In 1903 he began appointing inspectors whose job it was to visit the stores and report back at least once a week to his eldest son, John Benjamin, known as Mr John, who had become his father's deputy. Mr John was the most energetic and committed of the six brothers although they all worked in various aspects of the business.

When he was 25, John Benjamin married Mabel Van den Bergh, the daughter of Jacob Van den Bergh, founder of the Dutch margarine dynasty. He had arrived in Britain in 1879 to set up a London office. The rival margarine firm to Van den Bergh was Jurgens. In time the two groups merged, snapping up a number of Sainsbury's competitors such as Lipton's and Home & Colonial, all of which eventually became part of the Unilever empire.

From the vantage point of the early twenty-first century it looks like a strategic alliance, although Sainsbury shops did not sell much margarine, especially at the time of the marriage in 1896. Yet, the marriage is not mentioned in either of the official histories and it is possible that it caused some consternation in the family. The Van den Berghs were Jewish and John Benjamin would have had to convert to Judaism before he married Mabel at the West London Synagogue near Marble Arch on 8 January 1896. He would also have had to undertake to bring up any children of the union in the Jewish faith. Of his two sons, Robert married another Van den Bergh – his second cousin Lisa – but Alan married a young Englishwoman called Doreen Adams.

By the time Mr John reached 40, he was virtually running the business and in 1915 his father took him into partnership. At that point the company had 121 branches, 2,000 employees and annual sales of £2.7m.

As the company grew, so too did the sophistication of its systems. A rulebook, a tool that *The Times* had so decried in 1902, was introduced in 1914 with the aim of bringing about 'a universal form of management'.

The First World War put a number of strains on the business but also brought about some changes for the better. Most important was the employment of women in the shops, particularly in senior positions. Although the number of female staff dropped sharply once the war was over and many who had been running shops were demoted, some retained their managerial positions. Alice Hayes, for example, managed one of the Croydon stores from February 1922 to May 1928.

Mary Ann died on 9 June 1927 and, as is so often the case with close couples, John James did not survive long without her. He died six months later on 3 January 1928 at his house in Highgate aged 83, but not before uttering his final famous exhortation to his sons: 'Keep the shops well lit.'

On the day of his funeral every Sainsbury branch closed to allow the staff to join the long procession from Stamford House to Putney Vale cemetery.

In 1920 Sainsbury had annual sales of £5m from 129 shops and the tempo increased over the next two decades despite the Great Depression. By 1939 the number of stores had jumped to 255 and the turnover had more than doubled to £12.6m.

In 1922 J. Sainsbury entered a new phase of development when it was incorporated as a joint stock company. But in contrast to Lipton's and other rivals, there was no diversification of the ownership. The articles of association stipulated that only members of the family could become shareholders. John James became chairman and Mr John, Mr Arthur and Mr Alfred were made directors. The share capital of the company was valued at £1.3m.

While many of its rivals floundered, Sainsbury did well in the depression of the inter-war years because of the family's high standards, attention to detail and rigorous quality control. When the government put swingeing restrictions on free trade and duty on imports that did not come from countries within the British Empire, the policy hit Sainsbury's competitors hard. But Sainsbury, with its own farms and close relationships with British suppliers, did well. Advertisements of the day boast of 'Empire butter' and colonial mutton and cheese.

Sainsbury also had the edge on the other multiples through its larger, better-equipped stores and their correspondingly higher turnover. In 1939, while Sainsbury had sales of £12.6m from 255 stores, Home & Colonial's sales were £9.9m from 798 shops.

In recent years, Sainsbury has been criticised for being slow to expand into the north of England. But for many years the prosperous south-east provided more than enough demand, with the population of London and the Home Counties growing twice as fast as the rest of the country between 1921 and 1937.

Bridget Williams reports: 'The new housing estates of West London and Essex, and especially the rapidly growing suburban "Metroland" of Wembley and Harrow, offered ideal locations for Sainsbury stores.'

Although they were gentlemanly in their manners Mr John and his brothers could also be opportunistic. A former employee had set up a grocery chain in the Midlands called Thoroughgoods and when it eventually went bust in 1936 Sainsbury bought most of the shops, establishing footholds in Coventry, Derby, Kettering, Leicester, Northampton, Nottingham and Walsall.

A 1930s Sainsbury may not have had as many lines as a twenty-first-century superstore but, in food, the family clearly led the way with its range of fresh meat, game, pies and cheeses. Beef from Argentina, lamb from New Zealand and Devon, bacon from Canada, wild duck, widgeon, hazel hen, pheasant, grouse, partridge, hare and rabbit were all available in season. On the cooked-meat counter there were pies and sausages, brawn, chicken-and-ham loaf, boar's head, ox tongue and pressed pork. The cheese counter groaned with a wealth of Cheddars, Cheshires, Stiltons, Swiss Gruyère and a plethora of French cheeses.

True there were no chilled ready-meals but there was plenty with which to rustle up a quick supper or lunch. Despite the absence of tahini, taramasalata or the dozens of other world foods common today, few customers could have complained of wanting for choice – assuming they had money to pay.

Most Sainsbury branches offered a free delivery service by boys on bicycles and later by motor vans, particularly for larger orders. Reluctantly, Mr John eventually conceded that there should be a small delivery charge, which was introduced in 1934.

In 1938 John Benjamin retired after suffering a minor heart attack. Despite quadrupling sales and doubling the number of stores to 248 under his management, Mr John had an autocratic approach, something that was followed by future generations. After his retirement the *Grocers' Gazette* described him as 'an unapologetic dictator' who controlled the entire organisation 'from buying right through to the retail level in the branches'. The article went on to say: 'The orderliness of his nature plus the amazing organising ability he possessed, were the instruments he used to build up an unrivalled system of retail distribution which has been copied by the vast majority of multiple companies that have since come into existence.'

His heart attack spurred him to do what few business autocrats can bear to do – hand over the running of the company to somebody else while he was still alive. In this case it was made easier because he was handing over to his sons Alan and Robert, who became joint general managers – and from then on were known in the business as Mr Alan and Mr Robert.

Both boys were educated at Haileybury College, a boarding school in Hertfordshire, and had been imbued with the Jewish tradition of philanthropy and social liberalism. Mr Alan, who became involved in charity work in an East End mission as a young man, did not particularly want to work at Sainsbury. But while he was agonising, his mother told him that it would break his father's heart if he abandoned the family company, leaving him little option. He began working in stores – initially alongside his uncles Mr Arthur and Mr Alfred, buying eggs and dairy products. He then trained at the Boscombe store incognito – working under an alias so that the rest of the staff would not be intimidated. From these reluctant beginnings he became a flamboyant retailer and was by far the stronger personality of the two brothers.

The administration and finances fell to Mr Robert, who read history at Pembroke College Cambridge before training as an accountant. Quiet and scholarly on the one hand, he had a passion for the contemporary art of the time and it was he who began the tradition of arts patronage at Sainsbury. He became a patron to young artists, collecting the work of Henry Moore, Alberto Giacometti and Francis Bacon, all of whom he knew personally, at a time when their work was regarded as quite shocking. He also bought paintings by earlier artists whose reputations were already established.

Together the two men – the third generation - ran the company for the next thirty years. Their skills and personalities complemented each other during times that were far from easy. The Second World War and the severe food rationing that came with it were hardly conducive to growth.

The young Simon Marks had visited America in the 1920s in search of new ideas for his growing Marks & Spencer variety-store chain, and once the war was over Mr Alan also headed west on a corporate pilgrimage, taking with him Fred Salisbury, the first ever non-family director. Their mission, in March 1949, was to research the new phenomenon of frozen foods. But when they returned they were fired with enthusiasm for a new shopping concept that was taking off in the United States – self-service.

'We went to study the display and sale of frozen food,' Mr Alan later recalled. 'But we both came back so thrilled and stimulated at the potentiality of self-service trading that we became convinced that the future lay with what we thought were large stores of 10,000 square feet of selling space.'

Around the same time, a young street trader called Jack Cohen had made a similar voyage of discovery to America and had drawn much the same conclusions. Both Alan Sainsbury and Jack Cohen, however, were soon to discover that in introducing self-service into the UK they would need to take account of the vast differences between the two countries.

Self-service had taken off in America during the Depression, when vacant warehouses had been converted into big self-service stores selling groceries. Such stores were cheap to develop in America because land prices were much lower than in Britain. Wages, on the other hand, were higher, which meant food retailers found reducing staff levels extremely attractive.

But it was not yet feasible to construct warehouse-sized stores in Britain. Only 12 per cent of British households owned a car in 1950, compared with 59 per cent in America, so out-of-town shopping was impractical for most, and contemporary planning regulations prohibited large stores in urban centres.

Commentators of the day believed, as with so many innovations, that self-service would never catch on in Britain. One leading retail expert of the time, J. Edward Hammond, considered it was 'improbable that this class of emporium will ever be introduced into Great Britain'. Today he sounds as misguided as the man from Decca who turned down the Beatles. Even Alan Sainsbury's father, Mr John, voiced his doubts but, displaying true pioneering zeal, Mr Alan decided to convert the large Croydon store to self-service in 1950 – at 3,300 square feet it was one of the largest in the portfolio at the time.

Sainsbury was not the first UK retailer to open a self-service store – the Co-op had converted a few stores to self-service straight after the war – but the administration that went with post-war rationing made the shops difficult to run. Tesco also had a self-service store in the late 1940s and Allied Foods had some early self-service outlets. But the entry of Sainsbury into the sector, with its emphasis on design and quality, was the true birth of the self-service revolution. The Croydon store was arguably Britain's first real supermarket. By 1950, when it was relaunched, the worst rigours of rationing were over, so there was a wide range of non-rationed foods from which to choose.

Mr Alan had discovered his métier – innovation. The Croydon store, parts of which dated back to 1896, was refurbished under one of a hundred special building licences offered by the Ministry of Food to retailers who were brave enough to experiment with self-service – and were willing to share their experiences with others.

The refitting of 9–11 London Road, Croydon, spelt the death knell for marble countertops, mosaic floors and patterned tiles. It meant that the distinctive aura of the traditional store, that wonderful mingling of wire-cut cheese and machine-sliced bacon to order, of loose butter and of floors sprinkled with sawdust, would gradually disappear from Britain's high streets.

In its place came sanitised steel and perspex display counters stacked with pre-packaged goods. The friendly white-coated counter staff were replaced by checkout girls, although some counter-staff remained and far more assistants patrolled the aisles to help shoppers than today. Harsh fluorescent lighting took the place of old-fashioned lamps and, for the first time ever, open-topped refrigerated cabinets designed by the company's chief engineer, Ralph Hall, graced the store.

No wonder that much of the initial reaction was hostile, particularly among older people. One customer actually threw a wire basket back at Mr Alan after he handed her one at the store entrance.

Bridget Williams tells us that one competitor, although she does not mention who, told Mr Alan that the British public would never take to self-service. 'How wrong they were,' Mr Alan said later. 'How lucky we were that they were wrong.'

Two years later the first purpose-built self-service store was opened in Eastbourne, then another in Southampton in 1954. Planning restrictions were tight: new buildings had to be on former bombsites and many of Sainsbury's existing stores were too small to convert to self-service.

There was a long planning battle over the rebuilding of the bombed-out centre of Lewisham but in 1955 Sainsbury opened the largest self-service store in Europe – a 7,500-square-foot emporium – in the high street. By this time the press and public opinion had swung behind the concept of the new 'super markets'. It had become clear to everyone in food retailing that this was the way forward. The revolution proved immensely profitable. Between 1950 and 1960 Sainsbury's turnover quadrupled and profits soared from £560,000 to £2.6m.

Mr Alan's talent for innovation was given free rein and he pioneered the introduction of the RTC (ready to cook) frozen chicken into Britain, working with chicken producers such as Buxted Chicken and the Western Chicken Growers Association. Thanks to him, roast chicken ceased to be a luxury, served at family lunches only on Sundays, and became an affordable everyday item.

In 1950 the man who would become Sainsbury's most successful leader began work in the company. John Davan Sainsbury, the eldest of Mr Alan's three sons, was tall and imposing and had inherited his father's temper. Mr Alan could throw his weight around with the best and one former director recalled seeing him regularly 'incoherent with rage'. The young Mr John, or Mr JD as he became known, was much the same.

Mr JD also inherited his father's ferocious competitiveness and became a formidable adversary of Sainsbury's rivals. As the 1950s progressed and food became more plentiful it became clear that in the south-east of England the most energetic competitor, although totally different in style, was Tesco.

At that time few would ever have dreamed that Tesco, with its small untidy stores crammed with goods and its pile-it-high, sell-it-cheap philosophy, would one day gain a reputation as reliable as the respectable, trustworthy Sainsbury. Tesco certainly had more shops in the 1950s and 1960s, and higher sales, but the gulf in trading style was clear to see. The Sainsburys were the aristocrats of food retailing, purveyors of fine foods to ladies and gentlemen, Tesco was the Jack the Lad, flogging bargains to the masses.

The first time Sainsbury and Tesco publicly locked horns over an issue was the great trading stamps war of 1963. They discovered that a spirited public debate conducted through the press could be good for both sides.

Giving customers trading stamps with their groceries started, predictably enough, in America, where it found instant success. Shoppers loved collecting the stamps, pasting them in books and trading them in for a variety of products they could pick from an illustrated catalogue. In Britain the Co-op issued its 'divi' in fake lightweight money, but that could only be redeemed to buy more goods – like the first Tesco Clubcard, launched in 1995, which aimed to be an electronic divi.

Trading stamps seemed altogether more glamorous to the British public and caught the spirit of the time. In the UK some smaller chains began experimenting with trading stamps in 1961, the start of the swinging sixties when the consumer boom was revving up. Jack Cohen had been mulling over the pros and cons of trading stamps. He saw they initially drew in the shoppers, but he hung back. His biographer, Maurice Corina, depicts a man struggling with two quandaries. Firstly, Tesco was a member of the National Association of Multiple Grocers, which had warned against the use of trading stamps. 'Tesco was party to a gentleman's agreement with such chains as Allied Suppliers, International Tea, Moores Stores and J. Sainsbury, not to use stamps without notifying one another.' The agreement was to give three months' notice and was regarded as a de facto declaration against their use. Cohen also worried that if Tesco broke ranks and everyone else followed, then the competitive advantage of stamps would soon be lost – and all the promotional costs with it.

In June 1963 the Weston family, owners of Associated British Foods, Fortnum & Mason and the struggling Fine Fare supermarket chain, put in a new, aggressive Canadian retailer called George Metcalfe to head Fine Fare. Sainsbury, Tesco and the rest looked on keenly to see what tactics he would employ. On 21 August Metcalfe wrote to the chairman of the National Association of Multiple Grocers saying that Fine Fare intended to introduce Sperry and Hutchinson Pink Stamps into selected stores in November.

Alan Sainsbury led a volley of protests to Garfield Weston, the ABF chairman, which Tesco joined. But Cohen was wavering. Behind the scenes he had talks with the Green Shield Stamps chairman Richard Tompkins.

That did not prevent him from attending a 'secret' council of war at the Savoy Hotel. More than eighty leading figures from the grocery trade attended but representatives of Fine Fare were not allowed to be present and put their point of view.

Cohen dithered but his commercial instincts won out. 'If Fine Fare does open up with them [stamps] in a supermarket next to one of ours then we shall probably have to adopt them too,' he declared, adding: 'If this is the way to compete, we shall use them. I think the stamp companies will get rich in Britain.'

While the debate over trading stamps raged in the press and in Parliament, where the Labour MP John Stonehouse wrote to the President of the Board of Trade asking for an enquiry, the Pricerite chain fired the first real shot of the trading-stamp war. On Monday 14 October 1963 Pricerite announced that its twenty-seven stores would start giving away Green Shield Stamps immediately.

Pricerite's declaration made up Cohen's mind. 'This is it. I have absolutely no doubts now,' he told colleagues. His deputy Hyman Kreitman was dispatched to New York to research S&H Pink Stamps but in the end Cohen opted for Green Shield and Tesco quickly launched a Green Shield Stamps campaign accompanied by huge press coverage. Once more Jack Cohen showed his instinctive understanding of his customers' psyche. Whatever the strait-laced Sainsburys may have thought, the public adored them. The *Sunday Express*, reporting on the launch on 29 October 1963, said: 'In Leicester yesterday, the giant Tesco store was besieged by thousands of battling housewives. Twelve women fainted. The staff was completely overwhelmed. Finally, store manager John Eastoe cleared the shop and closed all the doors. Mr Eastoe said: "I have never seen anything like it in my life"…'

Despite the commercial success, Alan Sainsbury and his directors stood firm. As Baron Sainsbury of Drury Lane, he abhorred the idea of trading stamps, believing they stood for all the cheap and tacky ideas that Sainsbury opposed. He waged a vociferous 'anti-stamp' campaign, earning himself the title 'Lord of the anti-stamps'. His family and colleagues saw stamps as a gimmick and believed that the customer would see through the ploy and realise they were paying more for goods to finance the stamps.

Mr JD helped his father mastermind the counter-offensive campaign, which included full-page advertisements in national newspapers and leaflets explaining Sainsbury's opposition. One leaflet included this message: 'It would cost £2m a year for Sainsbury to give trading stamps … It would be impossible for Sainsbury to maintain their high standards of quality and freshness and give trading stamps without raising prices.' Mr JD also coined the advertising slogans 'Honest to goodness value' and the more enduring 'Good food costs less' as part of the company's 'SuperSavers' campaign.

Another line of attack was through politics. Alan Sainsbury unsuccessfully sponsored a bill in the House of Lords stipulating that stamps should be exchangeable for cash and urging that the wording of advertisements should be controlled.

Yet the huge publicity surrounding the launch of the stamps and the anti-stamp campaign boosted Sainsbury's sales as well as Tesco's. As John Sainsbury later admitted, 'It was actually a great thing for both groups because there was so much publicity for us both.'

The Sainsbury family continued to look down on Jack Cohen and Daisy Hyams at Tesco and their extravagant store openings with balloons, bunting and show-business celebrities. Their disdain was similar to the attitude of the exclusive Savoy hotels group towards the more downmarket but more profitable Trust House Forte hotel group. The Savoy had been built by the impresario Richard D'Oyly Carte, whose Gilbert and Sullivan operettas had been so successful he wanted somewhere for his audiences to stay. By comparison, they believed the Italian Fortes, who had started out with milk bars in London, to be upstarts with inferior hotels.

Alan Sainsbury stepped down as chairman in 1967 and his brother Robert took over. Quite why is as much of a mystery as why David Sainsbury took the chair in 1992. Both lacked the leadership skills required.

Perhaps Robert felt he should be given his turn as chairman. His son David appeared to have felt the same way in the 1990s. Robert could not have helped feeling overshadowed by his more extrovert brother. But whatever the reason, he lasted only two and half years before handing over to his brother's firstborn, Mr JD, in Sainsbury's centenary year.

It is said that families go 'from clogs to clogs in three generations'. The first generation makes the money, the second administers it and the third blows it on riotous living. The Sainsburys, like the Cadburys, are exceptions to the rule. Even though Tesco deposed the group as market leader in 1995 and its reputation has suffered in recent years, Sainsbury, like Marks & Spencer, remains a brand with a strong hold over the nation's psyche.

Alan Sainsbury proved to be one of Britain's finest retailers, building on the foundations of the past. Some observers doubted that his son had sufficient entrepreneurial drive to push Sainsbury forward. In the event Mr JD's drive and love of innovation took it to greater glories than his father ever could have imagined.

CHAPTER THREE

ENTER THE COSTERMONGER

'God Made the wicked Grocer
For a mystery and a sign
That men might shun the awful shops
And go to inns to dine.'

G. K. Chesterton

Despite its relative youth and upstart nature, Tesco had become a public company in December 1947, a quarter of a century before Sainsbury floated on the stormy seas of the 1973 stock market. By 1969 Tesco had 800 outlets, including nearly 300 stores acquired through the takeover of the Victor Value chain in 1968. But Jack Cohen's power over the company began to wane as he fell behind the changing times.

During the 1960s Sainsbury appealed to the upwardly mobile, aspiring, middle-class housewife in her quest for consistent quality, while Jack Cohen's Tesco provided the natural hunting ground for those people who had previously frequented street markets and relished shopping for the best deals. If someone like Julie Andrews was a typical Sainsbury customer – well spoken and squeaky clean – then Tesco shoppers were Barbara Windsor types – flamboyant fun-loving girls from working-class backgrounds who liked a bargain. Essex girls always loved Tesco.

In a Britain only just emerging from post-war austerity, there were more potential Tesco customers in Britain – more than half the population earned their living in manual and/or blue collar activities, according to the National Readership Survey. Throughout the 1960s Jack Cohen's creation led the market with higher sales and profits than Sainsbury, the Co-op, Fine Fare and a host of smaller rivals.

If the carry-on campers of Britain were more cost conscious than their singing-nun counterparts, their expectations during the 1960s were rising. The class system began to break down, but, even more important, women began campaigning for equality with men at work. The invention of the contraceptive pill meant women had more control over whether and when they had children than ever before.

Well-educated girls now expected a university education followed by a full-time career, and girls who left school at 16 were more ambitious too, often starting in banks and stores groups and working their way up to branch manager. The pre-war idea that work was a fill-in pastime between leaving school, walking up the aisle and becoming a mother was gone.

Even those women who still opted to have children early started working part time. Any inclination to shop every day disappeared along with Teddy Boys and Skiffle. If 'sexual intercourse began in 1963', as the poet Philip Larkin summed up the sexual revolution of the 1960s, then so did one-stop shopping along with mass ownership of cars, fridges and freezers. By then a proliferation of supermarket groups had opened their doors, led by Tesco and Sainsbury.

Supermarkets were, and continue to be, accused of destroying small shops. Yet those customers who opted for supermarket shopping were responsible for the closure of so many independent retailers. For most people, the advantages of one-stop shopping outweighed the pleasantries with the baker, butcher and greengrocer. And the food from the new super-markets was often fresher, of better quality and more hygienically prepared than that from smaller shops where turnover was lower and meat and fish sat in windows for too long. But the most important factor was that one-stop shopping was quicker. Women in the 1960s discovered better things to do with their time than chatting up the butcher.

Just as important as women's liberation and the accompanying social changes was the growth of foreign travel. The British took to the skies. Beguiled by guaranteed sunshine, warm seas, cheap alcohol and the blandishments of package-tour operators, families started to go abroad routinely for their holidays, developing tastes for new types of food and drink.

Elizabeth David published her first book, *Mediterranean Food*, in 1950, although it did not become a standard fixture in middle-class kitchens until the mid-1960s. Other cookery writers such as Robert Carrier and Jane Grigson followed with books full of recipes from France, Italy and Spain and regular recipe columns in newspapers and magazines. Luckily for Carrier, who delighted in the use of butter and cream, cholesterol had not then been identified as a killer. The British started to use herbs and garlic in cooking, chicken portions became everyday fare, cooked with peppers, with tomatoes, even with wine and cream. Green broccoli arrived from abroad – a different and more manageable beast from the purple-sprouting kind that appeared briefly each autumn. Olive oil graduated from ear-wax remover to cooking medium.

The people who bought those foods and read the new cookery books shopped mainly at Sainsbury, of course. But even the Essex girls were having their horizons extended, although they sometimes demanded fish and chips when they got to their destination and had yet to sample a glass of wine. For the moment most stayed loyal to Tesco, where Jack 'the housewife's friend' Cohen gave them the thrill of bargain hunting to spice up their shopping expeditions.

Cohen was an archetypal self-made man, driven by his desire to do the next deal, find the next site and open the next store. John James Sainsbury and his wife put quality and attention to detail before everything else; Jack Cohen cared about price, price and location.

His passionate belief in building sales volumes through low prices led him to mount a revolution in the early 1960s against the food manufacturers to pave the way for a free market in food retailing. Enraged by price controls on about 40 per cent of his products, Cohen and his secretary turned chief buyer, Daisy Hyams, lobbied ceaselessly against resale price maintenance, whereby manufacturers dictated the prices at which products should be sold, thus determining Cohen's own profits.

It was symptomatic of a world where the food manufacturer was king – an old-fashioned feudal king who had all the power. Cadbury Schweppes, Unilever and Procter & Gamble among others set a minimum price at which their goods could be sold – whether by a big powerful group or a small independent retailer. One argument put forward for resale price maintenance was that it ensured that even the smallest traders would be able to stock and sell the manufacturers' products.

Yet resale price maintenance kept prices artificially high and bolstered manufacturers' profits. Cohen believed it operated against the consumers' interests – and against everything 'Slasher Jack' stood for. How could he bring the housewife true bargains if his hands were bound by his suppliers, whom he described as 'robbing people monstrously'? In 1963 he and Daisy Hyams waged an aggressive campaign in the courts against the manufacturers, who fought back hard, recognising that the balance of power was shifting in favour of the retailers. Ironically, given their Quaker backgrounds and ethical stance, the chocolate producers Cadbury and Rowntree Mackintosh fought the abolishment of resale price maintenance most fiercely. On the other side, although other retailers joined the cause and free market groups such as the Institute of Economic Affairs published learned papers supporting the abolition, it was Cohen who led the fight.

He sensed triumph in 1964 when Edward Heath, then President of the Board of Trade, published his resale prices bill in February, although it took an almighty struggle to get it through the House of Commons. The government came close to defeat at the hands of Tory backbench MPs who feared for communities in their constituencies if small shopkeepers were put out of business. Finally in July the bill received Royal Assent, although Cohen still had many battles in the courts to fight as manufacturers sought to register their products for exemption.

The 1964 Resale Prices Act changed for ever the balance of power between supplier and retailer. It was a blow for freedom that was later recognised when Jack Cohen received a knighthood in the 1969 honours list.

According to its opponents, the act would sound the death knell of independent shopkeepers, and for some it did. Others were more inventive. In the new world, small shopkeepers would have to offer some advantage other than price to survive – and so the convenience shop that opened early and stayed open late was born, becoming an increasing feature of urban life during the next forty years.

Thus Cohen and Hyams became genuine social revolutionaries. Not only had they won carte blanche for the supermarket groups to cut prices to whatever level they deemed manageable, giving the customer a better financial deal, they also unwittingly spawned thousands of shops that opened when the customer needed them – albeit charging a higher price for the service.

Like John James Sainsbury a good half century before him, Jack Cohen grew up around London street markets, but his stamping ground was the East End – in Hackney, Hoxton and Whitechapel.

Cohen was born in 1898, the son of Avroam (Abraham) Koehen, a master tailor, and his wife Sime, who had fled from the pogroms in Poland at the end of the nineteenth century. Born two months premature, the newborn baby boy escaped an early death when an aunt noticed he was fighting for breath and loosened his traditional tight birth cowl. Little Jacob, as he was originally named, was the fifth child and second son in the family, which struggled to make ends meet on the earnings from his father's tailoring business run from a workshop in the family home in Rutland Street. Tragedy came to the family when a third son, Solomon, died from a fever in infancy. Avroam was an Orthodox Jew and an authoritarian father who set rules for his children and expected them to be obeyed. In the official biography of 'Sir John Cohen' published in 1971, the author, Maurice Corina, notes that: 'Jack always knew when things were going well – there would be a trip down to the Commercial Road to buy a new suit, topped by an Eton collar and set off with the mortar-board type of hat favoured for boys of East London Jewish families.'

Raised in a largely female household dominated by his patriarchal father, Jack sought his amusements outside the strict rules of his home. At the Rutland Street Elementary and Secondary Schools he performed only moderately in the classroom, but in the playground and the streets around the school he showed an early 'expertise at swapping and selling schoolboy possessions', a sign of things to come.

School bored him and by 13 he was desperate to leave. His parents decreed he stay until 14, when, for want of any other opportunities, he began working for his father, becoming so expert on the Singer buttonhole machine that he could dash off 100 in an hour, earning two shillings and sixpence in the process. Tragedy struck the family a second time when his mother died in 1915 and home life began to disintegrate. His father married again soon afterwards to a woman none of the children liked. They nicknamed her Mrs How-Do-You-Do, possibly because of her lack of domesticity. The children's beds went unmade and meals failed to appear.

By now Jack, as he had been called from early childhood, emerged as a young man with an irreverent sense of humour, an aptitude for work and a talent for trading. He was still innocent by modern standards and wanted to better himself – he had no wish to become a tailor like his father.

He turned 18 during the First World War and decided to enrol in the Royal Flying Corps, where he was joined by his brother, Morris, six months later. Initially the strictly brought-up Jewish boys found the rough and tumble of military life daunting and, for the first time, they encountered blatant anti-semitism.

According to his biographer, Cohen did not drink, smoke or swear as a young man but he had charm and his quick wit and easy way with people helped him to mix with the other recruits. After a posting in Marseilles he headed for Alexandria on the troop-carrier *Osmanieh*. Having dodged German submarines on the way, the ship was blown up by a mine at the entrance of Alexandria harbour on New Year's Eve 1917. Cohen had been peeling potatoes in the galley when the mine exploded and he struggled to the deck. There he was given a lifebelt and told to abandon ship. He fell into the water, where he survived for four hours, helped by a nurse who had jumped near him and had encouraged him to dog paddle to keep his circulation going. Unconscious when sailors from a Japanese destroyer finally rescued him, he came round in hospital and never saw the nurse again or knew whether she survived. He was lucky. Two hundred people from the *Osmanieh* died.

In Alexandria he was befriended by members of the Jewish community and for the first time became aware of the Zionist struggle to regain a Jewish homeland. He later became a generous supporter of Israel from its formation in 1948. In Alexandria he contracted malaria, which curtailed his military activities and helped him to get back home more quickly – all those who had suffered more than two bouts of malaria were given priority for the journey back once the armistice was signed.

Awarded the Victory and General Service medals for bravery, a tougher Jack Cohen returned to London to find there was no work. Signing up for the dole in 1919 to be told there were no jobs outraged him. 'I wanted work – something to rely on,' he told Corina. 'Unemployment is a useless, wasteful and almost immoral thing. Imagine healthy young men hanging about the streets. It was a hateful sight. I did not want the dole, just work. This was our due anyway after the war.'

As a schoolboy he had helped his brother-in-law, Morris Israel, on his drapery stall in a Hammersmith street market and a visit to see him inspired Cohen to set up his own stall. His father was dismayed, viewing market traders, or costermongers as they were known, as unsavoury, unskilled people. But Cohen pressed ahead and spent his time chatting with other market traders and discovered there were surplus NAAFI goods available from the wholesalers of Eastcheap, leading him to take the most important decision of his life; he quit the dole queue and invested his demobilisation gratuity of £30 on NAAFI groceries.

One spring morning in 1919 Cohen loaded a barrow with the goods and trundled them into the Well Street market in south Hackney. The street was already bustling with established traders and Cohen, with his easy manner, soon persuaded one of them to give him a pitch for a shilling. On the first day he sold £4 worth of Maconochie's Paste and Lyle's Golden Syrup at a 33 per cent markup – not a bad return by today's standards. Jack Cohen was on his way.

His father and sisters were appalled as the family home filled up with goods from a growing network of suppliers, but Cohen was undaunted. 'I felt it was good to make £1 in one day. It was money, something I needed if I was to make something of myself. Besides I found an excitement and thrill about market trading ...'

Within a few months he was carting his stall between two or three markets a day, drawing crowds of bargain-hunting headscarved housewives with his entertaining patter and attractive offers. He developed a reputation for mystery packs of assorted bargains for half a crown that included tins of metal polish, fish paste, canned jam and syrup. His nephews would help on the stall. 'Hold your hands over the money, and if necessary, be prepared to run,' he told them.

He hired a horse and cart to transport the increasing amount of goods from pitch to pitch and if he had any doubts about what his family and friends regarded as a dubious activity, they were quashed when he sold £100 worth of goods in just one day at the Caledonian market.

He opened his first bank account at the Joint Stock Bank, 47 King William Street, London EC4 in 1920 and by the age of 24 had established himself as one of the most successful traders around the London markets. He thrived on the hunt for good-value stock but, just as important, he knew how to sell. He had a 'silver tongue' and a friendly humour that customers found hard to resist.

Work took up most of his waking time but his sisters had romantic plans for their bachelor brother. His eldest sister pressured him into attending a relative's wedding, where he met a young woman called Sarah Fox, the only daughter of Benjamin Fox, a master tailor who made suits for Aquascutum in a small factory off Shaftesbury Avenue. Clearly a cut above him, Sarah – Cissie to her friends – presented a challenge that Cohen could not resist. Refined as well as beautiful, Cissie danced with Jack most of the night. She had another boyfriend at the time and for a while dithered between her two suitors, but eventually he won over both her and her parents. They married on 29 January 1924.

Even the most talented businessmen make some mistakes and Cohen was no exception. Despite his years on the markets he still had a naïve streak and perhaps wedded bliss blunted his usually razor-sharp instincts. Helped by a 'dowry' of £500 from Cissie's parents, he set up a new company called the Darnley Soap Works and bought up several tons of soap, which he had already been selling successfully in smaller quantities from his stall. He advertised for travelling agents to go out and sell what he could not manage from the stall. Plenty of 'agents' replied and were given samples and payment towards initial expenses. To begin with, everything went to plan: the agents sent in their orders, the soap was dispatched. But as the weeks went by no money came back and his 'agents' mysteriously disappeared. Jack Cohen had been taken for a ride. It was a lesson that would shape the way he ran his business in the future. For years he would employ family members in senior positions where possible and would trust only close colleagues.

Help for his bruised morale and finances came shortly afterwards when he came across a firm of tea importers and blenders in Mincing Lane called Torring and Stockwell. Mr T. E. Stockwell, one of the partners, began supplying him with tea at ninepence a pound. Cohen had the idea of repackaging it into half-pound packets and selling them for sixpence each. But he needed a name to put on the packaging. He and Mr Stockwell put their heads together and came up with the name Tesco from Stockwell's initials and the first two letters of Cohen. Tesco tea became his first 'own-brand' product. So was born a brand that would become first a household name in Britain and is now seen above shop entrances in a dozen countries around the world from Hungary to Taiwan and Thailand.

One market stall soon became two and in a few years he had a network of barrows throughout the street markets of east and north London. His assault on Croydon's Surrey Street market met with some resistance from locals. Luckily a local boy, Jim Harrow, became his first non-family assistant, rising at 4 a.m. to get the trestles for the goods ready by 6 a.m.

Jim marvelled at the weird and wonderful goods Cohen would bring to the market and was dazzled by his boss's ability to sell anything. 'He got away with it – only he could … I was never able to fathom out how Jack found such a variety of goods,' he recalled. There were Russian biscuits and James Keiller jams with torn parchment tops, which Jim was told to replace with greaseproof paper held firm with an elastic band. When cornflakes arrived from Australia, he bought them in bulk and packaged them up. Trade boomed and the stall was soon turning over £200 a day. Yet Cohen still did not keep books and Jim Harrow recalled sleeping with some of the takings under his pillow the night before his wedding. His wife, Peggy, became Jack's first female employee.

In May 1927 Jack bought Cissie her first house at 7 Gunton Road in Clapton for £1,517, stretching their finances considerably. But the rising cash flow from the business enabled her to employ a nurse after she gave birth to their first child, a daughter whom they named Irene.

By this time Cohen had moved into wholesaling, supplying rival stall-holders with tea and other goods. But the good times for the costermongers were coming to an end. In 1927 the London County Council passed a licensing law so restrictive it would drive many street traders out of business. Cohen responded by concentrating on his wholesaling business and by 1930 annual takings had passed £30,000 and he had amassed capital of nearly £5,000. But even then he still kept no books. It was time to take on an accountant and he charmed a meticulous bookkeeper, Arthur Albert Carpenter, into joining him and creating order out of chaos.

The year 1930, when his second daughter Shirley was born, proved a turning point for the business. Cohen recognised he had gone as far as he could supplying and running market stalls. He had successfully bought some big consignments of goods, notably many cases of Snowflake milk, which, although perfectly good, had turned out much thicker than the makers intended. Displaying his ability to turn a negative into a positive he marketed the evaporated milk as 'Extra thick, creamy Snowflake milk. Extra thick – extra value.' The tins flew off the market stalls. As the goods from his wheeling and dealing piled up in his warehouse, Cohen realised he needed more outlets from which to sell them.

A fellow market trader approached him with the idea of opening a joint venture in the covered market in Tooting Arcade in south London. The first outlet was called Bargain Centres of London. Cohen financed most of the start-up costs and within a few years he had a chain of small shops of no more than 500 square feet in places such as Chatham in Kent and Edmonton, north London.

Then at a venture at Burnt Oak he and his partner decided to convert the store into a proper shop rather than an interior market stall. For the first time Cohen put the name Tesco above the shop. They opened another Tesco at Becontree in Essex shortly afterwards. Turnover almost doubled under the new format and Cohen started to dream of owning 100 shops. Meanwhile the finances grew ever more complex and Albert Carpenter suggested they employ a girl to help him because it would be cheaper than employing another male clerk. They put the word out.

And so, one evening at 9 p.m., Dorothy Hyams arrived at the upper Clapton warehouse for an interview. She was 18 years old and had a job at the menswear retailer Hector Powe. Straight to the point as usual, Cohen asked her how much she earned a week. The answer was £1 5s. and he instantly offered her £2 with more to come if she worked hard and well.

Although bemused by the ramshackle stockyard, she took the job and earned her new pay, checking the cash daily with Carpenter and taking it to the bank on the bus. The hours were long and she was often driven home at midnight instead of her official 7 p.m. finishing time, especially on Fridays, but she thrived on the energetic atmosphere.

Known always as Daisy, she, like her boss, had left school as soon as she could and worked for Hector Powe for three years before joining Cohen. They had a rare chemistry and worked brilliantly together for many years. She rose to become the chief buyer with a reputation for formidable bargaining and much feared by suppliers.

She and Jack trusted few others in the company apart from each other. Her office had a window that overlooked the adjoining office where her four senior buyers worked, so that she could keep an eye on them. John Gildersleeve, who became the commercial and trading director in 2003, had the window bricked up when he moved into her old office in the Cheshunt headquarters. 'The culture then was less than trusting,' he remarked drily.

By January 1932 the business had grown sufficiently for Cohen to incorporate it as a limited company at Companies House. Six years later he had virtually achieved his dream of 100 shops. To celebrate, he took his family on their first Mediterranean cruise.

In essence those stores were little more than an extension of the market stall, a format with which he felt supremely confident. They had one advantage – the rents were low, which allowed Cohen to make money if he sold enough goods fast enough.

In the 1920s and 30s and during the Second World War, Britain was at a low ebb economically and the many unemployed had little spare cash. Tesco's pile-it-high, sell-it-cheap philosophy was perfect for those times. Cohen loved his soubriquet 'the housewife's friend', and even in later years he would collar bemused customers pushing their trolleys and declare: 'I did this all for you.'

Cohen had a gut instinct when it came to spotting suitable sites. He could always sense a good deal and he gradually developed an expertise in property. In the early days it was purely instinctive. One of his favourite family outings was to take his wife and two daughters for a picnic in the Essex countryside. On the way he led them in singing old music-hall and First World War songs such as 'When Father Papered the Parlour, You Couldn't See Him for Paste'.

The picnics served a dual purpose. As the family cruised through the outer London suburbs their father would often suddenly stop the car. 'This looks like a good little place,' he would say, meaning a good place for a Tesco store. And off he would go to see if there were any vacant shops. If he found one, he would do a deal to rent it there and then.

Inevitably the conversation at mealtimes was about the business – it permeated every aspect of their lives. If he had discovered a new line on a foreign trip the family had to test market it, whether it be tins of cherries from Italy or Appetito gherkins from Holland.

To his daughters, Shirley and Irene, he was a warm, expansive father with a large presence who would amuse them with strings of jokes and sayings. When they were sent off to boarding school during the rationing years of the Second World War, he would arrive on visits laden with Fry's chocolate bars, chocolate spread and other goodies.

Just after the Second World War Cohen, like Alan Sainsbury, took a trip to the United States and saw self-service stores for the first time. He returned to England declaring himself 'flabbergasted' by the gleaming emporiums he had seen and in late 1945 he opened a small shop with limited self-service that he called a 'super market', although another eleven years passed before he opened anything that could really support the name.

Indeed, as the company grew and the decades passed, Cohen's style remained the same. There was little evidence of the rigorous controls that were being put in place by Sainsbury and the newcomers Asda, or at Garfield Weston's Fine Fare, where a young James Gulliver, who later built up Safeway, was learning his trade.

Tesco's founder dreamed of a Cohen dynasty along the lines of the Sainsbury and Marks families but he and Cissie did not produce any more children after Shirley and Irene. A man of his era, he never considered inviting either of his daughters into the company, so he tried to create his family dynasty by inviting first Hyman Kreitman, husband of Irene, and some years later Leslie Porter, who had married Shirley, onto the board. Both men were modernisers and both, as a result, found themselves locked in terrible battles with their irascible father-in-law.

The first moderniser was Kreitman, who became Cohen's right-hand man from 1946, and the larger stores and modern systems in the group were the result of his foresight. Yet despite his efforts and those of the younger blades around him such as Ian MacLaurin, the joint architect of the modern Tesco, the company was still operating many small shops, albeit converted to self-service, as late as 1977. MacLaurin, who was by then managing director, describes them in his memoir *Tiger by the Tail* with some horror. 'Those shops were a disgrace – tiny and hugely busy but with no heating and no staff facilities apart from a loo out the back and a kettle somewhere.'

While Kreitman worried about store size, distribution systems and modern methods, Cohen waged war on resale price maintenance and looked for what would grab the public's attention. What would be the next 'new new thing' in supermarkets? He saw that in America trading stamps had gone down a storm with shoppers and yet he had joined the National Association of Multiple Grocers, led by the Sainsbury chairman Mr Alan and later his son Mr JD, whose members had agreed not to use them.

But Pricerite made the decision for him, and when he was still a vigorous 65, Cohen put up a metaphorical two fingers to his rivals and signed up Tesco with Green Shield Stamps.

John Sainsbury recognised that the subsequent high-profile 'war' between Tesco and Sainsbury over stamps boosted the profits of both companies: 'It did a lot of good for us because it emphasised that [Sainsbury] were all about quality and value and straightforward honest trading.' Sainsbury retaliated by advertising far more than ever before, using his slogan 'Honest to goodness'. 'It made national news and we were seen by our core customers to be on the right side.' In taking the moral high ground in its opposition to stamps Sainsbury had logic and reason on its side, but for many people logic and reason did not prevail.

Kreitman admired his father-in-law for his instinct, flair and drive but he could see that his seat-of-the-pants way of trading could not survive in an increasingly competitive world. Yet 'Slasher Jack' held fast to his belief that low prices and low prices alone drove his business – the quality of the product was secondary. Cash flow counted, systems did not. Store managers were left much to their own devices – as long as the cash was there at the end of the week. In his autobiography, MacLaurin describes the practice of 'buncing', which enabled managers to cover any shrinkage since the last stock check – usually eight to ten weeks previously. 'It was generally accepted that they could add a halfpenny to the price of any item under a shilling; a penny on anything between one shilling and two, and whatever they could raise at anything above that.'

But as in any business where the controls are lax, the system was abused and managers began creaming off a little for themselves. 'Managers used it for their own ends making an art form of the formula, one for him and two for me,' wrote MacLaurin. According to him, one store manager was even rumoured to have built a holiday home in Spain on the proceeds. Clearly, if a store started to do noticeably badly, Cohen would strike, but as long as the figures appeared to stack up he would tolerate such pilfering.

Cohen visited his shops regularly, some would say obsessively, especially when they were new. By the mid 1950s, Tesco store openings featured bands, balloons and celebrities. In the 1960s Kreitman got his way and persuaded Cohen to build new, larger, edge-of-town stores of up to 10,000 square feet.

Cohen shared with Sam Walton, Wal-Mart's founder, and Ken Morrison the understanding that retailing is part theatre. He loved the early television comedians such as Bob Monkhouse and Sid James. In the early 1960s they appeared regularly at store openings with the PG Tips chimpanzees, who had been trained to pour tea into cups. 'I wanted to give people the excitement and thrill I felt in the street markets,' said Cohen. 'The business of opening a new supermarket is like delivering a new baby. I have the same thrill today as each store opens.'

Such razzmatazz lit up the grey post-war years, attracting crowds in such numbers the doors of the shop often had to be closed to prevent accidents.

The opening of the Leicester showpiece superstore in 1961 was just such a spectacular. Sid James had the crowd rolling in the aisles – literally – before they went hunting for bargains in the new store. Although only 8,000 square feet, at the time it was huge compared with most other supermarkets.

Cohen had no illusions about the Sainsbury family's disdain for Tesco. For his part, he thought them unbearably smug. 'It was astonishing that when we came to town they sat and smirked. They did not see the excitement we brought along with a new style of service to the modern consumer. Behind all the balloons and the hired personalities to open the store and the publicity, we had put in hours of work and research', Cohen told his biographer, carrying on in damning tones: 'Too many of our competitors were sitting smugly behind their desks, out of touch with the consumer revolution and out of training when the real scramble began for sites and price leadership.'

Prophetically he added: 'Many of our rivals seemed to think we would bite the dust. Their complacency has been to their cost.'

Much of Cohen's brilliance lay in spotting bargain stock (and flogging it) and at finding good retailing sites, but he also had a wonderful eye for people. Spotting the talents of the teenage Daisy Hyams had been a coup, but just as important for the future of the group was the recruitment of Ian MacLaurin as his first 'graduate trainee'.

They met in 1959 at the Grand Hotel in Eastbourne. MacLaurin's version is that he had been playing cricket with an Old Malvernian XI and was having a drink in the bar before dinner. 'This stranger in evening dress drifted up and handed round his card, saying, "If any of you chaps ever want a job, just give me a call",' MacLaurin recounts. It was typical of Cohen's chutzpah.

MacLaurin knew of Cohen and the boardroom rows at Tesco through his father-in-law, Edgar Collar, who at the time was deputy chairman of the company. MacLaurin was a nice middle-class boy whose parents had professional ambitions for him, but he was intrigued by the tactics of this legendary entrepreneur who cared so little for convention. According to MacLaurin, Collar tried to warn him off: 'I don't want you even to think about joining the company. I have had so much of the Cohen family, I don't want any of my prospective family coming into the business.'

Yet, to his mother's dismay, he made that call and ended up in Cohen's office for a 'formal interview'. The conversation went much as the one with Daisy had. 'How much do you earn?' followed by the offer of a small increase on that – with more to come if things worked out. MacLaurin emerged with a starting salary of £900 with the promise of £1,000 a year and a company car in six months if, said Cohen, 'I like you and you like me'.

Some of those close to the Cohen family remember events rather differently. 'Ian MacLaurin got given a job at Tesco partly because Edgar Collar was his father-in-law,' said one family friend. It seems likely that the Eastbourne incident happened just the way MacLaurin described it but that, in fact, Cohen knew only too well the young man's relationship to his deputy chairman.

Whatever the origins, MacLaurin joined the board in 1972, became managing director in 1973 and executive chairman in 1985, before retiring and handing over the executive reins to Terry Leahy in 1997. Recruiting MacLaurin was a great example of Cohen's intuitive genius. Although he often fought the modernisation of the company, and particularly fought MacLaurin over the end of his beloved Green Shield Stamps in 1978, it was as if Cohen recognised that a different kind of person would be needed to take the company forward, even if he personally had to be dragged kicking and screaming into the future.

If Cohen selected well, he also commanded great loyalty among his staff as well as considerable fear. John Gildersleeve recalled working all night as a young manager to get the shelves filled by the Saturday morning when he was due to visit. 'The old man turned up with Daisy in his Rolls-Royce followed by an entourage of Jaguars. I was absolutely shattered by that time and I explained why I wasn't looking my very best but he didn't mind because the shop was heaving. Nothing pleased the old man more than taking money.'

Then Gildersleeve remarked to Cohen that the shop needed to be bigger. 'So he said, "I'll go and ask the man next door if he'll sell me his greengrocer's shop." And he did and the deal was done more or less then and there. So I got my bigger shop although it still wasn't very big.'

Cohen's trading skills ensured his stores were never short of product, although their provenance might sometimes be open to doubt. MacLaurin recalled Cohen producing some particularly doubtful 'plums'. 'The Governor, who could never resist a deal, once bought 100,000 cases of something called "gambos". The tins themselves certainly looked irresistible ... decorated with a plummy sort of thing … So in 200 stores they were stocked in the tinned-fruit section. By Monday morning,' recalled MacLaurin, 'we'd learned how wrong we had been. Gambos, it appeared, were a variety of seeded red pepper, which was how Jack's impetuosity came to ruin the delight of so many families' Sunday lunch.' Why nobody thought to open a tin and taste the contents before putting them on the shelves remains a mystery.

Another classic Cohen deal was a consignment of Flying Bird Danish cream from a half-sunken ship. The tins were dispatched to the shops with the instruction: 'Take off the labels, get a tin of Duraglit to clean off the rust and sell these for 2d. a tin.' They flew off the shelves.

Cohen built up Tesco trading out of small, ill-equipped shops – some no bigger than the early Sainsbury shops in Kentish Town – paying staff as little as possible and trading on paper-thin margins. Indeed in later years some journalists got the impression that both MacLaurin and his successor, Terry Leahy, would have liked to have airbrushed Cohen and his sons-in-law out of the history of Tesco. At one point, they even considered changing the name, in pursuit of throwing off the old Tesco image.

The founder's brand of instinctive, seat-of-the-pants trading may sit ill with the modern image of Tesco, professional to its fingertips, yet without him, the Tesco of today would not exist. Everyone who met him remembered his dominating vitality, his shrewd deal-doing and his Cockney wit. 'He was a people person,' said his daughter Shirley. 'He was touchy, feely and people just warmed to him.'

'You can't do business sitting on your arse' was one of his favourite sayings, so much so that he had the initials YCDBSOYA engraved on to tiepins, which he would give away to anyone he took a fancy to, including journalists.

The presence of Cohen, Kreitman and Porter in the boardroom was a combustible mixture. Cohen's combative style meant he argued ferociously with both his sons-in-law, occasionally even coming to blows with Leslie, who gave as good as he got. Kreitman, a thoughtful and measured character, regarded himself as a modern businessman. He could see that bigger stores would be necessary in the future and pushed through as many as he could. He also realised the potential of modern sophisticated systems powered by computers. Cohen, in later life, fought the future and disliked technology – 'I don't need a computer to tell me how much money is coming in' – along with modern management methods. Despite their differences – Kreitman resigned for the first time in 1960, though he later returned – Cohen and he worked together for twenty-five years. But as old age made Cohen increasingly unreasonable the relationship finally broke down and Kreitman retired for good in 1973 to step up his work supporting Israel and the Tate Gallery.

Through all the rows, Daisy Hyams continued to mastermind the buying, becoming managing director of Tesco (Wholesale) in 1965 and a main board director in 1969. A legend in her own right, she earned a reputation as the toughest buyer in the industry. 'Daisy revolutionised buying in Britain,' said one supplier. 'She showed that if you buy well, you make money. That is why Jack rated her so highly.'

Daisy Hyams also pioneered Tesco's own-label products. Although Sainsbury was the first to tread the own-label path – a more sotto voce blow in the war against the branded manufacturers – Tesco was not far behind. Cohen, however, chose not food as the weapon, but detergent. This was news: 'Jack Cohen intends to sell his own brand of washing powder in competition with the brands of Unilever and Procter & Gamble,' *The Times* informed its readers.

Daisy was famously loyal to Jack despite being underpaid compared with the men in the business. When MacLaurin joined the board he was surprised to discover that she was earning £5,000 a year while he received £7,500. When he tackled Cohen about this discrepancy he waved it aside. 'Oh, she's married, she doesn't need the money.' It showed how Cohen was stuck in the past.

As he grew older and suffered ill health, he became increasingly intolerant of new ideas, fearing the erosion of his power. Cohen was one of those entrepreneurs who found it hard to change his ways. A tyrannical control freak, he fought Tesco directors who told him the world was moving on, that something more sophisticated than gut feeling was needed to run a major business. Yet when they pulled something off, such as the success of increasing the number of bigger stores, he was thrilled.

On the surface the business appeared to be thriving and City investors adored him. Cohen loved to snap up companies as well as groceries. He expanded fast by buying up the smaller operators. In his City dealings he was in tune with the times – the heady bull market of the 1960s spawned the first post-war round of 'merger mania'. Food retailing was highly fragmented at the time and Cohen set about consolidating it. He embarked on a takeover trail with the approval of the City institutions who liked his strong personality and entrepreneurial style, not to mention the flow of rising profits the company generated. Journalists also liked him. He drove a Rolls-Royce, enjoyed horse racing and mixing with celebrities – and he was not too proud to talk to the press. Indeed, he was shrewd enough to understand how media coverage could help him win investor support for his deals, and his friendliness paid off. The business pages of the day were full of positive articles.

Cohen's personal popularity made it easy for Tesco to raise money for expansion from the City when it was needed. Even when in 1967 the group announced an £8.75m rights issue – asking existing investors to buy more shares at a discount to the existing share price – the coverage was relentlessly upbeat. 'There is no stopping Jack Cohen and Tesco supermarkets', wrote *The Times* business reporters. 'Always near the top of the list of a growth portfolio (in spite of warnings that the group has or is about to run out of steam), the board is now proposing a 1-for-20 rights issue at 15 shillings a share.'

Every acquisition received acclaim. Tesco bought both Irwins of Liverpool and Adsega, and Cohen even leaked his dream of bidding for a chain called Elmo Stores to *The Times*, which trumpeted the news. (In the end Tesco was outbid for Elmo by Fine Fare.) But his biggest leap forward was the acquisition of Victor Value in 1968 for £8.5m – his grandest transaction by a mile.

Cohen had been stalking Victor Value for several years. He and Victor Value's chairman Alex Cohen (no relation) had a series of clandestine meetings that had almost resulted in an agreed merger. But at the last moment Alex Cohen had pressed for total management control, and Jack Cohen pulled back.

But by 1967 Victor Value's profits were falling and the group could not even pay a dividend. Other predators began to circle, including Pricerite, Great Universal Stores and Fine Fare, where James Gulliver was keen to expand.

More clandestine talks – in a lay-by – were arranged between Hyman Kreitman and Alex Cohen's son Neville. The board deliberated – it was a big acquisition that might prove hard to digest. Kreitman could see the property potential of the shops and Leslie Porter envisaged a lot more space for his new Home 'n' Wear ranges of household linen, crockery and cookware. The risk-taking culture of Tesco won out and a deal was struck with the Victor Value board, which owned 54 per cent of the company between them. There was little the other shareholders could do but accept.

The smaller group added 280 stores and £45m of sales to Tesco, bringing the total number of self-service stores to 834. Tesco was now in fourth place (measured by number of shops) behind the Co-op, Fine Fare and Allied Suppliers, which boasted more than a thousand outlets.

As some had feared, Victor Value proved almost a deal too far. In the previous ten years Tesco had doubled in size and there was no strategy to merge the different cultures of the various acquisitions. It fell to MacLaurin to make sense of it all when Cohen promoted him to regional managing director that year. According to MacLaurin it took him eighteen months working fifteen-hour days to create some cohesion.

By the late 1960s the Tesco board was riven with family disputes. Kreitman succeeded in closing many small stores and opening up new and larger ones, sometimes without even asking Cohen in advance. But he had to fight at board level for plans to develop a big modern warehousing facility at Cheshunt in Hertfordshire. He won, but Cohen remained opposed.

Kreitman was the antithesis of Cohen. Described by Cohen's biographer Maurice Corina as a 'large, pipe-smoking enigmatic man – creative and cultured, courteous and calm', Kreitman rarely chose to confront Cohen in public, but he could not have been more different in outlook. Unlike his father-in-law he had been born into privilege as the youngest son of one of London's leading shoe manufacturers. Educated at Cordwainers College, a training ground for the shoe industry, he then served in the Royal Artillery during the Second World War.

Kreitman had met Cohen's elder daughter Irene after a riding accident while staying at the Selsdon Park Hotel in Surrey. Irene had also been staying there with her parents and tended him while he was recovering. They fell passionately in love and were married later that year. Cohen soon invited him to join Tesco, promoting him swiftly to become joint managing director.

Those halcyon days had long passed by the time Cohen reached his seventieth birthday showing no sign of wanting to relinquish the chairmanship. The arguments with Kreitman grew ever more bitter, and they did what board directors often do when they reach stalemate: they called in a firm of consultants.

The chosen arbiters were McKinsey, the alma mater of both Archie Norman, who was to revitalise Asda, and Roger Holmes, who attempted the same trick at Marks & Spencer. The team that did the assessment did not take long to reach the conclusion that 'The board should exercise more self-discipline in interpreting its role and conducting its meetings.' More important, they recommended that Sir Jack Cohen, founder of the company and chairman for the previous twenty-eight years, retire to be replaced by Kreitman.

The McKinsey findings enabled Kreitman to reshuffle the board and 'elevate' Cohen to the post of life president. Cohen was under no illusion as to what that meant and phoned up Brian Basham, a friendly journalist on *The Times*. ''Ere, they've fired me.' 'What?' gasped an incredulous Basham. 'Yes, we've had McKinsey's in and they've sacked me.' Even on the record he was disarmingly honest. 'It was quite a shock when the management consultants decided I should go as senior executive,' he told Basham, who rewarded him for the scoop with a glowing tribute.

But if the new chairman thought that was the last he would see of Jack Cohen in the business, he was mistaken. Cohen kept his office, went in nearly every day and insisted on attending all board meetings, sitting at the head of the table. In one desperate ploy, the directors moved the meeting to 7.30 a.m. without telling him only to find him waiting in the boardroom as usual when they arrived. 'You're late,' he said with a satisfied smile, tapping his watch. Other times he would arrive after the meeting had started and Kreitman would have to vacate his seat. Kreitman may have been in the forefront of modern business methods but he was no match for Cohen when it came to psychological warfare.

When Ian MacLaurin joined the board in 1971 he was amazed at the way board meetings were conducted. 'It really was an extraordinary set-up, like a meeting of the Chicago mafia, with Jack in the role of the Godfather, all the while scheming to curb Hyman's power.'

Leslie Porter had joined the board by that time. Kreitman felt in desperate need of support on the board and, ten years after he had married Shirley, Leslie Porter finally agreed against his better judgement to become a director. 'It will be easier to handle our father-in-law if there's two of us working together with him,' said Kreitman. Porter was unafraid of a good argument with Cohen and the boardroom rows grew ever louder. But Porter proved himself much more than a mere foil for Cohen. He introduced non-food items into Tesco for the first time, using the tag Home 'n' Wear. Today Tesco's strength in selling a vast range of products from children's pyjamas to TV sets has become the engine of its growth.

It all began with tea towels. Porter ran a small household-textile business started by his father. In his memoir, *Life According to Leslie* (2003), he set out the story:

'One morning I called my father-in-law and suggested he introduce a line of tea towels. "When you come round Friday, you can bring me a few bundles," he replied … On Saturday he took about twelve of these bundles to the different branches and asked the managers to call Daisy Hyams and tell her if the tea towels were selling. The following Monday my phone rang. Daisy was on the line. "How many tea towels have you got?" she asked. "About ten thousand dozen," I replied. "Send them all in," she said. And that was how I introduced non-food products to Tesco.'

As Porter gained in influence Cohen agreed to let him expand into small items of furniture and other household items. An in-house competition produced the name Home 'n' Wear, possibly the first time 'n' had ever been used in retail marketing this side of the Atlantic.

When Kreitman resigned in 1973 having spent twenty-five years attempting to instil some discipline into the company, he was a defeated man. Cohen was jubilant, believing that in Porter he had found his true successor.

He was right. Before Porter's chairmanship the Tesco philosophy had been that of a wholesaler rather than a retailer. David Malpas, the strategist and thinker in MacLaurin's regime, credited Porter with turning Tesco into a true retailer.

'Jack Cohen had founded a wholesale business, even though he was essentially wholesaling to his own retail outlets. The shops were seen as an appendage to the buying/distribution business. Even up to the early 1980s invoices were sent out to suppliers from 'JE Cohen (Wholesale) Ltd', said Malpas. 'Sir Leslie's philosophy was "what does the customer want?" – a market-led approach, rather than "what can we sell?"'

The last years under his father-in-law had become a chase after gross margin – the company had lost its way in the search for profit and a blizzard of property deals. Porter's approach – spotting consumer trends and riding with them – was different from Jack Cohen's tactics and represented a huge change for the company. Under Porter, the customer came first.

While building up the non-food side of the business Porter recruited Raymond Turner from a drapery shop in Kilburn, persuading him to manage a new prototype store on the outskirts of Leicester where, said Porter, 'they would sell everything at discounted prices'. Turner's initial reaction was that Porter was crazy – 'nobody would come to this Godforsaken place'. Nevertheless he accepted the challenge. 'Some months later on opening day,' Turner later recalled, 'the crowds had to be controlled by the police. The fact that we were undercutting other stores hit all the newspaper headlines – some of the publicity was not exactly complimentary, but Sir Leslie assured me, saying, "Raymond, don't worry, we could never afford to buy front-page publicity in all the nationals – let it run."'

An energetic trader, Porter was flamboyant and amiable unless provoked – and nobody provoked him like Cohen. On one occasion, so MacLaurin recounts, the pair grabbed the Wilkinson swords that decorated the boardroom wall and started to duel. 'One more crack like that and I'll kill him,' yelled Cohen.

At 76, Cohen's age began to tell he became even more vindictive, growing increasingly jealous of Porter's power. On one hair-raising occasion Cohen actually began punching Porter while he was driving his Rolls-Royce. Five directors including MacLaurin had been to a lunch at Unilever, where Porter had been presented with a carriage clock. So jealous was Cohen that afterwards, sitting in the front seat next to Porter, he suddenly exploded. 'You are nothing but a thief and a crook,' he cried, and he hit him on the shoulder. The second time Porter hit back and, with the car veering all over the A3, Cohen opened the passenger door, shouting, 'I know when I'm not wanted.' Luckily Porter was able to pull over and avert disaster.

Such stories show how Cohen found difficulty in moving on. He desperately wanted, as had Sainsbury and the Marks & Spencer founders, to keep the business in the family, but he had no sons. Bringing in both his sons-in-law was not quite the same. Divide and rule was the order of the day and the result was mayhem.

Cohen may have revelled in the cut and thrust of bitter debate but he rarely carried arguments over to the next day. 'You could not help but love him,' recalled MacLaurin. 'We would have the most ferocious rows during the day, but he'd always come into my office before going home and say: "Goodnight, Ian. Tomorrow's another day."'

By the early 1970s Tesco's profits had begun to reflect the turmoil within the company. The novelty of trading stamps had worn thin and customers were tired of the mostly tatty, badly run shops. Increasingly there was somewhere more pleasant to go – Sainsbury, Safeway or even one of the smaller groups such as Budgens.

Customers wanted better all-round value – a combination of price and quality. Inflation was rising and the price of goods in the shops mattered more than sticking stamps in books. At the same time Tesco had split the management between the north and the south of England, a dangerous move that created two fiefdoms.

By then Asda, which had been created by the Associated Dairies group in the north of England, was beginning to build superstores on the edges of towns, a move that many food retailers dismissed as being unsuitable for the British market.

Tesco's northern managing director Jim Grundy joined in the ridicule, reinforcing Cohen's own opinion. He still felt more comfortable in stores of less than 4,000 square feet. Grundy reported back to London that the larger stores were nothing but an aberration and that to copy them would only 'put an economic rope around our necks'.

Such an ostrich-like attitude only made matters worse. In 1974 Tesco's half-year profits dropped unexpectedly by 20 per cent and the City pundits began to waver. Articles were written questioning Tesco's ability to survive. After a second fall at the year end the City institutions, which had suffered the worst bear market in shares since the 1930s, fell out of love with the group and the shares began to tumble. Increasingly Tesco was being written off as poorly managed and downmarket.

MacLaurin came to the rescue, taking on Grundy's job in the north and effecting such a turnround that he was made managing director of the whole group. Behind the scenes he had recruited a band of bright young men around him. They included Colin Goodfellow, who had worked as a butcher's boy at the start of his career, and Mike Darnell, whom MacLaurin poached from Key Markets. Most significantly he signed up David Malpas, a Liverpool University graduate who, with his pipe and impressive intellect, became known as the brains of the MacLaurin era.

MacLaurin and Malpas became one of those complementary partnerships that sweep companies to greatness. Contemporaries of MacLaurin say that although he was not an intellectual, he was a formidable operator. Malpas, on the other hand, was much more of a thinker and an introvert. He would come up with the ideas and the strategy; MacLaurin would make it happen.

MacLaurin knew how to lead. Like so many other successful business people, he had honed his natural leadership skills on the school sports field. He seemed to know instinctively how to lift people's spirits. He turned store visits into performance art. Before he arrived, he would know the names not just of the store manager and his deputy but of several of the checkout girls and floor staff. He had a talent for remembering whether they had children, or a mother in hospital.

He created a powerful esprit de corps through the use of sport at Tesco that still exists today. At Malvern he had captained the school cricket team and later played for Kent. He had also played football for the Chelsea Combination XI. In later years he became a keen golfer, inspiring him to organise golfing weekends with senior management. He used the same ploy to draw closer to his suppliers, hosting similar weekends for them in Valderrama in Spain complete with professional instructors.

All this helped him to do what seemed impossible, to galvanise his managers into taking the old low-price, low-quality Tesco and refashioning it as a supermarket group on a par with Sainsbury. It took dedication, time and effort and in the process he shamelessly copied his main rival. Taking a downmarket product up market is arguably the most difficult task in business. This challenge led to an agonising discussion about whether the company should abandon the name Tesco. Ultimately, it was decided that the positive messages the name conjured outweighed the negative.

The MacLaurin/Malpas axis began to bear fruit as early as 1975 when profits hit £23m, rising to £25m the following year. Yet the duo realised that more radical action was needed.

MacLaurin and his team were clear that Green Shield Stamps, which were by then costing £20m a year for no appreciable increase in trade, had to go. Cohen remained emotionally wedded to them and despite his ill health and lack of executive power, he was still the company's founder and a force with which to be reckoned. But MacLaurin did his research. His supermarket contacts in America told him stamps were yesterday's news, yet that was nothing like enough to convince Cohen. Meanwhile Tesco House began to leak like a sieve and rumours flew that the company was on the brink of abandoning stamps. MacLaurin admits that 'by the spring of 1977 we were actively involved in a campaign of disinformation, which led Elinor Goodman, then retail correspondent of the *Financial Times*, to speculate: 'Few people expect Tesco to abandon stamps altogether. A more likely course of action would be for the company to renegotiate a new contract which would allow it to dispense with stamps in situations where they are seen not to help trade.'

She was partly right. Cohen was attempting to cut a new deal with Richard Tompkins at Green Shield. But at the same time MacLaurin had been test marketing deep discounting in a few of the Midlands stores. The results were conclusive: customers wanted cheap prices. Stamps had become an irritating irrelevance in that inflationary era. Even so, Leslie Porter and the older Tesco directors loyal to Cohen wavered. An advertising agency, McCann Erickson, was engaged to research customers' views. Their results confirmed that Green Shield Stamps were past their sell-by date.

Finally, MacLaurin took the decision to put the proposal to ditch trading stamps to a full board meeting. The vote in favour was close, and Cohen tried four times to reverse it, but in the end he had to concede defeat.

MacLaurin and the four directors who had voted with him now had a vacuum to fill. If Tesco was to abandon stamps, it had to give the customer something else. The Tesco image was a long way downmarket and the products were no longer particularly good value when compared with the competition. Tesco had to be relaunched. MacLaurin's fizzy team of new, bright boys decided on a campaign that would offer discounts on key products. McCann Erickson came up with the slogan 'Operation Checkout'.

On 8 May 1977 Richard Tompkins, the chairman of Green Shield Stamps, received a letter from Leslie Porter terminating his lucrative contract with Tesco. He reacted immediately by claiming Tesco was bound for a year – but in fact the small print of the contract stated it was only a month. The next day Tesco took full-page advertisements in the *Daily Mirror, Daily Express, Daily Mail* and the *Sun* announcing an end to Green Shield Stamps and heralding a new dawn. The ad included a statement from Jack Cohen. Like the showman he was, despite his misgivings he made it look as though it was his own idea. 'Tesco has always done what its customers want. That's why we are going to change our trading policies', he declared.

In that short statement he enshrined both the old and new philosophies of the company. In the early days Jack Cohen was the 'housewife's friend' with arrays of bargains; then trading stamps with their rewards of consumer products appealed to the emerging aspirant shoppers of the 1960s. He hung on too long, but fortunately for Tesco, MacLaurin and Malpas had the courage to push for what customers of the 1970s wanted.

By 1977 Tesco's profits and market share were both just ahead of Sainsbury's. Relinquishing stamps released around 2 per cent of turnover – or £20m – with which to change the whole look of the stores and orchestrate a price-cutting campaign. Daisy Hyams got the job of working out on just which items to cut prices for the greatest effect.

Market research showed that Tesco's reputation for low prices was better than the reality, while the quality of goods was actually better than its reputation. Much of the 'cheap and nasty' image came from the small cluttered shops rather than the products they sold. MacLaurin and Malpas seized the opportunity. 'This was a marketing gap that was to provide the platform for the re-launch of Tesco: to refine our image whilst discounting on prices,' wrote MacLaurin. In other words they would lower prices at the same time as improving the look and feel of the stores.

MacLaurin knew that for such a sea change in policy to succeed he had to convince all the staff that the repositioning was the right course. In his early days Cohen had been an inspirational 'on the hoof' communicator but latterly the staff had felt excluded and morale was at rock bottom. Staff turnover was in 1977 running at 180 per cent. But with only weeks to go until the biggest switch in trading policy in the company's history, MacLaurin needed to carry the staff with him. He summoned 250 top managers to the Cheshunt headquarters and set out a three-point plan that aimed:

1. To increase Tesco's sales and market share.
2. To generate customer loyalty.
3. Most important of all, and most difficult, to reposition the company and transform Tesco's image.

He and Malpas spent the next week travelling the country selling the aggressive new strategy to staff in every sizeable store. That done, they took a small group to the United States to find out how American supermarkets that had dropped stamps had managed the switch. They visited Giant in Washington and Stop and Shop in Boston, where the manager revealed how all the display windows had been whitewashed the day before the change-over – a device that appealed to MacLaurin's sense of theatre.

The launch date was initially set for Wednesday, 8 June 1977, three days after the Queen's Silver Jubilee celebrations. On the preceding Saturday night all Tesco's shops were closed and the windows whitewashed so that the competition and the public could not see what was happening, creating an atmosphere of intrigue and mystery.

Tesco let it be known that the shops would reopen on the Wednesday with a price-cutting campaign. Sainsbury and the smaller chains responded by advertising their price cuts on the Tuesday and Wednesday. But Tesco outsmarted them by delaying the relaunch by one day so that their rivals' advertising lost its power. Teams of Tesco staff worked through three days and four nights to 'remerchandise' the stores and change the prices on individual products – an arduous task before electronic pricing.

For MacLaurin, the run-up to the launch was hectic and fraught. What if he had got it wrong? Cohen would be unforgiving. He knew that his job and possibly those of his close colleagues who had pushed the vote through would be on the line. His fears proved groundless.

So much excitement was generated that when the doors of Tesco's 1,000 or so stores were thrown open on the Thursday morning the staff were almost mown down by the throng. Inside, customers found a new look. Gone were the brash Day-Glo posters and Green Shield advertising. In its place was business-like red and white signage and posters everywhere announcing Operation Checkout.

Once again Tesco took full-page advertisements in the press displaying the best of the price cuts and backed this up with a television campaign. Heinz baked beans and Chivers marmalade, both at half price, were two of the more spectacular offers. When Cohen saw the uplift in sales he was once again happy to take the credit. 'He was thrilled at the upturn in trading,' recalls MacLaurin. 'The money came rolling in and he loved it.'

Two years later, when he was seriously ill, Cohen planned a surprise visit to a big new store at Pitsea in Essex, but his chauffeur alerted MacLaurin. The store manager and MacLaurin were ready to greet the old man when he arrived and after a triumphal tour of the store in his wheelchair, where hosts of customers came up to shake his hand, he asked to go up in the lift and be pushed onto the balcony overlooking the shop floor.

'How long we were there, I can't say,' wrote MacLaurin. 'All that I do know is that when I finally turned to him, there were tears rolling down his cheeks. I said, "Are you all right, Governor?" and almost inaudibly he replied, "I never imagined that this was how it would be." ... The following day, the Governor died.'

Operation Checkout was to kick-start a new-style Tesco on the way to the top of the supermarket league, not just in sales, but also in public perception.

CHAPTER FOUR

THE NORTHERN WARS

'Oh wherefore come ye forth, in triumph from the north?'

Thomas Babington Macaulay

If one single factor facilitated the rise of the supermarket as we know it today, it was the motorcar. By 1961 there were 6.2m cars in use in the UK – one for every ten people. By 1971 the number had risen to 11.5m and in 2004 there were 25m cars registered. The desire of newly mobile families to drive to the supermarket for the novelty of a 'one-stop shop' gave the new boys on the block, Asda and William Morrison, a head start.

In the north of England these two youthful companies were able to leapfrog the development from small high-street shops to 30,000-square-foot or even larger stores, with car parking and petrol stations. Both Asda, originally a part of Associated Dairies, and Morrison, the relatively small but beautifully profitable acquirer of Safeway, started supermarket businesses in the mid 1960s. Unlike Sainsbury and Tesco, they never had to carry the burden of a portfolio of high-street stores.

Asda sprang from the brains of two men: Noel Stockdale, the vice-chairman of Associated Dairies, and Peter Asquith, an entrepreneurial butcher. In the early 1960s Asquith and his brother Fred had set up a small butcher's shop in Pontefract. When they sold it they made enough money to convert a cinema in Castleford into a food store where they offered a wide range of groceries as well as meat.

But although they were experienced butchers, as well as great characters with natural retailing flair, they soon realised they could not expand into chilled and frozen foods without significant capital. They also recognised their lack of experience at running large stores.

They looked around for a richer and wiser partner and, after a number of rejections, struck lucky with Associated Dairies. From their first meeting Noel Stockdale and Peter Asquith hit it off and in 1965 they formed a joint company called Asda Stores Ltd.

Not only were they a good combination, they were also lucky. The abolition of resale price maintenance in 1964 had come just at the right time, while the opportunity to purchase two superstores for a song gave them an early introduction to mixing food and non-food under the same roof.

The story goes that Peter Asquith discovered the attractions of price discounting early on in his Pontefract store when a cut-price promotion brought the customers flooding in as never before. The experience turned him into a northern Jack Cohen with his eyes set on volume rather than margin. 'Nothing we sell will be at full, normally expected prices. Our aim is to sell as much as possible at a smaller profit margin, rather than a little bit at a large profit', stated an early company report. It was a wordier way of saying, 'Pile it high and sell it cheap'.

But unlike Cohen, Asquith and Stockdale, who had become chairman of the new company, quickly saw the virtue of big spaces. Again fortune played into their hands when an American company called Gem International put up for sale its only two British stores, a 70,000-square-foot purpose-built emporium in Nottingham and another two-storey building in Leeds. Only part of the stores was devoted to food as the rest of the space was rented to franchisees selling everything from fashions to pharmacy. But the food and non-food experiment had proved a disaster for the American management, who had believed retailing would be much the same on both sides of the Atlantic. According to Andrew Seth and Geoffrey Randall, the authors of *The Grocers*, the venture was running at a loss of more than £300,000 and they wanted an exit. When Stockdale and Asquith visited the Nottingham store for the first time they saw 'almost as many staff as customers' and grocery takings were just £6,000 a week.

Asquith told Stockdale he could boost the food takings to £25,000 a week and tax concessions meant that effectively they acquired the stores for next to nothing. Within weeks the customers came pouring in. The success of those two stores formed the basis for Asda's philosophy of selling cut-price branded goods in a big space. From then on they never opened any store smaller than 30,000 square feet.

The franchisees selling non-food were gradually phased out, but as they disappeared Asda developed its own expertise in selling clothing, electrical items and books, mirroring what Tesco was doing in the south. It also put petrol stations alongside the stores.

The combined talents of Stockdale and the Asquith brothers proved an almost instant success in a largely industrialised region starved of variety and bargains. The people of north-east England rushed to shop at the stores with such enthusiasm that at times the crowds had to be held back and customers allowed in a few at a time. The Leeds store, which ironically they had not really wanted, became the headquarters of Asda. The Asquiths were soon snapping up sites, taking big premises such as cinemas and factories and changing their use. For a few years they had the concept to themselves as the competition was wary of such large spaces and tied in to their existing leases, which were still mainly on the high street. 'We had a seven-year start,' said Stockdale later.

Fate had put the Gem stores in their way and, having found a formula that worked, they had a rich parent in Associated Dairies prepared to fund rapid expansion. Asda also strengthened the management team by recruiting the talented Peter Firmston-Williams from Key Markets. For the next ten years Asda powered ahead, building its portfolio to more than a hundred stores and floating on the London stock market in 1978. The City was impressed and by 1980 the company boasted a higher price–earnings ratio – the main stock market measure of a company's likely progress – than Sainsbury.

The 1980s was boom time for retailing with relatively little pressure on prices. Sainsbury and Tesco made great strides forward, investing not just in stores but also in depots, transport networks and computer systems.

But in 1980, when Asda's able chief executive Firmston-Williams retired, Noel Stockdale and his fellow directors chose an ineffective successor. Perhaps there was a shortage of suitable candidates or a reluctance to poach from within the supermarket sector, but John Fletcher, the man they chose to replace him in 1981, proved to be a man more of form than substance. He had risen to the senior ranks at Warburton, the bakery company, but had then taken time out to study at Harvard Business School. Charming, bright and arrogant, he believed that all he had to do was to continue doing what had worked before and all would be well. Hence he continued buying stores (probably a good decision) but he held back from producing own-label products in the way that Sainsbury and Tesco were doing (certainly a bad decision).

Fletcher's eye appeared to be on the glory of expansion into the more prosperous south and boosting short-term profits by cutting investment and raising prices.

He began to antagonise his boardroom colleagues by either making big decisions such as cancelling the purchase of two sites without their knowledge, or simply steamrollering his policies through.

While profits continued to increase along with the Asda share price, it was hard for the rest of the board to convince Fletcher that his strategy was flawed. The warning sign was the rise in profit margins to a level far above those of the competition. In 1984 Asda's margins – return on sales – were approaching 6 per cent compared with less than 5 per cent at Sainsbury and 3 per cent at Tesco.

Stockdale finally became suspicious and put his finance director on the case. After some detective work in the stores he discovered that Asda's food prices had been quietly rising and were fast approaching an uncompetitive level. In future years both John Sainsbury in the 1980s and Sir Richard Greenbury when he was Marks & Spencer chairman in the 1990s became too ambitious, fixing their eyes on short-term profits and raising margins rather than keeping margins level and prices competitive to help boost sales. As happened with Asda, when customers started to notice they began drifting away. Under pressure from the institutions, the board asked Fletcher to resign in 1984, but Stockdale failed to stop the rot.

In 1985 not only did Asda have the highest margins in the business at six per cent, but also return on capital employed had risen to 32 per cent compared with 25 per cent at Sainsbury and 21 per cent at Tesco and it soared to 41 per cent in 1986. Any business student will know that such figures meant that either there was simply not enough capital being invested, or that the prices of goods were unsustainably high. In Asda's case it was a bit of both and in the way that cartoon characters continue running in midair before noticing there is nothing underneath, so did Asda's profits. And, like Wile E. Coyote, Asda fell to earth with an almighty bump.

The rot could have been stopped if a strong, modern-minded chief executive had been appointed but Stockdale promoted the finance director John Hardman to the post. Like his predecessor, Fletcher, Hardman suffered from grandiosity and enjoyed the perks of life at the top. He loved to use the company jet, particularly for corporate entertaining of suppliers on golfing parties to Spain and other such frolics. Such lavish spending may be condoned if the profits and the share price are heading upwards, but not when a company is in trouble.

Even Stockdale felt that Hardman was not the right man to take over from him as chairman and so he looked outside for a strong leader. His eye fell on Derek Hunt, a former policeman running the flat-pack furniture retailer MFI who also enjoyed a colourful lifestyle. The City thinker behind the deal was Gerald Horner at the stockbroker Scrimgeour Kemp Gee, later subsumed into Citigroup. His fertile imagination and persuasive manner made him a star mergers-and-acquisitions fee generator, and he came up with the idea of putting the two companies together. (Horner also dreamed up the merger between the retailers Burton Group and Debenhams.)

Morgan Grenfell advised Asda while David Reed, who headed the corporate-finance division at County Bank, advised MFI. County had made its name advising fast-growing, non-establishment entrepreneurs and Reed took the ball and ran with it. These were heady days for mergers and acquisitions. The stock market was riding high and 'merger mania' was in full flow. Reed later recalled having dinner with Derek Hunt at the County offices in Old Broad Street. When Hunt told him about a call he had received from Stockdale, but had not yet returned, Reed exclaimed: 'I bet he wants you to merge with Asda' – and so the next day it proved.

Horner convinced Stockdale and Hunt that, together, the two floundering companies would be stronger. Just as important for Stockdale, he felt Hunt was capable of leading Asda out of the mire into which it had sunk.

On the surface the commercial logic of putting the two groups together looked just about plausible to uncritical eyes. Asda had bought some furniture stores in its early days and by the mid 1980s it owned Allied Carpets, Wades and Ukay. These chains were, according to the official view, a second source of growth now that big supermarket sites were hard to acquire because of tighter planning regulations. The unofficial view was that nobody knew how to get rid of them.

Like Asda, MFI had large sites and aimed at the lower end of the market – the aspiring blue-collar workers, or CDs, in socio-economic grouping parlance. So the merger with MFI was not without some spurious synergy, although even amid the hype one analyst described it as 'a merger of the challenged'.

The mistake was to keep Hardman in place as chief executive of the merged businesses. In the same year as the ill-fated union he announced a new management plan to reposition the business, which in essence involved throwing money at the problems. The first step was to open more stores, mainly in the south of England. The second was to introduce an own-label range – rather late in the day. The third was to install a new distribution system. The fourth was to redesign the stores. All this was extremely costly – each store refurbishment came in at between £2m and £4m – and the company, with its many-layered management structure, became weighed down by costs.

The new distribution system, though necessary, suffered many teething problems – just as the new distribution system at Sainsbury did more than a decade later. One or two of these ideas on their own would have been sound, but Hardman attempted to push through all four at once. As if that was not enough, seduced once again by the takeover frenzy of the mid 1980s Hardman made another acquisition – sixty Gateway superstores for £704.3m – an amazing price by anyone's standards. As a result, Asda's debts piled up although ironically those stores would later prove crucial to Asda's recovery.

According to insiders, Hunt and Hardman fell out almost immediately. 'It didn't take Derek long to realise he had made a terrible mistake,' said one adviser, and the group demerged in 1987. 'It was an extremely costly exercise in trying to find a new leader,' said the same source. 'The companies were like two drunks leaning against each other for support.'

But Asda's problems were even more fundamental than getting its acquisition strategy wrong. By 1988 Asda had developed two boards of directors. The management board, which oversaw non-food, reported to the chairman. The second board oversaw the grocery operation and reported to the chief executive. In other words, there were effectively two companies with some directors in common. A Harvard Business School case history published in 1998 reported that, 'The bureaucracy had reached a point where it was difficult to get anything done. Subordinates called their superiors "Mr" and authority was never questioned.'

Asda had somehow acquired a swish London headquarters plus three separate offices in Leeds employing 2,500 people. Senior executives had their offices well away from the troops. One manager told the Harvard researchers that the executives seemed 'more interested in hunting and partying than in addressing the serious issues faced by the company. They knew the company had lost focus, but they didn't seem to care.' The result was an exodus of talented executives and managers.

The Harvard case study reported: 'There were some very good regional and store managers: entrepreneurial people who had been attracted to Asda during the 1970s and early 1980s when Asda was an exciting place. When John Hardman became chief executive we entered a period where there was a lot of control from the top and the entrepreneurial people were not allowed to act entrepreneurial.' So they left.

One redeeming decision Hardman took during this time was to recruit George Davies in 1989 to design and market a range of clothes aimed at Asda customers. Davies had just been ousted from Next, the company he had created, and he was looking for a new platform. In twelve years the George clothing range gained almost 3 per cent of the UK clothing market – an outstanding achievement from a standing start. When Wal-Mart bought Asda, it threw its weight behind expanding and promoting the George brand, even though in 2001 Davies moved on to create the successful Per Una range of clothes for younger women at Marks & Spencer.

In 1988 the Prime Minister, Margaret Thatcher, attended the opening of Asda's new state-of-the-art corporate headquarters. Such grandiose events so often signal problems ahead. While Hardman threw shareholders' money at his problems, ignored the grass roots and jetted around hosting parties – occasionally even taking the corporate jet to the United States – Asda's customers noticed that its food was no longer particularly cheap. Hardman had deliberately introduced more upmarket, higher-margin items into the stores and the traditional Asda customers were not impressed. Nor were they impressed by the lack of value in the basic range of foods. And so they started to shop elsewhere.

In Asda's homeland of Northern England that 'elsewhere' was increasingly a supermarket chain called Morrison. Like Jack Cohen, Ken Morrison, the Yorkshireman who founded Morrison, began his business career trading in street markets after serving in the forces. In 1950, when Morrison was coming to the end of his army national service in Germany, his mother rang to tell him his father had become too ill to carry on running the family market stall in Bradford. Did Ken want to run it when he returned, or should she sell it?

Morrison, who was still running the family business more than fifty years later, decided to have a go. He ran a growing network of stalls for the next twelve years. Like Cohen he loved to provide his customers with bargains. One of his tricks was to buy up all the dented cans of vegetables and fruit that were sold off for next to nothing by the manufacturers and sell them to bargain-hungry customers.

But there the comparisons with Cohen end. When Morrison made the leap into the growing new world of self-service stores, he made it into big spaces with his eye on providing a bargain. Unlike Cohen, he hated publicity. Although the group floated on the stock market in 1967, he had little truck with the City or the world of public relations, preferring to let the results speak for themselves. Even when he bid for Safeway in January 2003, he kept communications with analysts and journalists to the minimum, although the BBC's *Money Programme* seduced him into appearing in a documentary about the bid.

Among his fellow retailers, though, he is almost universally liked and admired. Allan Leighton, the man who helped turn Asda round after it had veered towards bankruptcy under Fletcher and Hardman, rated him highly: 'He is streets ahead of everybody in terms of food retailing,' he told the *Independent* in 2002. 'When I was running Asda, who were we looking to copy and envy? It was Morrison.'

Like the Asquith brothers at Asda, Ken Morrison's eye fell upon a disused cinema for his first big space. He noticed a for sale sign on an old Odeon in Bradford and put in a bid. But almost immediately he realised he needed a lot more money than merely the purchase price. The floor sloped – as cinema floors do – and it would cost at least £1,000 to level it. The architect he consulted not only arranged the work but also found him a bigger site on the market for £3,000. By now, what had been an idea became a passion and Morrison realised that if he was to be serious about setting up supermarkets he needed about £100,000 to get the two stores up and running. Legend has it that he simply walked into his local Midland Bank and asked the branch manager to lend him £70,000 for the project. To his surprise the manager agreed and that was that. In *The Grocers* Seth and Randall wrote: 'Nothing had been or indeed ever was written down. No business plan of any kind had been presented. Walking out in amazement, Morrison realised he didn't even know what interest rate he might be paying and, as it happened, he didn't ever use the facility, so he never did find out what it might have been. But this was how Morrison got started.'

While Asda was losing sight of its main customer proposition – value for money – Morrison's 40,000-square-foot stores provided just that. Well positioned, they offered good-quality basic food at prices thrifty northerners appreciated. As Ken Morrison says, 'The poor need bargains and the rich appreciate them.'

What distinguishes Morrison from the competition is simplicity. Not for him marketing tools such as trading stamps or loyalty cards. 'I'd rather you tripped up over a pile of cheap cream crackers than give you a loyalty card,' he once said. Neither did he follow Asda and Tesco into selling clothing or electrical goods on any scale. His aim has always been to sell good food at 'outstanding value'.

He also enjoys the 'theatre' of food retailing. In his early shops he would place a meat pie in the window with an appetising trail of steam coming out of it. The steam came from a kettle in the basement below attached to a rubber tube. Later, he invented his 'market-street' format, which guides customers through the store past 'the butcher', 'the pie shop' and so on. In his only TV appearance during the bid for Safeway, which showed the gruff Yorkshireman, pink shirted, greeting his customers like a benevolent uncle, Morrison emphasised the point. 'It's a little touch of nostalgia,' he said, describing the fresh-fish counter. 'You can choose the fish, the fishmonger will bone it, skin it, put a bit of parsley with it. It's activity and theatre, it's an interchange.'

Morrison preferred to own his sites outright, eschewing fancy sale-and-leaseback transactions. Also, unfashionably, he owned or part-owned some of his suppliers, as Sainsbury had done many decades before. Woodhead, the butcher he used from early days, eventually became part of his business. He resisted the temptation to contract out his distribution – and owned much of the packing operation for his fruit and vegetables, cheese and bacon in the belief that this gave the group better cost and quality control.

A Yorkshireman to his fingertips, who is fond of saying that today's sirloin steak is tomorrow's rissole, he always disliked taking on debt and was famous for inspecting the rubbish bins to make sure there was no unnecessary waste. Yet surprisingly he paid his staff better than his mainstream competitors in the North.

Morrison built the company into 119 stores, nearly all of 40,000 square feet or more, without the benefit of non-executive directors, permanently retained investment bankers or public relations consultants. When asked on his seventieth birthday if he would take things a little easier, he replied that, yes, he would now work only five days a week instead of seven, which would give him the weekend to visit his stores. He still loved visiting his stores and chatting to staff and customers and showing his detestation of bureaucracy. In short, while Asda suffered from poor management, Ken Morrison's company was becoming a textbook case for excellence.

As the 1990s began Asda's profits and share price headed downwards, with City investors becoming increasingly critical of the management. In July 1991 the groundswell of City hostility pushed Hardman to resign along with Graham Stow, who had been chief executive of the Asda Stores subsidiary. Into the resulting vacuum stepped one of the non-executive directors, Sir Godfrey Messervy, who became interim chairman. He swiftly appointed the headhunter, Anna Mann, to find a new top team. Her first job was to find a chairman the City would recognise as a safe pair of hands.

True to her reputation she came up with the right man for the job in Sir Patrick Gillam, who became chairman in 1991. Gillam was a tough professional with a wealth of experience as a managing director at BP, deputy chairman of Standard Chartered Bank and a director of Commercial Union.

Although Gillam liked to keep a low profile, his appointment at least signalled that someone serious was in charge. He could scarcely believe what he found; the contrast with the immaculately run BP could not have been starker. The portfolio of 204 stores was impressive, with an average selling space of 40,000 square feet, but most of them needed a facelift. Yet the money had run out. A £1bn cash surplus in 1987 following the sale of MFI had vanished, with much of the money spent on Hardman's purchase of the Gateway stores in 1989. By 1991 the firm's debt had soared to £1bn as interest rates shot up. And as shareholders took fright at the stream of profit warnings, the shares plummeted from 100p to 30p. The loan covenants were in danger of being breached, which, in simple language, meant bankruptcy was on the cards.

'The company has an unbelievable debt profile; it is a recipe for disaster', Gillam declared in a statement in October 1991. A £354m emergency rights issue was launched to save the company from ruin.

Finding a competent chief executive with experience in retail became paramount. Once again Anna Mann turned up trumps. Reviving an ailing supermarket group in the north of England was not to many Young Turks' taste in 1991, but in one of her most astute pieces of work she came up with an energetic ambitious executive called Archie Norman. Not only did he have the talent to do the job, he also had the motivation. At the time Norman was the somewhat frustrated finance director at Kingfisher, the Woolworth, B&Q and Comet conglomerate.

An alumnus of McKinsey, Norman at 37 burned with ambition for a top job, and it was no secret that he felt constrained by the Kingfisher chairman and chief executive, Geoff Mulcahy. Mulcahy had headed the team that had bought the UK arm of Woolworth from its American parent, and had already transformed it into a multi-headed profit machine, renaming it Kingfisher. But although Mulcahy consulted widely with his fellow directors and multiple advisers on every decision, he liked to be in total control. Most important, he trusted no one, and certainly not someone as ambitious as Norman.

In the autumn of 1989, soon after the Gateway purchase, when it became clear that Asda was in trouble, Mulcahy had toyed with the idea of bidding for it but when he put the idea to Norman, then finance director, he met a wall of resistance. Mulcahy abandoned the idea, although there were other factors apart from Norman's antipathy behind his decision at that time. Thus he was stunned when Norman walked into his office one day in 1991 and told him he had been headhunted to rescue Asda, and that he was seriously considering going. If Norman had believed Asda was worth rescuing, thought Mulcahy, why had he opposed a bid from Kingfisher?

They had lunch to talk things through and Norman told him the only thing that would stop him leaving Kingfisher was if Mulcahy would split his roles and appoint him as chief executive. 'In that case, Archie, I suggest you go to Asda,' Mulcahy is believed to have told him in his dry way.

Norman faced an age-old dilemma. Should he pursue his successful but frustrating career at Kingfisher or take on a challenge that might end in glory or disaster when he knew so little about the company? Owing to the secrecy surrounding his appointment he had been allowed to meet only Gillam and two non-executive directors during the interview process, so he had little in the way of reliable information. But Gillam and Mann put on a lot of pressure. Gillam was desperately encouraging shareholders to support his rights issue, at a time when rivals were saying the group could not survive. Worse still, Asda had no chief executive.

Norman finally accepted the offer of the job by facsimile when Gillam was ten minutes away from going on stage to face 1,000 angry investors at the meeting to approve the rights issue. Grasping the fax in his hand, Gillam was able to announce that Norman had agreed to be the group's new chief executive.

Two months later on a grey, rainy morning in December, Norman arrived in Leeds. A southerner to his fingertips, who had been educated at Cambridge, he was hit by the full force of his decision to leave Kingfisher with its pleasant offices in the Marylebone Road, a stone's throw from the West End. 'I had never been to Leeds in my life. When I got off the train it was horrible,' he told Harvard Business School researchers. 'There was rain, and there was fog; you couldn't see more than three hundred yards. It was all so depressing.'

Norman still had to face the trauma of moving his family up to Leeds with him and putting his children into new schools. Suddenly the way ahead seemed more daunting than he had imagined. 'Leeds is not far from London, but it seemed far on that day. I had no contacts there; I was completely isolated and it was a bit lonely. I began to wonder what I had gotten myself into.'

The company secretary arrived at his hotel to take him to Asda's head office. He had organised his arrival for 8 a.m. but when he went to the executives' floor he found 'not a soul in the place'. At Kingfisher the board directors regularly played squash together at 7 a.m. before their first meeting of the day an hour or so later. Norman was used to the relatively easy-going atmosphere at Kingfisher, where directors and secretaries called each other by their first names and there was constant debate and interaction between staff. When he met the Asda board for the first time he introduced himself as Archie but his new colleagues used only their surnames. 'At Asda they were used to the big corporate manager, the big suit, and they thought they were going to have this guy come in and tell them all what to do,' Norman said.

He called together the twenty-five senior managers for a meeting at 9 a.m. and introduced himself. 'My name is Archie and this is how I work ...' He went on to give a rousing speech, concluding with the words: 'There is room on this boat for everyone who can pull on an oar.'

Norman did not promise them that everything was going to be fine from then on, but neither did he suggest that huge numbers of them were for the firing squad. Instead he spoke to them as people with something to contribute – probably the first time that had happened at Asda for more than a decade – but he did make it clear that the company was in a mess and the priority was to survive. In order to survive, costs would have to be cut, but he also wanted to bring innovation back into the company.

The story of Asda's revival has become a textbook case. It was possible partly because, once the extent of the crisis was spelt out to the workforce, they were willing to learn and change. Norman said that he was not interested in the past. 'This is day zero', he told them. 'The business is in poor shape and must change sharply in order to survive. There are no sacred cows and nothing that can't be examined. Our first objective is to secure value for our shareholders and secure the trading future of the business.'

He then listed six priorities: first, the need for cash; second, a return to core values; third, setting up two experimental store formats; fourth, management reorganisation to build one team; fifth, a need to build a culture around common ideas, and sixth, 'We must love the stores to death, that is our business.'

Norman's preliminary store visits showed him they were managed by men and women who cared passionately about their work but were intensely frustrated by the lack of communication with head office. One manager approached him and said he could not believe he was the new chief executive because he had no entourage. 'I asked them questions about what they thought we should do and they found it all very surprising,' said Norman. 'One store manager was amazed when I started listening to what he had to say and taking notes, because no one had ever done that before.'

During his first week, Norman brought in Peter Samuel, a psychologist and consultant he knew from Kingfisher, to meet the top forty managers and write a profile of each one. He wanted to know who still had 'some fuel in the tank' and who was burned out.

Although Norman knew many people would have to go, he wanted to use as many as possible of the existing managers to bring about change. 'You don't have the option of sweeping everybody away, you have to work with what you have got and turn round those people who may not be confident or motivated,' he said.

Norman thought he understood the situation at Asda, but not until he asked the finance team for cash flow forecasts did he realise just how dire it was. The finance team sent him figures that showed cash going out and debt rising, but the forecasts stopped at May 1992, just five months away. He asked them for the following financial year's forecasts but they said there were none because, astonishingly to him, they only did their business plan once a year. He pushed them to say what they thought the situation would be by the following September. After some prodding they replied that the company would have run out of cash and would again be in breach of some of the loan covenants. They were chilling words, but highly motivating.

Drastic action was called for and Norman set about selling assets to raise cash. 'I said, we are stopping the spending and we will throw the luggage overboard and sell everything we can.'

In early 1992 the disposals started. He sold a prime site in Scotland to Safeway for £25m, a record price at the time, another in the Midlands to Sainsbury for £20m and another four to Safeway and Sainsbury. Altogether £70m was raised from the sale of store sites. He also vetoed the £40m budgeted for investment in the furniture business Allied-Maples, halted all store refurbishments and put a moratorium on new-store development. In 1993 he sold Asda's residual interest in MFI for £72m and closed the Lofthouse food manufacturing operation with a loss of 1,300 jobs.

By January 1993 he and Gillam had captured the confidence of the City to such an extent that investors stumped up another £350m through a second rights issue. He also closed three of the four 'head offices', halving the number of staff to 1,200, all based in Leeds.

Norman brought in his old employer McKinsey to put together a plan while Arthur Andersen was hired to undertake a profitability study to pinpoint exactly where Asda was making money, and where it was losing it.

There was also the problem of what to do with Allied-Maples, which Norman believed could be turned round, even though he could not afford to pour money into it. Allied was reorganised into a separate company, financed by venture capitalists with Asda holding a minority stake. He put in a separate management with Phil Cox on the board to report back. His strategy paid off when Allied floated on the stock market in 1996, netting Asda £73m for its stake.

Norman knew he could not transform Asda on his own. Even before he joined he had hired Phil Cox as finance director and by April, Allan Leighton had joined them from Mars as the marketing director.

Leighton, who used to describe himself jokingly as 'the man from Mars', had spent his entire career at the American confectioner's British operations and had become a devout believer in its management philosophy. While many British companies had based themselves on a military-style command-and-control structure with graduated privileges for staff and executives, Mars had an egalitarian culture. In the early 1980s visitors to the Mars plants, as well as being intrigued by the huge vats of goo, were surprised by the staff dining room where 'even the directors' ate – revolutionary in Britain at the time.

At Mars, Leighton had been in charge of marketing for Pedigree, the pet-food arm, whose biggest customers were the supermarket groups. Such experience meant he brought both effective management philosophy and knowledge of food retailing to the group. His extrovert, jokey manner was a perfect foil for Norman's reserved upper-middle-class Englishness.

Almost as soon as he arrived, Norman removed a layer of management by collapsing the group board and stores board into one management board – so that all managers reported directly to the chief executive. A new philosophy was born – that people's jobs were whatever was required at the time, not what was in their job specification. Staff – now renamed 'colleagues' – were deliberately moved around the company into new positions. Phil Cox explained it to the Harvard team thus: 'It was task oriented rather than positional. You will never hear anyone say, "That's not my responsibility".'

Once the new structure was complete, department managers were given the task of cutting back on staff. In May, Asda cut 500 in-store middle managers – roughly 10 per cent of people at that level.

Norman and his team did, however, realise that there had to be an injection of new people from a different culture. They looked around them and saw – it was not that difficult – that the best food retailer north of Birmingham was William Morrison.

For many years Asda had been driven by a bureaucratic head office where the directors held the stores in contempt. Norman wanted to turn the business on its head so management, as it was at Morrison, became focused on the stores. 'We hired a lot of people out of Morrison because they had good instincts and were real shopkeepers and that is what a lot of our people lacked,' he said later.

Morrison had developed its market-street format, with fruit and vegetables piled high either side until the customer reached the meat counter, the delicatessen counter, or the cheese counter, which were all staffed. Northerners enjoyed the human contact and felt it added enjoyment to the chore of food shopping.

Such personal service within a supermarket was unheard of at Asda until then, but Norman, Cox and Leighton embraced the idea and copied it unashamedly. They were not alone. By the mid 1990s all four major supermarket groups had personal counter service for meat, fish and delicatessen – harking back to the original Sainsbury stores with their separate counters.

Sir Richard Greenbury at Marks & Spencer resisted the idea for many years but when he heard that a rival as downmarket as Asda was to provide it, he gave the go-ahead for investment in bakery and fresh meat counters at its stores – at considerable expense.

The idea is simple – make shopping in a supermarket more personal. In fact, most of the goods on sale at these counters are available pre-packed, so it becomes a matter of personal preference whether the customer wants to buy a ticket and stand in a queue, or just whisk round with a trolley.

The injection of Morrison people together with the can-do attitude of the management team began to lift the morale and confidence of the Asda 'colleagues', as Norman restyled his staff in imitation of America's Wal-Mart, who for so long had felt ignored and undervalued. Now directors were walking among them, asking their opinions and taking heed. Norman and Leighton knew that people with poor attitudes and no motivation would never deliver. So they put in place a system of goals and recognition that would make everybody feel part of the business. The checkout operators suddenly felt important. When they hit productivity targets they were awarded 'wings' and when they exceeded them they began training others. When they did not do well on the checkout they were moved to somewhere more suitable. 'Tell Archie' suggestion boxes for the staff appeared in every store and everything from morale to attitude, absenteeism and checkout throughput was measured. Everyone who worked for Asda was a 'colleague' whether they cleaned the toilets or negotiated with Unilever.

The enclosed office became a thing of the past. Leighton had all internal walls knocked down making the head office open plan, as it had been at Mars. He positioned himself at a desk in one corner to show his faith in the principle, but spent most of his time in the Leeds headquarters pacing the floors talking through problems, encouraging people and cracking jokes. 'Allan has that ability to make whoever he is talking to feel they are the most important person in his life at that moment,' said one colleague.

As far as was possible, Asda became a single-status company. Individual offices and allocated car parking spaces disappeared and every colleague who stayed with the company for a year received share options. The effect on morale was dramatic.

Meanwhile, Norman set about getting the best he could out of George Davies. Asda had plenty of space and with Norman's encouragement Davies began expanding his clothing lines. His mission was to bring stylish clothes to all the family at low, low prices. Within ten years, sales of the George range hit £500m. By 1997 Norman was even talking of becoming number two in clothing after Marks & Spencer. It was an ambition that would not be realised in the face of Arcadia (the old Burton) and Davies's own creation Next. Even so, the George brand was spectacularly successful, particularly in children's wear, blending fashion, easy care and low prices. Parents loved the convenience of being able to throw children's clothes into the trolley along with the Hula Hoops and Pampers. Between 1995 and 1997 George children's clothing more than doubled its market share to 6.3 per cent. It was one area where Asda beat Tesco hands down.

In October 1995 the board paid Davies £15.9m for the ownership of the George business and the brand name. It was a shrewd move by Norman and, although it may have seemed a great deal of money at the time, it was one that Davies, always a big spender, was later to regret.

By the mid 1990s Leighton had emerged as a star. From a much humbler background than Norman, Leighton grew up with his heart set on becoming a professional footballer. Then, at 15, he broke his leg badly and in the same year his father died suddenly. These two catastrophes at a crucial time in his life proved great motivators, feeding his drive and ambition.

He and Norman became a great partnership. After a couple of years in marketing Leighton moved on to operations, running the stores, where his energy and enthusiasm made him a powerful motivator of the troops, from the checkout assistants to the cleaners. 'How do you make the person who cleans the toilets feel they are important? You come up with a golden mop award,' he recalled.

The next step was a course at Harvard Business School and when he returned 'humming with ideas' it became clear to Norman that Leighton should be his successor. So in 1996 Norman stepped up to be chairman while Leighton assumed the mantle of chief executive. For the next four years they were one of the most successful duos in retailing. But both became restless, one for new challenges in business, the other for the world of politics. Both saw that release from their successful partnership could come only from a merger or takeover that would give Asda the critical mass necessary to compete with Tesco. Four years after Norman took the chair, they sold Asda to the world's most powerful retailer, Wal-Mart – but not before a serious flirtation with Safeway.

CHAPTER FIVE

THE SCOTTISH INVADERS

'All for one, one for all.'

Alexandre Dumas

Safeway was built by three Scotsmen. James Gulliver and Alistair Grant learned food retailing in the 1960s at Fine Fare, a supermarket chain owned by the Weston family's Associated British Foods group. The youngest of the three, David Webster, began his career as an investment banker. Their daring acquisitions in the 1970s and 1980s while they were building up Argyll Foods, which they later renamed Safeway, earned them the nickname 'the three musketeers', or sometimes 'the gang of three'.

They were opportunists. Had fate dealt them a different hand in 1986, when Argyll lost out to Guinness in the battle for the Scottish spirits company Distillers, they would have headed Britain's biggest drinks group, and Safeway might never have become one of the UK's main supermarket players. Later that year, however, the New York private equity firm Kohlberg Kravis Roberts, which had backed a management buy-out of the American supermarket group Safeway, put the UK division up for sale. On the rebound from the bruising loss of Distillers, Argyll bought the chain from KKR in an auction, and merged it with its existing business before renaming the enlarged group Safeway. It was the best brand.

Argyll already had more than 4 per cent of British supermarket sales in 1986 and in the next three years it transformed all seven of the other Argyll supermarket chains such as Presto and Lipton's into Safeway stores, introducing wide aisles, in-store bakeries and delicatessen counters where store size allowed. By 1990, Safeway had become the third largest supermarket group in Britain.

The roots of the Safeway story go back to the autumn of 1972, when David Webster met the mercurial James Gulliver and the urbane Alistair Grant in London. There was instant chemistry. Gulliver and Webster came from the west of Scotland, near Glasgow, and Grant from the east. They were three young men in a hurry, keen to make some money out of the heady bull market raging at the time. They also had a common ambition to bring prosperity to Scotland.

When they met, Gulliver was running Fine Fare. A short, pugnacious graduate of Glasgow University, Gulliver cast a spell on both Webster and Grant. His powerful personality, intellect and seniority made him indisputably the leader in the early years of the various businesses they set up. In 1972 Gulliver was already 42, while Grant was six years younger and Webster, at just 28, was, initially at least, the junior partner. Gulliver would even refer to him as 'the boy'.

Those who knew them in those days recall how Gulliver dominated the other two, rather as a father might dominate his sons. He enthused them with his prodigious energy, beguiled them with his lavish lifestyle and, already ostentatiously rich, gave them something for which to aim. He also cajoled them into huge effort and they would occasionally grumble that they did all the work while Gulliver – who loved to schmooze with City journalists and analysts – basked in the glory. As time went on and the age differences became less important the trio's relationship evolved to become more equal. Grant described it as a three-legged stool.

For many years Gulliver's business star shone so bright that both colleagues and investors accepted his flaws as merely the foibles of an entrepreneurial character. Gulliver had three weaknesses: women, vanity and drink. Of these, vanity was the certainly most damaging. Vanity caused him to state that he had a business degree from Harvard Business School in his *Who's Who* entry when in fact he had studied at Georgia Technical College in the United States after graduating from Glasgow. While he appeared to get away with misbehaviour such as drunken fights at parties and running a wife and sometimes two mistresses at once, the discovery of this lie during the Distillers battle irretrievably damaged his reputation and soured his relationship with Grant and Webster.

But back in 1972 Gulliver was still in his prime and hungry to build his own business, assisted by his young willing colleagues. 'We had a wonderful time together for many years,' recalls Webster.

During Gulliver's seven years at Fine Fare, which he joined as manager of a shop-fitting subsidiary, he transformed the company into a modern profitable supermarket group, introducing information technology at an early stage and bringing in modern management techniques. In 1972 he was named the Young Businessman of the Year by the *Guardian* newspaper, an award that was said by cynics to carry a curse. Gulliver proved the exception for many years, although it caught up with him eventually. Not long afterwards he became discontented, believing Associated British Foods did not reward his talents sufficiently or give him the resources to expand Fine Fare as he would like.

Gulliver had recruited Grant from Unilever to head marketing at Fine Fare and the two men formed a strong friendship as well as a good working relationship. Webster had trained as a lawyer before joining the merchant bank Samuel Montagu. He then moved to another bank, Brandts, where his boss, Mike Andrews, a Harvard MBA, introduced him to Gulliver. Outwardly reserved, Webster had ambitions to break out of banking into the broader commercial world and make some serious money. So when Gulliver told him that he and Grant were looking for a shell company – a small enterprise that was already listed on the stock market – he leapt at the opportunity to join them.

Gulliver was barred in his severance contract from ABF from working in food retailing for two years, although it was clear that any business the three men bought was likely to be closely related. By January 1973 they had found Oriel Foods, an old edible-oil processing and bacon-wholesaling business in Liverpool controlled by Malcolm Horsman, an entrepreneur from the circle of young men who surrounded Jim Slater, the entrepreneur behind the Slater Walker investment empire. In order to buy a significant stake in Oriel, Gulliver borrowed about £600,000 and Grant £100,000. Despite his conservative demeanour Webster also borrowed £100,000 – equivalent to more than £1 million in today's money. The lender was his old boss Mike Andrews.

True, the times were wild. In 1973 the stock market was coming to the end of a bull run that had made many fortunes but there were still a host of young men snapping up shell companies and dreaming of instant riches.

Gulliver may have been barred from food retailing, but not from wholesaling. In short order Oriel snapped up three small companies including a small chain of cash-and-carry outlets based in Nottingham. Within a few months the group was on track to make profits of £1m and such progress caught the eye of the American RCA Corporation, one of the world's biggest conglomerates, which made an £11m cash offer for Oriel, valuing it at twenty-eight times its profits, a sky-high rating even in those heady times.

No sooner had the price been agreed than the Yom Kippur war broke out in Israel and Opec nearly doubled oil prices. Interest rates soared and it looked as though RCA would back off, but the Americans held firm and the deal was closed, giving the three musketeers heavyweight resources to expand the business and, more important at the time, a secure future. 'Our bacon was saved,' recalled Webster with feeling. 'God knows what would have happened otherwise.'

Eight months later they bid for another public company, Morris & David Jones of Liverpool, more than doubling Oriel's size and giving it a £3m profit base. It comprised cash and carry, tea and coffee blending and some 'own-label' manufacturing for Marks & Spencer.

'Although we were only producing about 1 per cent of RCA's profits, we were one of the few parts of the group performing to plan by 1975,' Webster recalled. But by 1976 RCA's directors had become distracted by problems in their mainstream business. Then the dollar/sterling exchange rate dropped from $2.40 to $1.70, leaving RCA with significant capital losses.

The trio tried to buy the company back but when their offers were rejected they began to make plans to leave Oriel, meeting every Sunday morning in Gulliver's house in Welwyn, Hertfordshire, to discuss new ventures.

They hired a clutch of new talent, including a young Harvard MBA called Martin Sorrell, who became Gulliver's personal assistant. Sorrell, who went on to create the global advertising giant WPP, has largely affectionate recollections of those days. His main job was to manage Gulliver's finances. 'James used to say that there were two types of money – my money and other people's money,' he said. 'He was a very shrewd operator.'

At one point, through an acquisition, Gulliver, Grant and Webster had found themselves holding 5 per cent of a new advertising agency called Saatchi and Saatchi but Gulliver had sold the shares at a time when they had plummeted to 8p. If he had kept them he could have made another fortune. Sorrell, meanwhile, became Saatchi's finance director.

The trio finally left Oriel and set up James Gulliver Associates in what appeared to be the riskiest venture yet. They injected £500,000 into it and arranged bank borrowings for a lot more. Never short on style, Gulliver found offices in 1 Charles Street, Mayfair, opposite Mark's Club, which was owned by Mark Birley and was a favoured dining place for movers and shakers.

There was just one problem. For the next three years they were barred by their RCA contracts from any business activity involving food. They survived by wheeling and dealing, snapping up 29 per cent of the double-glazing specialist Alpine Holdings and adding Dolphin Showers two years later. 'We were just bloody active,' said Webster, now chairman of InterContinental Hotels.

When the three years finally came to a close, they bought a stake in a crisis-torn food wholesaler and retailer called Morgan Edwards, based in Shrewsbury, bought Louis C. Edwards and used them as a platform for acquisitions. Within a year they had a mixture of butchers, freezer centres, fifty grocery stores and a Spar wholesaler – in short, it was a hotch-potch.

By the summer of 1979, as Tesco and Sainsbury continued their price war, James Gulliver Associates had interests in four listed companies producing a stream of deals. In early 1980 they merged the two largest companies, Louis C. Edwards and Morgan Edwards, to form Argyll Foods. Then Gulliver finally persuaded RCA to sell him Oriel Foods, giving the trio a sound base and a business they knew intimately. Within four years Argyll had become a significant force in food distribution with turnover of £230m and profits of £7m. Argyll was a darling of the early 1980s stock market, with the shares rocketing from 10p to 100p between 1978 and 1982 and giving Gulliver just what he wanted – valuable currency to buy other companies. Along the way, in February 1983, Webster sold Alpine Holdings to Michael Ashcroft for 148p per share, up from the 19p they had paid and valuing the company at £17m.

Gulliver and co. were not the only entrepreneurs trying to build new food retailing empires. Alec Monk, a likeable businessman, had taken over a company called Linfood, which he built into a medium-sized food retailer and dreamed of it overtaking Sainsbury and Tesco. Gulliver, whose ambitions were shaping up the same way, saw Linfood as just the thing to give Argyll a leap forward into the mainstream.

Lord Kissin, an elderly industrialist and president of Guinness Peat, a merchant bank, had acquired 20 per cent of Linfood, which he happily sold to Gulliver. Armed with that stake Argyll made an audacious £90m bid for Linfood, which was twice its size. Monk, who saw all his dreams of building a market leader disappearing, was furious but Gulliver looked set to win. Then disaster struck. The Office of Fair Trading decided to refer the bid to the Monopolies Commission.

The Argyll management was baffled as the normal criterion for a referral was that the two companies would hold a market share in their sector approaching 25 per cent. When Webster pointed out to the OFT official who rang to tell him the news that the market share of the two companies was less than 3 per cent between them, the official replied blandly, 'We thought it would be interesting to look at what happens when two distribution companies were merged.' In the smash-and-grab days of the early 1980s, Gulliver was not prepared to wait for the Monopolies Commission to trawl laboriously through the activities and trading details of both companies. Instead, Argyll wrote off the £1.6m bid costs and retreated.

And that was that. Linfood was saved and Monk went on to build it up through acquisitions. It was later taken private in a highly geared transaction that led to financial crisis. The company that eventually emerged from the wreckage was called Somerfield, a chain of smallish supermarkets that limped along for many years until it was revitalised in 2003 by new management led by John von Spreckelsen.

In that era of rapidly opening and closing doors another bigger and better opportunity soon presented itself to the three musketeers. In 1982 Sir James Goldsmith rang Gulliver to say he was putting his company, Allied Suppliers, up for sale. Goldsmith, a friend of Jim Slater and an old-fashioned tycoon, had grown bored with food retailing and wanted to walk on a wider, or at least different, stage. Allied had been formed in 1929 by the merger of Home & Colonial, Lipton's and Maypole Dairies into a group that became Britain's biggest food retailer apart from the Co-op. By the 1980s Allied had 923 stores throughout Britain, 795 trading as Lipton's and 128 as Presto. Rated by then as the fourth biggest food retailing multiple, Allied had built up its market share to 4.6 per cent and was strong in Scotland.

Almost twice Argyll's size, Allied was a big bite, but Gulliver loved to live dangerously. Argyll bought Allied for £101m, raising £81m through a share issue and borrowing the rest.

The company's debt was now dangerously high at 100 per cent of its net assets, and many in the City feared it was a deal too far. But they reckoned without the team's managerial talent. The economic climate remained grim but the arrival of the Thatcher government in 1979 had given the business community hope. The economy hit bottom in 1981 but by 1983 Thatcher's policies were starting to take effect and the economy began to recover.

Argyll's directors set about knocking the combined group into some kind of order. They sold their surplus property to release cash and set some goals. The main one was to increase the profit margin from 1.6 per cent to 3 per cent within three years. The increased buying power of the expanded group enabled it to negotiate keener prices from suppliers and to introduce detailed profit planning. By mid 1985 Argyll had begun to look relatively streamlined and was making pre-tax profits of £53m on sales of £1.8bn.

Even so, the group still lagged behind Sainsbury and Tesco, both in size and, more crucially, in the way it was structured. By the mid 1980s, when other supermarket groups had introduced central warehousing and distribution and computerised ordering, Argyll's stores received only a third of their goods from central warehouses and its systems were as diverse as its seven trading names – Presto, Lipton's, Templeton, Galbraith, Hintons, Lo-Cost and Cordon Bleu. All these formats and fascias resulted in Argyll juggling three own-label ranges, several different pricing policies and no end of internal conflicts.

In 1985 Argyll announced plans for modern distribution centres and that Presto should be the main trading name, subsuming Hintons, Templeton and the larger Lipton's. The Lo-Cost name would be used for the smaller discount shops. Argyll also invested in large modern distribution centres. As a result the company more than doubled the proportion of goods distributed through its own warehouses and profit margins rose steadily towards the 3 per cent target.

The scene was now set for one of the most audacious takeover bids the London stock market had ever witnessed. If it had succeeded, the three Scotsmen would have created one of the most powerful drinks companies in the world. The Safeway of the 1990s would not have existed.

In the late summer of 1985 rumours started to swirl in the City that Argyll was going to bid for Distillers, the giant of the Scotch whisky industry. Distillers was a sleeping giant, overmanned and undermanaged. Hence it was valued at a low price–earnings ratio of only seven and was viewed as ripe for takeover.

Gulliver described it as 'a dripping roast', so tempting did it seem to him. The team began gathering information in February 1985, trawling through every available document in Companies House, which contained a wealth of financial detail, through industry files and through brokers' research. 'It was amazing how much information was available if you looked for it,' Webster later reflected. 'The board of Distillers suspected we had an inside source, but we certainly did not.'

In July and August they put the financial plan together. Although Argyll had a stock-market value of just £600m, the value of the first offer it prepared for Distillers was £1.9bn. But the plans leaked into the press and in September Gulliver was panicked into saying Argyll had 'no present intention of bidding', which, under the rules of the Takeover Panel, meant that he could not launch his bid until December.

The drinks group Guinness also had its eye on Distillers, and the delay gave it a chance to prepare its own bid at a higher price. Several books have been written about what then happened. In short, through many twists and turns, share ramping and other skulduggery, Guinness finally won the day although, despite the dirty dealing, it was a close-run thing. Ernest Saunders, Gerald Ronson, founder of Heron Corporation, and a stockbroker, Tony Parnes, ended up in jail and others involved in the affair had their reputations severely tarnished. In 1992 Argyll received £100m compensation following legal action.

Losing the bid cleanly would on its own have put great strain on the relationship between Gulliver, Grant and Webster. But when, towards the end of the battle, one of the public relations men for Guinness leaked to the press that, contrary to his *Who's Who* entry, James Gulliver had never attended Harvard Business School, it was the beginning of the end for the three musketeers. Grant and Webster may have put up with a great deal from Gulliver over the years but their relationship was a close one. When Neil Collins, the acerbic City editor of the *Sunday Times*, rang Webster for confirmation, Webster said the story was nonsense because he and Grant had never doubted Gulliver. But Collins seemed so confident that Webster checked it out with Gulliver, who eventually confessed the truth.

For Webster and Grant, the revelation that such an oft-repeated story that they had believed from the very beginning of the musketeers' adventures together was a lie was too much. Their patience with their onetime hero, leader and good friend ran out. They closed ranks and never really forgave him. Gulliver never recovered from the failure to acquire Distillers or the loss of his own credibility and his partners' loyalty and close friendship. From then on Grant and Webster headed Argyll, Gulliver continuing as chairman in name only until he retired in 1988.

Grant became chief executive and deputy chairman in 1986 while Webster kept his crucial role as finance director. Like executors after a funeral they set about dismantling the drinks business, selling it off piecemeal. They also disposed of food manufacturing, leaving Argyll as a relatively streamlined food retailer, but one that lacked scale. The scene was now set for the creation of Safeway.

The opportunity to build on their supermarket base came from the other side of the Atlantic. In the middle of 1986 Dart Corporation made a hostile bid for the American supermarket group Safeway. In response, its management launched its own highly leveraged offer for the company backed by Kohlberg Kravis Roberts.

Safeway had set up operations in Britain in 1962 with the acquisition of seven supermarkets and a few small food stores around London. The first purpose-built Safeway opened in Bedford in June 1963.

By 1978 it had expanded to sixty-nine stores with a management base in Aylesford, Kent. Nine years later Safeway operated 133 stores with 2m square feet of sales area. Its large stores made their mark in the south-east with their wide aisles, in-store bakeries and delicatessen counters. The group also sold more than a third of its products under a strong own-label brand. By 1987 Safeway ranked number six in the UK food retailing industry with a national market share of 3.4 per cent. It was particularly strong in London, the south of England and Scotland. Sales topped £1bn in 1986 when the company reported pre-tax profits of £43.8m.

In early 1987 the Safeway managers, backed by KKR, emerged as the successful bidders for the business. But in order to service the debt taken on to finance the deal, they put the UK arm up for sale. Grant and Webster needed no convincing that Safeway and Argyll made the perfect fit. Safeway's stores were mostly in similar but not overlapping geographical areas to those of Argyll, which now had state-of-the-art systems and distribution centres. Most importantly, during its short life in Britain, Safeway had established a brand that stood for quality fresh food, innovation and a pleasant shopping experience for the customer.

Argyll clinched the deal in February 1987 for £681m, a much more digestible meal than Distillers would have been, and Grant and Webster set off in hot pursuit of Sainsbury, Tesco and Asda. Their objective, they said, was, 'To establish Argyll as a retail group of enduring quality with Safeway as one of the most successful and respected UK food retailers of the 1990s.' Although

Safeway had a strong presence in Scotland it had relatively little in the north of England, where Asda and Morrison had the game to themselves.

They set themselves a target of tripling the Safeway sales area by converting more than a hundred of the larger Presto stores to Safeway and going hell for leather after new sites for purpose-built stores. At the time a Safeway store had more than 50 per cent more sales per square foot than the same size Presto and 75 per cent better operating profit.

Once again they were able to use the superior buying power of a bigger group to drive down prices from suppliers and push up profit margins. They also capitalised on the Safeway name and focused on its strengths such as fresh food, its good-quality own-label range and customer service. In response to the farming lobby they set up regional boards to help make the group more sensitive to local suppliers.

In 1990 a splendid new 37,000-square-foot prototype Safeway opened in Coventry. Fresh produce was arranged around the outer walls while groceries, dairy and frozen food were displayed on the inner aisles. The pride and joy was the food court offering a delicatessen, a fresh-fish counter, fresh bread, made-to-order pizzas and a butchery department.

At that time Sainsbury was well ahead of Tesco and was comfortably the market leader in both profits and perception. Under Ian MacLaurin and David Malpas, however, Tesco had made up much lost ground. In terms of sales Asda took the number three place, even though rumours of the northern group's imminent demise surfaced weekly. Asda's business model was based on huge low-cost shed-like stores and when it moved south and had to pay vastly more for store sites, the numbers ceased to add up to a profit. In response it moved away from what it was known for by increasing prices, and lost the confidence of customers as a result. In terms of profits Argyll was well ahead of Asda and in 1990 it seemed inconceivable that Asda could recreate itself and overtake Argyll to become the third biggest group.

Among the smaller players in food retailing Marks & Spencer maintained its reputation for brilliant innovation, particularly in chilled recipe dishes, and for superior quality at a price. Customers also liked the good-quality food and service found in Waitrose stores, but there were not yet enough of them to be any real threat and their owner, the John Lewis Partnership, appeared content to progress at a sedate pace.

The integration and development of Argyll and Safeway took nearly four years and cost more than £1bn, most of which was spent on building new stores and converting old ones and on modern distribution centres. Yet Grant and Webster put off changing the company name to Safeway until 1996. The number of stores rose from 133 in 1987 to 310 in 1991 and the sales area tripled as planned to 6m square feet. In May 1991 Argyll proudly reported pre-tax profits of £291m, more than three times the profit for 1987. Turnover had soared from £1.1bn in 1987 to £3.5bn and the all-important profit margin had risen to 6.7 per cent.

Taken in isolation, Argyll was powering ahead. Yet without Gulliver, the group lacked an important element. The three men had previously been likened to a three-legged stool, and without Gulliver a crucial element was missing. While Webster and Grant understood professional management and complex finance, Gulliver had been the instinctive, entrepreneurial risk taker.

In retailing, the competition never sleeps and while Sainsbury gradually lost impetus, Tesco started buying up large out-of-town sites in the teeth of a recession. Meanwhile Anna Mann was working on finding new talent to breathe life into Asda.

What happened next could have redrawn the map of supermarket expansion in Britain. Asda's beleaguered chief executive John Hardman secretly approached Webster and Grant to sound them out about making a bid for Asda. They met one Sunday evening at the home of a stockbroking friend. For once Webster and Grant had differing views. Webster felt that such a takeover would be highly risky at a time when Safeway was undertaking a dynamic store-development programme, opening twenty-five new state-of-the-art superstores a year under the Conservative government's relaxed planning regulations.

Asda's 200 stores were of variable quality and a big investment would be necessary to bring them up to the standard of Safeway stores. Grant was tempted by the deal but Webster cautioned against. If Gulliver had still been chairman, many believe he would have taken the leap. As it was, Asda stayed independent and eventually returned to a price-focused strategy.

What few foresaw at the time was that John Gummer, a keen new environment minister, would in 1993 pass planning regulation PPG6 designed to protect the provincial high streets of Britain. The new regulation would stop the building of new superstores in out-of-town retail parks dead in its tracks.

CHAPTER SIX

SAINSBURY'S BIG GUN

'The reasonable man adapts himself to circumstances; the unreasonable man expects circumstances to adapt to him. Therefore, for all progress, we must look to the unreasonable man.'

George Bernard Shaw

John Davan Sainsbury was the patrician leader from central casting. He was about as different in background and style from Jack Cohen as it was possible to be. Born on 2 November 1927 in Chelsea, he was the eldest of Alan Sainsbury's three sons – and it showed. Tall and commanding, he could be outwardly courteous and charming, particularly to the lower-ranking store staff, yet his outbursts of temper, usually over minor details, were notorious. 'He may be grey now, but do not forget he was born a redhead,' warned a director to a new recruit. His store visits could be terrifying occasions for the managers, who called him Mr JD or just JD.

Every Sainsbury shop had a store plan, laid out meticulously by Mr JD or his father before him, showing precisely which products went where. A full store inspection by JD and the entourage of executives who usually accompanied him could take three hours. He did not just stroll around: with his team in tow he would walk imperiously along the aisles, black notebook in hand, jotting down comments. Staff felt that he could almost smell problems. Whenever he suspected that a store plan had not been followed to the letter he would call for the copy that his executives always brought with them. If his instinct proved correct – and it usually did – the errant manager would receive a dressing down in front of his staff. Prices and labelling were all scrutinised. The worst offence of all was a gap on the shelves where stock had run out – this he found insufferable and he showed no mercy to any shelf-stacker who attempted to disguise it using another product. He also visited the competition, and if a Waitrose or Marks & Spencer store had better displays than the next branch of Sainsbury he visited, the manager would be told. Uncomfortable though he made them feel, the staff admired his passion for excellence, and it was he who coined the phrase 'retail is detail'.

Tyrant and martinet, Mr JD may have been called unpleasant names behind his back by his executives, but nobody ever accused him of being a bad or mediocre retailer. He personified George Bernard Shaw's definition of 'The unreasonable man'. His chairmanship of Sainsbury took the company to undreamed of heights. In the twenty years from 1972, three years after he became chairman, and 1992, when he retired, pre-tax profits grew at a staggering 23 per cent a year. Sales grew by slightly less, 19 per cent, reflecting a steady increase in profit margins. The company never made his longed for profit target of £1bn, but profits in 1992 were £628m on sales of £9.2bn, making Sainsbury Britain's most profitable retailer that year. For the first time Sainsbury beat Marks & Spencer, realising one of his long held ambitions.

To colleagues he was both hero and villain. 'He was passionate about giving customers what they wanted. He was innovative; he pioneered brown bread, tights instead of stockings, and ready-to-cook chickens and was thought quite eccentric. But he was a passionate merchant,' said one.

Steven Esom, the managing director of Waitrose, who used to be Mr JD's personal assistant, takes a more mellow view. 'Everyone knew what he expected, his standards were clear and highly structured. Retail is about command and control. It is run on the principles of an army.'

Despite Mr JD's reputation for arrogance he was often open to new ideas, as Louise Davies, then a young nutritionist and presenter of a postwar radio programme *Shopping List*, found when she lobbied the supermarkets to produce smaller portions. The early supermarkets targeted families by selling family-sized packs, but Davies, author of the book *Easy Cooking for One or Two*, believed passionately that to lure older and single people into supermarkets they must provide portions suitable for one or at most two people. 'When they began they didn't have the concept of singles, but Sainsbury and Marks & Spencer were very responsive to my ideas,' she recalled.

Yet Mr JD rarely delegated anything concerning the stores. For most of his chairmanship he vetted every single piece of advertising, every pack design and every promotional flash on every pack.

His combative personality thrived on competition. When he took over the running of the company it was far smaller than Tesco, whose profits in 1969 were two and a half times those of Sainsbury. Even as late as 1982 Tesco's market share at 11 per cent was still 1 per cent ahead of Sainsbury's. It took him until 1986 to push Sainsbury into the lead – a lead that he then built on until most people forgot that Tesco had ever been bigger. As the heady 1980s progressed Sainsbury continued to expand geographically, with new locations as far north as Yorkshire and Lancashire.

Once Tesco had been overtaken, JD set his sights on becoming the most profitable retailer – a title that regularly went to Marks & Spencer, which had many similarities with Sainsbury. It was a venerated family firm that had become an institution in British life and although Marks & Spencer never set out to be a full-scale supermarket, its product innovation set the standard for all food retailers, and the company philosophy of quality, value and service had much in common with that of Sainsbury.

Part of the decline in fortunes of both companies in the second half of the 1990s can be laid at the door of the visceral rivalry between them. Such was the desire to hit profits of £1bn first that insiders believe it caused both firms to under-invest in existing stores, deferring maintenance and training programmes while pushing up margins to unsustainable levels in order to increase profits.

In the end both institutions suffered the same fate; the products ceased to be good value, the stores became tired and the pace of innovation slowed. The customers noticed and began to drift away to competitors. The resulting damage to profits, infrastructure and morale proved hard to mend.

But when he retired in 1992 JD could look back on a glittering career. He received a knighthood in 1980, one of the first bestowed by the Thatcher administration. Then in 1989 he was created Lord Sainsbury of Preston Candover, after the village in which he lived and to differentiate him from his father Alan, Lord Sainsbury of Drury Lane. Alan Sainsbury sat on the Labour benches in the House of Lords and his son on the Conservative side.

John Sainsbury's spectacular success was extraordinary in the fourth generation of a dynastic family. He had the same talent for retailing as his parents and grandparents. But his drive to prove himself found its roots in his disrupted childhood. As the eldest of Alan Sainsbury's three sons, he should have been set fair for a life of privilege and certainty. But divorce and the Second World War intervened. Shortly after he turned eleven years old in 1938 his world shattered when his father left his mother, Doreen Davan Adams, for Elizabeth Lewy, whom he married in 1944.

Soon afterwards the war broke out and John and his two brothers, Simon and Tim, were moved down to Bexhill-on-Sea to live with their paternal grandparents. Tim, the youngest, recalled that they stayed there until 'we could hear the guns across the Channel and planes overhead', whereupon they went to live with their maternal grandparents before, finally, in 1941 settling with their mother at her house near Windsor. All three were sent to boarding school – and for much of their middle and later childhood their father became a somewhat remote if still powerful force in their lives. 'He would occasionally come down to the school to see what we were up to or we would visit him for the day.' Tim remembered on one occasion going to tea at his father's office and being served biscuits from the Co-op. His incensed father demanded their instant removal.

As children they came under the influence of their eccentric grand-mother Mabel, née Van den Bergh, the daughter of the Dutch margarine company's founder, who married John Benjamin, the father of Alan and Robert Sainsbury. According to the *London Illustrated News* she had a liking for fast cars and would sit in the back of her latest indulgence, regularly leaning forward to tap on the glass, urging the chauffeur to drive faster. 'A little bit of Dutch/Jewish blood does wonders for the commercial instinct,' John Sainsbury told the magazine in 1983.

So, unlike his father, neither he nor his brothers grew up with the distinctive Sainsbury shop smell of bacon and cheese in his nostrils. Nor did they take part in constant family discussions about the business as the children of Simon Marks or Jack Cohen did.

John went to Stowe, his brothers to Eton. 'We were all supposed to go to different schools, but when we moved to Windsor, Simon was already there and the headmaster said he had a place for me,' said Tim.

If John resented this, he never admitted it. At Stowe he enjoyed drama and even dreamed of becoming a professional actor. One Easter holiday he landed himself and his friend a week's experience at the Windsor Repertory Company. But, as he told Sue Lawley on *Desert Island Discs*, 'I learned I was not a very good actor'. Instead he spent his national service as a member of the Life Guards in Palestine and then went to Worcester College Oxford, where he read history.

He enjoyed Oxford 'more than the army' and flirted with becoming a full-time academic. Instead he decided to join the business and become 'a first-class businessman rather than a second-class don'. 'I did not know a lot about it but I felt I would be crazy not to give it a try,' he said. 'After all, I had to earn a living some way, so why not at Sainsbury?'

His timing was spot on for a member of the younger generation. He joined the general grocery buying office in 1950, the same year as the Croydon store was converted to self-service, making it the first ever Sainsbury supermarket.

He soon became the company biscuit buyer and experienced for the first time the intoxicating thrill of seeing sales increase dramatically. 'We grew the trade very fast and I found tremendous excitement and pleasure in the art of negotiating with suppliers.' For much of the 1950s supplies were still limited and retailers had to plead and cajole to increase their allocations. JD, as he was called to differentiate him from his still-active grandfather Mr John Benjamin, showed himself a pretty forceful negotiator right from the start.

His obsession for detail became legendary and inevitably braver souls in the organisation would occasionally make fun of him. Ross McLaren, who headed the dairy division before going to America to run the successful Shaws supermarket chain, recalled the chairman returning to his Stamford Street office with a pot of yoghurt he deemed unsatisfactory and summoning McLaren to his office. 'This yoghurt is runny,' he thundered. 'It should be much thicker.'

'Well, JD', said McLaren, a robust Scot with a lively sense of humour, 'yoghurt is a live culture and it is very sensitive. If you shout at it, it goes runny.'

To his credit, JD saw the joke, although what McLaren called the 'runny yoghurt war' continued for several years.

Colleagues at Sainsbury compare JD to Prince Charles in many of his attitudes. When travelling he detested any delay and would grow impatient if he had to wait in a queue for more than a few seconds. As he normally travelled first class or in private planes this was rarely a problem. But his lofty manner towards airline staff made his fellow directors squirm with embarrassment.

On one occasion, shortly after airlines had banned smoking, he lit up a small cigar in the first-class cabin, where he and his fellow directors were the only passengers. After the cabin crew made repeated requests for him to put the cigar out, the pilot emerged from his cockpit and threatened to turn the plane round and return to the airport if the cigar were not extinguished. Finally, JD acquiesced.

Difficult he may have been, but he had an inspired touch when it came to food retailing. Along with a hawk's eye for detail – a wrong price here, a bruised apple there – his personality also encompassed great vision. He saw that Sainsbury could be the leading retailer as well as providing the best butter in the world.

At the company's annual meetings, JD would invariably be the only director of those on the stage to answer questions. But he did not transform the company alone. The recruitment of Roy Griffiths, a brilliant strategist who had his total confidence, was crucial. Griffiths took a long-term strategic view of business and was a steadying hand on his chairman. He and JD's wife Anya were regarded as the only people JD really respected. Griffiths, together with Simon and Tim Sainsbury, helped him re-invent the company.

Tim Sainsbury, the director in charge of property, recognised the potential of large out-of-town stores and set about capitalising on the existing property portfolio. Sainsbury owned most of its collection of stores in prime positions in Middle England's high streets. They were able to sell the least profitable of these at high prices and use the money to build something three times the size on the edge of town. The phrase inside the company was 'old shops for new'.

JD also capitalised on the reservoir of talent the group contained – men and women rigorously trained, steeped in the company's values, but never before allowed to stretch themselves. Now the opportunity was theirs and they responded valiantly under his command.

But if his twenty-three years as chairman were the most glorious in the history of Sainsbury, the last ten of them also saw better times for Tesco and Safeway. When JD stepped into the chair in 1969 Tesco was ahead in sales, although Sainsbury had the middle-class food market much to itself. Marks & Spencer and Waitrose, although highly regarded, were much smaller players acting almost as test marketers for new ideas.

By the time JD retired in 1992, Tesco still lagged two percentage points behind Sainsbury's 19 per cent of the market but Ian MacLaurin and his team had transformed the 'cheap-and-cheerful' company into an increasingly credible alternative to Sainsbury. Just as important for Tesco's future growth, they had bought up so many out-of-town supermarket sites at high prices that the Sainsbury directors wondered just what they would put in all that space.

'At Sainsbury we always had to be sure exactly how a store would work,' said one. 'We would evaluate new openings in huge detail and when we replicated those sums on the new Tesco stores, there was no way that we could make the investment pay off.'

The competition was gaining strength all round. Safeway was surging forward in the south and Scotland, and at Asda's demoralised Leeds head-quarters Archie Norman and Allan Leighton were ripping down office walls along with the old hierarchical culture in order to transform the group into a new and formidable entity. On top of this Continental discounters such as Netto and Lidl had arrived, forcing all the big groups to cut prices to compete.

During the 1970s and early 1980s JD's command-and-control style of management worked perfectly. Riding the wave of a consumer boom he recast the sleepy family company he had inherited into a dynamic force and made his relatives rich beyond their wildest dreams. After the company floated on the stock market in 1973 many of the sixty or so extended family members became multi-millionaires. As Alan Sainsbury once told his children at one of the regular family gatherings, 'You have always been well off, but you must thank your elder brother John for making you super-rich.'

Such a generous comment conceals Alan Sainsbury's reluctance to let go of the reins. At the beginning, Alan used to change the prices of some products in the stores without JD knowing and there was uproar when he found out. 'There was a lot of antler clashing,' said one colleague.

It was all kept out of the public eye. To the outside world the Sainsbury family presented a seamlessly united front. Internally they were like most families, a seething cauldron of emotion, jealousy and resentment. Although David, the three brothers' cerebral scientific cousin, worked at the company, they would only encounter him socially at family weddings and funerals.

JD had learned about innovation from his father and constantly looked to the future, ensuring Sainsbury stayed ahead of the trend. In some ways the most radical change he made was to turn the company from a private one to a public one listed on the London stock market. Without that break with tradition, the spectacular growth of the 1970s and 1980s could not have taken place, although the initial offering was more about releasing cash than raising capital. He promised the flotation would 'in no way affect the control of the company, its established trading policy or its style and philosophy of management'.

Much of the arrogance of the Sainsbury culture stemmed from its long-standing private ownership. By the time the family was ready to countenance putting its precious shares in other people's hands the company was four years past its 1969 centenary year and its members had become used to answering to no one outside. Suppliers could count themselves fortunate to be suppliers while customers, albeit valued in general, did not count for much as individuals.

By the 1970s the Sainsbury clan had multiplied and there was some pressure on the board to put a value on their shareholdings and a desire, partly whipped up by the frenzied bull run in the stock market from 1969 onwards, to turn their holdings into something more spendable.

Most successful companies float within the first twenty years of existence in a quest for new capital. They are typically hungry young firms in need of expansionary capital – Tesco was a classic example. Sainsbury, in contrast, was a dowager coming to market, confident and well presented with more than a century of successful trading under her bodice. Its flotation was the biggest ever seen on the London Stock Exchange, valuing the company at £117m.

Few doubted it would go well – the brand that was so valued in the high street would be valued in the City, where everyone's wife shopped at Sainsbury. Coming during a wild bull market – the imminent end to which was anticipated by nobody at the time – the flotation excited the imagination of private and institutional investors alike. There was only one snag. Intent on keeping control, the family would sell only 15 per cent of its precious heritage.

The result was a stampede of would-be-investors at the Midland Bank's Austin Friars new issue department on Thursday, 12 July 1973. Within minutes the list of applications was closed, £495m having been offered for £14.5m worth of shares. One pension fund bid for the entire issue.

Sainsbury punished the greedy and rewarded its staff and small share-holders. Anyone who had applied for more than 15,000 shares was scaled down to 2 per cent of the amount applied for, allowing even the smallest applicants to receive some shares. Of the 147,577 individual applications, 4,772 came from members of Sainsbury's staff – a large number at a time when 'ordinary' people rarely thought of investing in the stock market.

Every member of staff had received a priority application form and JD later lobbied the government to introduce legislation that would encourage other types of profit sharing. When trading in Sainsbury shares opened the following week, the stock market opened its doors fifteen minutes early so that dealers could prepare for the rush. Sainsbury shares jumped from 145p to 165p in early trading. The *Yorkshire Evening Post* remarked wittily that 'Good shares cost more ... at Sainsbury's.'

Public or not, Sainsbury was still very much a family business. Five out of ten main-board directors still came from the family in 1973, down from seven in 1960. Under John came Simon, who was deputy chairman and oversaw the finances, and Tim, who masterminded property. Astonishingly they operated from separate offices – John in Stamford Street, Simon in Streatham and Tim in Clapham.

In the early days Tim would make all the decisions on new sites, construction and fitting out. Sainsbury folklore had it that when a new store was complete he would hand the keys to his eldest brother, who could like it or lump it. It may not have been quite that clear cut, but the property and retailing functions were certainly separate.

Was there intense sibling rivalry between the three brothers? It was more a case of JD poaching increasing amounts of territory from Simon and Tim until they decided that working outside the company might be preferable.

The three brothers' first cousin David, son of Robert, worked with Simon as financial controller while James Sainsbury was in charge of cooked meats. Of non-family managers at the time of flotation, Roy Griffiths was the most significant, advising and calming his red-haired chairman. Once the company became public the board structure gradually changed as new outside talent came in and Simon and Tim left. Tim went into politics, becoming a Conservative MP, and Simon pursued other business interests and patronage of the arts.

The family also learned the hard way that shares could go down in value as well as up. By the end of 1973 the stock market had begun to fall owing to industrial unrest and rising inflation and interest rates. The oil crisis sent it into free-fall until the FT30 index hit 146 in January 1975 compared with a peak of 543 in May 1972 and Sainsbury shares halved to 74p. Simon Sainsbury assured the small shareholders, many of whom were Sainsbury staff, that the fall was a result of market forces, not the company's performance, and wisely advised them to hang on to their shares for the long term.

As the 1970s progressed, Sainsbury found the greatest barriers to expansion were erected not by rivals – Tesco was floundering in the early part of the decade – but by the trade unions and the Labour government. Trade unions dominated Sainsbury depots and their leaders, not so different from the shop steward Peter Sellers played in the film *I'm All Right Jack*, relished timing their strikes to cause maximum inconvenience. They would call a strike on a Wednesday, with the implicit threat that if management refused to meet their demands, the shelves would be bare on a Saturday. Most of the early action was piecemeal and short lived, however, and easily settled with a concession.

The Sainsbury family, paternalistic by nature, put off a confrontation with the unions, hoping that reason would somehow prevail. Meanwhile trading was tough; sales were well below Tesco's, even though rampant inflation disguised just how much the company was struggling. JD and Roy Griffiths began to fear for Sainsbury's future if the power of the unions was not curtailed.

The crunch came in 1977 when Tesco launched Operation Checkout – the beginning of its repositioning under Ian MacLaurin – to coincide with the Queen's Jubilee celebrations.

The unions decided to launch a strike for the same week to paralyse Sainsbury's distribution network. The action was, unusually, across the whole company and the prospect of empty shelves loomed.

As customers flocked to Tesco, lured by deep discounts on key items, the humiliation at Sainsbury became too much too bear. Paternalism was one thing, allowing the unions to ruin your business was another. It was time to respond. 'The Jubilee strike was a watershed in our dealings with unionised staff,' recalled a former director. 'Tesco was motoring and we were struggling.'

JD and Roy Griffiths, the director in charge of distribution, kept the shelves stocked by contracting out most of the distribution to firms such as

Tibbett & Britten. And when the strike was finally over after six long weeks Griffiths made sure that more than a third of the distribution stayed with the outside contractors. Sainsbury could never again be held hostage by its workers to the same extent, although it took the arrival of Margaret Thatcher in 1979 to curb the unions' power altogether.

When the success of Operation Checkout became clear, Sainsbury's managers realised they had to fight on price – although there was to be no unseemly rush. JD put an energetic young director called Peter Davis in charge of masterminding a counter-offensive. Seven months later in January 1978 Davis launched Discount 78 – the first time Sainsbury had engaged in an all-out price war. It was so successful that it pulled the company up close to its old rival. By 1982 the two leaders both had sales of nearly £2bn but Sainsbury's profits of £89m were more than twice those of Tesco with £42.7m.

The early 1980s also witnessed some takeover skirmishes among the smaller players. In 1982 James Gulliver's Argyll Foods bought Allied Suppliers from Cavenham Foods. Then Linfood Holdings bid £72m for Fitch Lovell, owner of the Key Market stores.

Sainsbury found town planners almost as big a problem as the trade unions. 'It was taking almost three years to get planning permission for a single new shop,' JD remarked acidly. Tesco was usually the main competitor for sites. What amused executives in the two companies was that a quirk of fate linked Tim Sainsbury, development director from 1962 to 1973, with Robin Behar, the head of Tesco's property team at the same time.

Before the war the Sainsburys employed a governess called Muriel Fox Hill, whom the children called Foxy. After the war she went to work for the Behar family, tutoring young Robin. At her wedding two decades later Tim took delight in proposing the toast to the bride and groom, announcing that 'Foxy had more influence on the location of supermarkets than almost anyone else in the country.'

Sainsbury might have struggled with the planners because Tim had no interest in cosying up to local councils, believing it was in their interests to have a Sainsbury store in their area. 'I have walked out of one or two meetings before now,' he told one reporter.

Tesco was different and once MacLaurin had become managing director the competition intensified, with MacLaurin's team searching the country for new sites. To many they seemed more streetwise, more approachable and perhaps better at negotiating with local councils.

Innately conservative, Sainsbury resisted embarking on any really sizeable developments. Although JD recognised the potential of edge-of-town and out-of-town locations, he rarely authorised stores of more than 18,000 square feet, and never one of more than 25,000.

At the time Asda was opening 40,000-square-foot monster sheds in the north of England and developing a reputation for low prices. But when JD voiced his concern about the group if it moved south, Tim told him the costs would escalate and the model would not be as profitable.

Another reason Sainsbury avoided larger sites was that JD and his directors saw the company as essentially a food retailer. He viewed the idea of selling 'non-food' items with disdain, possibly fearing it would blur the focus on food and confuse the customer. He failed to see how selling clothes, toys, beauty products and electrical goods, most of which earned much higher margins, alongside food could please customers intent on their food shopping. While he kept Sainsbury aloof from such practices, Tesco and Asda filled up their extra space with clothing and household goods that could become 'impulse purchases' for customers making their way round the store.

Asda and Tesco had already grasped the synergies between the two types of shopping although it is doubtful in the 1980s that either foresaw a time when televisions, designer make-up and gardening equipment would all be on sale in supermarkets.

But if JD missed an opportunity in non-foods he stole a march on Tesco and the rest of the competition in the 1970s by aggressively expanding own-label products. For him it was 'The most important innovation of the lot.'

Ironically, considering that Jack Cohen's Tesco tea had been a pioneering own-label product, Sainsbury leapt ahead, capitalising on the trust inherent in its brand. For more than 100 years Sainsbury had symbolised quality and consistency. Customers knew what they were getting and butter or biscuits in Sainsbury wrapping were often just as acceptable as established brands – especially as they were a little cheaper. It even worked with champagne. Tesco customers might pick up bargains, but the quality of what they took home was less assured.

JD laid out the rules for what he always called 'private label'. 'The products had to be as good as the leading brand and they had to be cheaper.' This was achieved through cost savings. 'It had very basic economics. There were no advertising or marketing costs and distribution costs were far lower.'

By 1980, more than half of Sainsbury lines carried the company's label, an astonishing proportion by international standards and way ahead of Tesco or Asda. True, Marks & Spencer never sold anything that did not bear its St Michael brand, but it was a niche player in food with premium prices and a limited range.

Sainsbury's development of its own label enraged the owners of well-known food brands, who saw sales suffer even though some made money by manufacturing Sainsbury own-label products. JD fought many battles with such giants as Unilever, Heinz and Procter & Gamble. But some small manufacturers were prepared to cooperate with such a valuable client in return for more business than they had ever dreamed of, and many achieved great success as a result. Sir Gulam Noon, whose company supplies Sainsbury with a wide range of Indian chilled dishes, was one example. Noon, as everyone calls him, made his fortune by selling 'authentic' curry to Sainsbury. He started with four or five dishes and by 2004 made 105 dishes for Sainsbury as well as the Indian food to take away from the deli counter. He also supplied Waitrose and Morrison, though never Tesco.

JD fell in love with North America as a young man, and he never ceased to look there for the next new thing. Not long after he had joined the company an opportunity to revitalise the way Sainsbury sold bacon presented itself. The head of Canada Packers, a bacon supplier, came to see him about expanding trade with Sainsbury and told him of the new ways his company was curing and pre-packing bacon. To find out more JD tagged a visit to Canada on to a holiday in America and spent much of his time at the bacon plant or investigating North American supermarkets.

The traditional Wiltshire bacon business was trimmed back and Canada Packers became one of Sainsbury's leading suppliers. New techniques of milder curing and pre-packing proved a hit with customers. By 1960, ten years after he joined the company, sales of the bacon business had gone up from £15.8m to £68m.

The bacon expedition was the first of many business trips and holidays to America. JD soon became a member of the Supermarket Institute of America, which met in a glamorous location each year for its annual jamboree at which ideas, gossip and business cards were swapped.

In the late 1970s JD's American contacts alerted him to scanning, the new technology for ordering goods, adding them up at the till and allocating merchandising space. Roy Griffiths investigated these new and at the time hugely expensive techniques. British and European supermarkets were in general suspicious of new technology but Sainsbury introduced it at least two years before its rivals. The company may have had to endure the teething problems that occur with new technology, but the customers liked scanning and it resulted in much greater efficiency at the checkout.

Sainsbury may have missed the boat, and continued to miss it, on selling non-foods but it slayed the competition when it came to high-quality own-label items and had a head start on technology and the new 'just-in-time' procedure where suppliers' goods arrived at the depots in the morning and went out to the stores in the afternoon. Another area in which it took advantage of growing consumer sophistication was wine, where Alan Cheeseman, a young executive, led the way. Aware that many of its customers had developed a liking for wine while on holiday but had limited knowledge of it, Sainsbury was the first supermarket whose wine labels both described the contents and suggested what food it would best accompany. It also focused on stocking good, inexpensive wines, and by 2004 sales had reached 3 million bottles a week.

During the 1980s – an era when company takeovers took on a gladiatorial aspect for directors of public companies – Sainsbury expanded into America with the purchase of a New England supermarket chain called Shaws and into the home DIY market with Homebase, a DIY and gardening joint venture set up in 1979. To this Texas Homecare was added in 1996 under David Sainsbury's chairmanship. It was, however, sold for £969m in December 2000 as part of Peter Davis's first-year clear-out.

Surprisingly for such a quintessentially English company, Sainsbury's foray into America with the purchase of Shaws proved a sustained success until Shaws was sold in 2004. The Sainsbury scouts had looked at several states, including Texas. 'Thank God we decided not to go to Texas,' declared JD later.

In some ways it might be compared to Lord Rayner's disastrous purchase for Marks & Spencer of Brooks Brothers, a modish menswear retailer on the east coast of America. But Shaws worked in a way that Brooks Brothers did not. Shaws was a family business that was even older than

1. Replica of Tesco founder Jack Cohen's first stall

2. Early Bradford store

3. Interior of Sainsbury's Chelmsford branch, 1931

4. Home delivery *c.* 1930

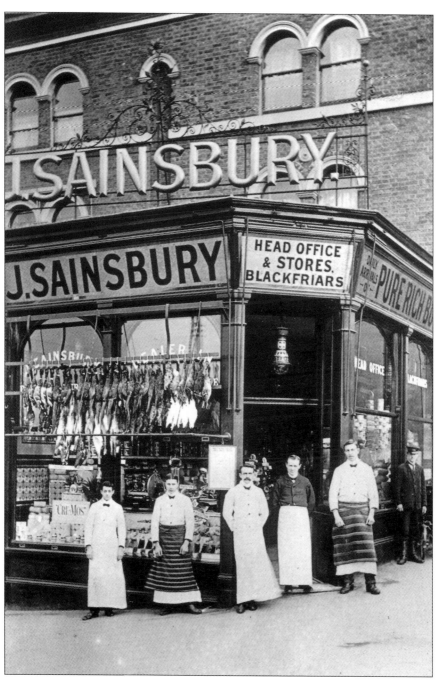

5. A rare corner shop; Blackheath Village *c.* 1902

6. John James Sainsbury with his six sons:
John Benjamin, Arthur, Frank, Alfred (back row, left to right),
Paul and George (front row)

7. John James and his wife Mary Ann, the founders of Sainsbury

8. David Sainsbury in the Cromwell Road delicatessen, 1994

9. Sir Peter Davis, Sainsbury chairman, 2004

10. Allan Leighton, part of the turn-round team at Asda

11. Justin King, Sainsbury's bright new hope, appointed in 2004

12. Keeping it in the family, 1969. From left to right: Mr Alan, Mr Robert, Mr JD, Mr James, Mr Simon, Mr Timothy and Mr David

13. Out for a stroll: Jack Cohen, Tesco founder, his wife 'Cissie' and their daughters, Irene (right) and Shirley *c.* 1935

14. Sir Jack Cohen with Daisy Hyams (left) and his daughter Shirley *c.* 1975

15. Ian MacLaurin (left) and Mike Darnell at Sir Leslie Porter's retirement party 1985

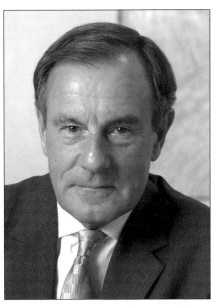

16. Sir Leslie Porter, who liked to spar
with the chairman

17. Lord MacLaurin, the man who
modernised Tesco

18. David Reid, Tesco chairman 2004,
who likes to party

19. Sir Terry Leahy, Tesco chief executive
since 1997 – who does not like to party

20. Bentonville, Arkansas,
home of the brave

21. Sainsbury's gleaming HQ,
Holborn Circus, London

22. Asda House in Leeds, home
of the blue sofa

23. Modern Morrison's,
no pretensions

24. Sir Ken Morrison doing it the Yorkshire way

25. David Webster,
Safeway chairman, the last
musketeer

26. The three musketeers, Alistair Grant, James Gulliver and David Webster
at the Savoy, 1983

27. Archie Norman, seated, turning Asda round

28. Part of the Wal-Mart family: Tony de Nunzio, Asda chief executive

29. George at Asda children's clothes

30. Asda's wide open aisles

31/32. Two firsts:
Mr JD showing Her
Majesty the Queen
Mother round
Sainsbury's first wine
selection, Cromwell
Road, 1985 (above).
Tesco sells toads
for the cooking pot
in Hymall, a joint
venture in Shanghai,
October 2004 (right)

Sainsbury. It had been founded in 1859, ten years before the Drury Lane dairy shop, but that did not stop the management being at the cutting edge of modern technology. And it was the electronic scanning technology they were pioneering that attracted Sainsbury to them. The Shaw family had been looking for a non-American partner and Sainsbury seemed the perfect fit.

Unlike Brooks Brothers, which had cost too much and was badly run, Shaws made money quietly and consistently. Between the twice-yearly state visits from JD the management were left to get on with it, freed of the constant interference experienced by the UK stores. It also provided Sainsbury directors with a perfect excuse to fly first class to the United States to visit a company not so far from New York, where a wealth of opera and art beckoned.

In his private life JD was always a passionate supporter of the arts, although his heart belonged to Sainsbury. 'It's extraordinary staying with him,' recounted one house guest. 'There are Monets on the walls but squeezy Sainsbury soap in the bathroom.' A keen collector of Impressionist paintings, he was also a great opera lover and bon viveur. He sat on the board of the Royal Opera House from 1969, chaired it from 1987 to 1991 and remained an enthusiastic supporter. He and his brothers financed the Sainsbury Wing of the National Gallery.

His devotion to his wife Anya Linden, a former ballerina, was clear. After meeting her briefly he went to see her dance in 1962 and persuaded her to have dinner with him after the performance. 'Anya and I had a marvellous dinner together and I fell in love immediately,' he told Sue Lawley on *Desert Island Discs*. They married in 1963 and set up a joint charitable trust that they called Linbury – an amalgamation of their last names. When her husband's personality caused anger or distress, her gentle charm often acted as a soothing balm on hurt feelings. When Peter Davis would arrive home furious at yet again being over-ruled by JD, his wife, Sue, would say 'Think of Anya. He can't be that bad if he's married to her.'

In 2004 knowledgeable customers were amused to see that Sainsbury was selling a type of new potato called the Anya, recommended for use in salads.

It took Sainsbury until 1986 to overtake Tesco in terms of market share. In that year Tesco had 14.2 per cent of the market compared with Sainsbury's 14.6. Asda was way behind with 7.4 per cent followed by Safeway with 4.2 per cent and Morrison with just 1.5 per cent. Sainsbury sailed on serenely as the undisputed leader of the sector for nearly a decade. When the time came for JD, by then Lord Sainsbury of Preston Candover, to hand over the reins, nobody foresaw the calamity ahead even though there were clues.

One of them was his reluctance to discuss succession. In 1986 Peter Davis quit his number three position in the company as assistant managing director. In theory he was running UK stores, but in practice he found his role was simply to obey orders. 'I was not allowed to set the price of Gordon's Gin,' he said later. JD, it seemed, would not give even his most able directors the slightest autonomy. It was also made clear to Davis that when JD retired, he would not get the top job to himself.

At that time, JD – unwilling to contemplate his own departure – disliked any discussions about succession but eventually he outlined his plans to the inner circle. He wanted Davis and Roy Griffiths to be made joint managing directors under him and when Griffiths retired, David Quarmby would take his place. Davis and Quarmby would remain as joint managing directors under David Sainsbury when he became chairman. Quarmby's previous job had been running London's buses and, although he had a dazzling intellect, his experience had been largely outside the retail sector. Davis felt his experience at running supermarkets was far superior and that it was time to move on from the old-fashioned idea of having two managing directors. After some argument he eventually told JD he wanted to resign.

JD may not have wanted Davis as sole managing director, but he was outraged that a hitherto loyal servant should dare to leave the company. He also reckoned Davis was too valuable an asset to lose and too able, not to mention too full of Sainsbury secrets, to be allowed to work for a rival. He pulled out all the big legal guns at his disposal to prevent Davis from leaving. The Sainsbury lawyers told Davis he was on a seven-year contract and that if he did leave he would be barred from working for another food retailer. It was an uncomfortable time. For a few weeks after he tendered his resignation, Davis still chaired the trading committee every Wednesday and went about his daily duties. But the chairman refused to speak to him, behaving as if he was invisible.

'There was a lot of bad blood,' recalled Davis. Finally he managed to extricate himself and secure a new job as managing director of Reed International.

On the Friday he was due to leave, some of his colleagues threw a small party for him, but the security men broke it up on the grounds that it was

not 'authorised'. They then escorted Davis off the premises and took possession of his company car keys and his company credit card, which was cut up
in front of him. He was also frisked to ensure he had no sensitive papers on
him.

JD did not speak to him for eight years. 'John viewed Sainsbury as his train
set and he was the equivalent of the Fat Controller,' one director said. 'Nobody
had the right to decide whether they wanted to get off or stay aboard.'

Sainsbury viewed Marks & Spencer as its most able competitor – each put
quality and value at the top of their priorities. For more than a decade they
vied for the position of Britain's most profitable retailer. Colleagues recall
Lord Rayner, then chairman of Marks & Spencer, arriving at a supplier in a
vicious temper because the morning papers had run the story that Sainsbury
had overtaken Marks & Spencer for the title. By 1991–2, the year JD retired,
Sainsbury's profit margins had risen to 7.9 per cent compared with 4–6
per cent for the rest of the industry. This was almost as high as margins in
clothes retailing.

In order to achieve this level of profit JD had quietly cut back on investment in the stores. He trimmed capital spending and he cut spending on
everyday maintenance, training and information technology. Fond of the
limelight, he devoted increasing amounts of time to the Royal Opera House,
the Sainsbury Wing of the National Gallery and the Linbury charitable trust.
By the time he handed over the company to his cousin David, colleagues
believe it was something of a poisoned chalice. There is also no doubt that
David Sainsbury, a mild-mannered scientist-cum-politician with little
interest in the nitty gritty of retailing, drank deeply. Even so, the notion that
JD, an autocrat who had ruled the company for twenty-three years, could
move out of his office and that the business would keep on running in the
same way without him smacks of collective delusion.

Things might have been different if Margaret Thatcher's secret plans to
parachute JD in as chairman of British Telecommunications in 1986, six
years before his eventual retirement from Sainsbury, had been successful. BT
had been privatised in 1984 but Thatcher and her business-minded advisers

felt it needed a strong injection of private-sector expertise. JD agreed that when the chairman Sir George Jefferson retired, he would step into the role and shake things up.

But such a move struck fear into the BT hierarchy, a close-knit group steeped in the ways of the public sector. They objected strongly to the idea of appointing a forceful free-enterprise spirit such as JD and in the ensuing row with the government Jefferson suddenly decided to quit early owing to stress.

JD could not leave Sainsbury at such short notice and Thatcher had to accept the internal candidate, Iain Vallance. Had JD taken the BT job in 1986, Peter Davis might have stayed, albeit as joint managing director, and might have proved himself capable of running the company alone under David Sainsbury. BT, on the other hand, would probably have made a much more competitive fist of the telecoms market than it did.

In 1986 David Sainsbury might also have been more motivated to make a success of the retail challenge he was eventually given. In the event, by 1992 his interests had gone down a very different track from flogging food from superstores.

Under David Sainsbury's chairmanship, the company's fortunes went rapidly downhill. There was, however, little sign of the nightmares to come when JD announced that he was going to retire. Indeed, JD pulled out all the stops in the last year of his reign and in 1992 he announced record profits of £632m, up by 25 per cent, 'including the benefits of a rights issue', and snatching the title of Britain's most profitable retailer from Marks & Spencer. Sainsbury had also been voted the most popular supermarket in a Consumers' Association survey in which 41 per cent of those questioned said they would choose to shop at Sainsbury 'if there was one convenient' compared with only 28 per cent who chose Tesco.

This extract from his statement to shareholders speaks volumes: 'Looking back over the last 20 years you might be interested to know that our compound rate of profit growth has been 23 per cent a year ... Our return on capital employed was 21.4 per cent. This was certainly a satisfactory return, but I suggest a far from excessive one. It is in fact just ahead of Marks & Spencer's and the average of all UK food retailers by around 2 points.'

He also pointed out that Sainsbury had increased market share over its 'principal competitors' and that its prices were lower than the competition: 'Fundamental to our growth in market share is the excellent value we offer.

We have maintained our 2 per cent competitive advantage over the average of our principal competitors and retained our position as the lowest priced supermarket retailer.'

Furthermore, the company was forging ahead on choice: 'We launched some 1,500 new lines last year ... New lines include the Boboki pizza range, Ciabatta bread, Condiverde pasta sauces, yogurt duet and almost 50 new ready-meals from Indian Rogan Gosh to British bread-and-butter pudding. New fruit, vegetables and salads included Frais de Bois, pink currants and baby coconuts.'

JD made sure he left Sainsbury on a high note and it seemed that not even he understood just how important his leadership had been. 'I am delighted that my cousin David is to be my successor and that the company is going to be led by him and our two very able managing directors, Tom Vyner and David Quarmby,' he said. 'I know that the future leadership of the company could not be in better hands and under them we will continue to go from strength to strength.' How very wrong he was.

CHAPTER SEVEN

THE FIGHT FOR SUPREMACY

'By method and discipline are to be understood the marshalling of the army in its proper subdivisions, the graduations of rank among the officers, the maintenance of roads by which supplies may reach the army, and the control of military expenditure.'

Sun Tzu, *The Art of War*

The battle lines were being drawn as JD's reign drew to a close. In February 1991, Tesco launched a £572m rights issue to help pay for an ambitious store opening and renovation programme then running at almost £1bn a year. Ian MacLaurin wowed City investors with plans to open twenty-five new superstores a year for the next four years at an average cost of £35m each. The City lapped it up and Tesco's successful reception cleared the way for a fund-raising fest. Within weeks, Sainsbury, Argyll, Morrison and Asda had all announced rights issues raising £1.8bn between them. Armed with these funds, they went to war.

But for once it was not just each other they were fighting. A new threat had arrived from Germany and Scandinavia – the discounters. Aldi, Lidl and Netto had targeted Britain, believing it to be a vulnerable market for their no-frills formula of a narrow range of cheap goods sold from unprepossessing sites in tertiary locations. The UK big four set about seeing them off their territory, often helped by their suppliers, who saw little value in their brands being on sale in such downmarket shops.

For the previous ten years MacLaurin and his team at Tesco had relentlessly copied Sainsbury – or benchmarked it, as they called it – in a highly successful effort to turn Tesco's image round. David Malpas, the quiet pipe-smoking deputy chairman, was the perfect foil for MacLaurin, especially as he was happy to play his strategic role behind the scenes. Neither, insiders felt, could have done the job without the other.

Tesco scouts reported back from Sainsbury stores daily on prices, displays and new products – there are few real secrets in retailing. One young marketing manager found himself at the heart of the action. Terry Leahy had joined Tesco in 1979 after graduating from the University of Manchester Institute of Science and Technology (UMIST). He had also worked at the Manchester branch of the Co-op and had travelled all over the country visiting the 270 societies. 'The management [of the Co-op] was more sophisticated then than at Tesco, but the ownership structure made growth impossible,' recalled Leahy. 'It was clear, even then, that the lads at Tesco were the coming thing.'

The future chief executive was turned down for the job he applied for, which went to another young hopeful. But then the recruitment team decided to give the successful applicant a more senior job and called Leahy back in.

Leahy spent a miserable first year beavering away in an embryonic marketing department that operated from a windowless office in the bowels of the Cheshunt headquarters. A couple of years later the department had developed and he became involved in the benchmarking of Sainsbury. 'I provided the first building blocks of how to copy Sainsbury. We had to take Sainsbury apart, find out what things were important to customers and how we rated.'

Always keen on research, he borrowed the trade-off model that Ford used when it researched how to combat the Volkswagen Golf and Polo and came up with the Fiesta. People rarely tell the truth in surveys so the idea was to force them to trade one possibility against another by posing a string of questions such as 'Is quality more important than price?' 'Eventually they get lost and start telling the truth,' said Leahy. Armed with the answers the senior management worked ceaselessly to implement them and throughout the 1980s the Tesco brand image steadily improved. MacLaurin was hailed as a hero and received a knighthood in 1989 for his achievements as chairman while, to the outside world, Malpas was nowhere to be seen. Between 1986 and 1991 pre-tax profits more than doubled to £546m. In 1991 Sainsbury's profits were behind at £505m, although they leapt ahead the following year.

Archie Norman and Allan Leighton had begun to make an impact at Asda.

Norman's strategy and Leighton's brilliance in implementing it together with expansion into the south of England began to reinvigorate the company.

At Argyll, Alistair Grant and David Webster had shaken off the bitter memories of the Guinness affair and had converted every food retail outlet they owned to the Safeway fascia. The big suppliers such as Unilever, Northern Foods and Associated Biscuits welcomed the revitalised Asda and Safeway, delighted that there were now four strong players.

At Sainsbury, JD's legacy was one of arrogance. 'The management there never questioned themselves because they had had the high-margin areas of south-east England to themselves for so long,' said one former Tesco director. 'Fifteen years ago no one in Esher would have dreamed of going to Tesco.'

JD made it clear that he regarded Tesco as beneath both him and his company: 'I remember going to lunch at the Ritz with a bunch of Tesco directors and Lord Sainsbury was at another table,' recounted the same director. 'He looked at us as though we were something the cat had brought in.' Yet three years after David Sainsbury took the chair in November 1992, the mighty Sainsbury group had lost its way. Sales and profits fell and in 1995 Tesco soared past it to become Britain's biggest supermarket by market share.

Tesco had recovered well from difficult times in 1992 when the sector came under attack from the discounters at the bottom of the market. The arrival of the German chain Aldi in 1990 and its headline-grabbing cheap lines of food drew the smaller UK operators KwikSave and Gateway into a tit-for-tat action. What became known as the baked bean war drove the price of a can of baked beans down to 4p.

Tesco had fought back hard, defending its turf when the continental discounters arrived. In retaliation it launched its Value range of low-priced items in blue and white 'prison uniform' packaging. Everyone then joined the price war – Asda, Safeway and Sainsbury all cut prices across swathes of products and the growth of the discounters was halted. David Sainsbury, the new chairman, appeared content. 'We have really hurt the discounters. They have no room to cut prices further,' he told the *Financial Times*. Yet analysts were questioning whether he understood the gravity of Sainsbury's problems.

Before becoming chairman, David Sainsbury had always worked in the finance office, away from the hurly burly of baked beans and low-fat yoghurt. In his early days he worked for Simon Sainsbury, JD's younger brother. From this position he had observed the trading side of the company from afar, but he had never been involved – and it was made clear he would not have been welcome.

He and his three cousins were as different in outlook as Margaret Thatcher and Neil Kinnock and they rarely met outside the business. One Sainsbury wife said she had never seen JD and David at the same social function.

So it was hardly surprising that the Thatcherite JD, who relinquished the chairmanship with mixed feelings, made little attempt to tutor his intellectual cousin, who had backed David Owen's Social Democrats before moving to Labour. What is perhaps more surprising is that David did so little to play himself in, despite holding the somewhat meaningless title of deputy chairman for four years before moving into the chair.

He seemed at first to believe that the team he inherited would continue to run the business as they had always done without the leader they had served for so long. And unlike most 'new brooms' he did not bring in many new people from outside the company – people who might have new ideas and would owe him their loyalty rather than JD. The Sainsbury family behaved as if they were medieval monarchs and once a new king was crowned, all the subjects would swear allegiance and that would be that. They soon discovered differently.

So sure of the market leadership had the management become that in 1992 David Sainsbury seemed blissfully unaware of any changes in the air. The three most powerful of the old guard had gone – Roy Griffiths, JD himself and Joe Barnes – and the team he inherited, while skilled and competent, operated on a command-and-control basis. The commander in chief, JD, spoke and the lieutenants performed with unquestioning obedience. Without their leader they went off the rails. When David Sainsbury promoted Tom Vyner, the chief buyer, to be joint managing director with David Quarmby the directors of Tesco chortled with delight and broke open several bottles of champagne. 'He was an amazingly tough buyer, but he had always been under JD's domination and he knew nothing about management,' said one. 'John Sainsbury would pass him the gun and he would fire the bullet.'

Without JD as his leader, power appeared to go to Vyner's head. Brutal behaviour antagonised manufacturers to such an extent that some even took their best people off the Sainsbury account, diverting them into servicing Tesco, Asda and the smaller chains. 'I could not see why I should put my best talent into dealing with Sainsbury, when the experience was always so unpleasant,' said one. If David Sainsbury even knew of this behaviour he did nothing to reverse it.

There has been much made of the legendary negotiating style of Daisy Hyams and her successor John Gildersleeve at Tesco. Yet by all accounts they were pussycats compared with Sainsbury buyers. 'They were hateful to deal with,' one former supplier said, 'far nastier than Tesco or the others.'

Many suppliers despised Vyner for his bully-boy behaviour, although they were pleasant to his face. He was quicker than most to threaten to delist products or drastically reduce their shelf space if the supplier did not lower the price or stump up money for a promotion.

Vyner and all the Sainsbury buyers had a 'massive inferiority complex about Marks & Spencer', according to one supplier. When one biscuit and ready-meals manufacturer refused to make sandwiches for Sainsbury because it had an exclusive contract with Marks & Spencer, Vyner was incensed. 'He cut us out of own-label contracts for biscuits and crisps as a punishment,' recalled a director of the company.

But in other instances Sainsbury and Marks & Spencer would both use companies such as Northern Foods and Hillsdown Holdings to supply chilled meals – although they might have to provide separate 'dedicated' factories.

Why David Sainsbury ever took on the job of chairman, when he would have been far happier sponsoring scientific endeavours and engaged in political initiatives, is a mystery. Friends of the family have said that he viewed it as his duty and that he had long felt a sense of frustration at being kept so far away from the trading side of the business. JD, Simon and Tim rarely met him socially. Insiders also believe that David's wife, Susy, encouraged her husband on the grounds that 'it was his turn' to chair the mighty dynasty.

From his viewpoint in the finance department he felt he had a mission to modernise the company. His MBA at Columbia Business School in New York had taught him about modern management theories – flatter structures and more consensus, all of which in his view meant empowering management down the line. He may have been right in theory, yet he had little idea how to bring this about in a company run for so long on hierarchical lines. Bringing in a modern-minded chief executive with a good track record from outside the company would have been one practical course. Instead he opted to retain the status quo.

With hindsight it is easy to say that David Sainsbury should have refused the chairmanship and opted instead to concentrate on his political career. Having been a founder member of the Social Democratic Party he became minister for science and innovation in Tony Blair's New Labour government when he left Sainsbury in 2000. His promotion of genetically modified foods caused a storm among the British public that spilled over into suspicion of the company. The public finds it difficult to differentiate between David Sainsbury the scientist and government adviser and David Sainsbury the scion of the eponymous company. He also made headlines because of his wealth – a million-pound donation to the Labour Party resulted in allega-tions of sleaze, particularly when they were linked to a relaxation in planning permission for out-of-town stores.

As the holder of almost a quarter of the company's shares he was by far the richest Sainsbury, even though he was more liberal and less grand than many of his cousins. Rather than being called 'Mr David' in the family tradition, he asked staff to call him David. None of this endeared him to a culture where the boss had until then held kingly status. The store staff who had lived in awe and admiration of JD quickly lost respect for a new chairman who had little idea of how the shelves should be stacked and kept asking for their opinions. Although he seemed like a nice guy, he lacked charisma and leadership.

If he had not been a Sainsbury, it is unlikely he would ever have been considered for the chairmanship. His financial experience and his academic and scientific prowess were valuable but he was clearly not up to running the nation's leading supermarket group. By all accounts, his management skills were minimal. Intellectually he was arguably superior to his predecessor, but as a retailer he was not in the same league.

Initially, the City welcomed the new leader, admiring David Sainsbury's cleverness, while his generosity to the arts and science was universally applauded. Investors believed there was a need to modernise and that change necessitated upheaval. A bedding-in period was to be expected and short-term disturbances would be tolerated. But Sainsbury's rivals were making too much progress for them to be tolerated for long.

His lack of interest in the day-to-day business soon became clear. When he became chairman in November 1992, he was best known as bankroller of the SDP and for his Gatsby charitable trust, named after the hero of Scott Fitzgerald's novel. The trust donated £30m a year towards the developing countries and scientific research.

At lunches with those eager to hear about his new strategy for modernising Sainsbury he talked at length on the wonders of genetically modifying a tomato and of the benefits that genetically modified foods would bring to developing countries. In plans for the future of Sainsbury, he appeared to be profoundly disinterested. 'The trouble with David was that he was no grocer at all, and not much of a leader', wrote Martin Vander Weyer in the *New Statesman.*

City investors, analysts and financial journalists returned from their initial meetings with him underwhelmed and concerned. A shy man, he perhaps felt it was too early to set out his plans for the company, although he did have some.

David Sainsbury's big idea was revealed a year later when he introduced a general management restructuring. 'Project Genesis', as it was called, led to the loss of 650 middle-management jobs and encouraged anyone over 50 to take advantage of a generous retirement package. 'What better way to destroy a business than to get rid of its most experienced people?' recalled one director later. Marks & Spencer made much the same mistake seven years later, ridding the company of what one director called 'one thousand years of experience' and with similar disastrous results.

By 1995 Sainsbury's customer complaints were rising and sales were falling. 'David threw everything up in the air. He tried to change too many things all at once,' said the same director. The result was chaos at a time when Tesco, Asda and even Safeway were gaining ground.

David Quarmby took the blame and resigned. Once again the chairman looked inside rather than outside the company for a replacement and made Dino Adriano chief executive. Adriano was a popular executive, but not a retailer, having served Sainsbury all his life on the finance side. Adriano resisted taking the job, sensing the problems that lay ahead, but David Sainsbury flattered and cajoled him into it. Tom Vyner became deputy chairman. He was meant to be a link between the older and younger generations, between the old outlook and the new, but even he admitted he made a rather weak bridge. 'I warned them Genesis was wrong, but I didn't resist hard enough,' he told a colleague later.

In the event, nobody was strong enough or sufficiently skilled in managing change to pull it off.

Competitors, meanwhile, had been limbering up for a fight. Argyll's conversion of all its Presto stores into Safeway gave a huge shot in the arm to sales and profits. The first two Presto converted stores, including retrained staff, boosted sales by 55 per cent and doubled profits. The way ahead was clear. In a £90-million programme the whole of Presto was converted to trade under the Safeway fascia. By May 1991 pre-tax profits were three and a half times higher than 1987 levels, at £191m, while sales had grown from £1.1bn to £3.5bn in the same period.

The new big boy on the block quickly rose to become joint fourth player with Asda. Safeway's image was quite different from Asda's. It eschewed the cut-throat world of non-foods, which required bigger sites than it owned, going for quality fresh produce with a green edge to it and ready-meals that were almost as good as those at Marks & Spencer. It also tailored its stores to local tastes, courting farmers and other suppliers.

Safeway's problem was scale. Having spent more than £1bn it did not have much left in the kitty for aggressive store expansion. Like JD at Sainsbury, Alistair Grant and David Webster refrained from bidding for big new sites, a mistake all three would come to regret.

In fact the only group aggressively buying up large sites in the recession of the early 1990s was Tesco. After the success of the 1980s some directors had put forward a plan to build a glitzy head office to replace the dreary Cheshunt monstrosity. Instead they decided to build three new superstores.

In the Cohen–Porter era the property director Francis Kreicher worked ceaselessly with Tesco's estate agent Healey & Baker to improve and increase the portfolio. But even by the early 1980s MacLaurin and Malpas could see that although they had far more stores than the competition most of them were far too small.

Kreicher was an old-fashioned property man with a brilliant eye for location and a talent for successfully appealing against planning application rejections. When he retired there was a gap until John Gildersleeve (JG as he was known throughout Tesco) set up a site research unit to evaluate the property portfolio and how it should change.

Throughout the late 1980s and early 1990s Tesco opened many superstores at £35m a throw, some in areas deemed too unpromising by the competition. The Surrey Quays store on the south side of the Thames in London's docklands was a prime example of brownfield development. Until Tesco opened its doors in 1989, the people of Bermondsey and Rotherhithe had to journey several miles to Lewisham or to the Sainsbury at Nine Elms in Vauxhall to find a decent-sized supermarket. Tesco provided one on their doorstep and the middle-class customers who bought up the new houses on the riverfront had little option but to learn to love shopping there. The store served two markets – the indigenous community of low earners, many of whom lived in public sector housing although some had bought their houses during the boom of the late 1980s, and the newcomers – a mixture of City types, doctors, midwives and other young professionals with families.

Tesco bought the whole of the Surrey Quays shopping centre and developed it, a risky venture that took some years to come right. Although WHSmith and Boots took space at the beginning, other retailers such as Marks & Spencer stayed away. 'We just did not think the catchment area was right for us,' said a Marks & Spencer director. Several spaces remained unlet for the first couple of years until retailers such as Top Shop and River Island were enticed by attractive rents.

For Tesco the 30,000-square-foot store with its huge car park was an instant success, demonstrating the amount of pent-up demand. Gradually the shops in the dismal small parade in Rotherhithe disappeared. When Tesco opened at Surrey Quays there were two butchers, a greengrocer, a general grocer, a convenience store, a newsagent and a chemist. Ten years later only the newsagent and the convenience store still survived. The local vicar declaimed against Tesco in his sermons, calling it on one occasion a temple of Mammon, but his congregation voted with their wallets. They found that the airy Surrey Quays shopping centre provided a more dynamic focus for the community with a children's activity area, cafés, a hairdresser and a Burger King. Many local people found jobs there, preferring the conditions to working in the cold local shops.

Surrey Quays was a big gamble and it paid off for Tesco eventually – although the other retailers struggled through the difficult years of the early 1990s and shops regularly changed hands. Similar stories were unfolding all over the country. By 2002 Tesco had 50 per cent more store space than Sainsbury, giving it an unassailable advantage.

The new-image Tesco required better-trained staff. 'It was clear that Tesco staff were less professional than those at Sainsbury and Safeway,' recalled one director. The MacLaurin team introduced a new training programme and inter-store competition. Staff were given ten criteria to aim for, including making eye contact with customers, saying hello and giving clear directions to where products could be found.

Yet in 1992, all was not well at Tesco. Pendulums in business usually swing too far one way or the other and in Tesco's pursuit of Sainsbury it had swung too far upmarket. MacLaurin had taken it ahead of its customer base and at just the wrong time. Its prices were, for a while, higher than those at Sainsbury and by 1991–2, when the country found itself gripped by a vicious recession, particularly in the south-east where property prices plunged, Tesco's sales and profits wavered. Between June and September 1992 the share price began to slide, losing 15 per cent as a series of nasty rumours fuelled by news of flat sales volumes circulated through the City for the entire industry from the Institute of Grocery Distribution. A Harvard Business School study published in 2003 stated: 'The lower-priced continental discounters attracted the value conscious and Sainsbury did a better job of attracting the quality conscious.'

Caught up in the economic euphoria of the late 1980s – a time when anything seemed possible – many people had believed in Margaret Thatcher's exhortations to become part of a property-owning democracy and bought their own homes. Now they laboured under rising mortgage payments as interest rates rose relentlessly.

Despite Tesco's modernising strides, its customers – dubbed 'Thatcher's children' – were still younger, less well educated and less financially secure than Sainsbury's. Tesco began to lose ground for the first time in a decade. In 2004 Tim Mason, the marketing director, put it this way: 'We missed the turn in the road and kept going on the road of upgrading. But when you live with negative equity you don't actually give much of a stuff where the smoked salmon comes from.'

When MacLaurin announced first-half results in September 1992 City fears were confirmed when he revealed that the growth in Tesco's profits had slowed to 10 per cent compared with 22 per cent for the same six months in 1991. Profit margins may have widened to nearly 7 per cent compared with

3 per cent in Jack Cohen's day, but Tesco's products had become a little too expensive for its customers and sales has slowed as a result.

Although retailing generally was struggling, Tesco had lost ground against Sainsbury. Many of its new superstores were, like Surrey Quays, located in areas worst hit by the recession. Ian MacLaurin made an impassioned speech blaming Tesco's slowdown on the grim economic picture. 'I have been in this industry for thirty years and I have never experienced trading conditions like this before,' he told investors. 'Consumers have been shot to pieces. Confidence is at zero in this country. The government has to regenerate confidence.'

There was little sympathy, though, for a man whose salary had risen by 55 per cent to £606,000 the year before. Since 1988 Tesco's market share had risen from 14.2 to 17.6 per cent but Sainsbury's had just kept ahead, moving from 15.3 to 18.8 per cent. Behind MacLaurin's rhetoric lay a market share barely holding its own in the face of a flight to trusted names during the recession. The fact that in the last year of his reign JD had taken all possible short-term steps to push profits as high as possible before he left had yet to be appreciated.

Yet the Tesco team recognised that the blame lay as much with them as with the tough conditions. Any sign of creeping complacency was crushed with the company's characteristic toughness.

During the MacLaurin era, the business had achieved what many thought impossible – it had taken a downmarket brand upmarket – but he had overshot the mark and it was time for a rethink. From then on his influence began to wane. A gifted leader, he enjoyed the limelight, but he had also built a team of able and experienced men around him – David Malpas the strategist, David Reid the diplomat. The head of buying John Gildersleeve was affectionately described by suppliers as a thug, pirate and astute negotiator. They had been together during the crucial years of Tesco's modernisation. They also had some wise non-executive directors such as Victor Benjamin, a veteran from the Leslie Porter era, and John Padovan, the former chairman of County NatWest, both of whom lent objectivity.

Together Tesco's management moved swiftly to stem the impending crisis. They recognised that too much attention had been paid to their main competitor at the expense of their core customers, and that new initiatives were required in order to win them back. When they looked within Tesco for the right person to take the business forward their eyes alighted on Terry

Leahy, the tense, hardworking young man from Liverpool who by then was heading the marketing/fresh foods department. At just 36, Leahy was promoted to the main board, where he set about analysing what exactly had gone wrong.

True to form, before acting, Leahy commissioned detailed focus-group research to find out why customers were leaving. 'Tesco had squandered a lot of goodwill with its core customers', stated a Harvard study. 'Their anger had less to do with a rational comparison of what the company had to offer but rather that Tesco had so obviously been chasing Sainsbury, copying them on this, copying them on that, instead of trying to satisfy its own customers.'

Tesco's customers wanted a return to better value as well as the better service and all the innovations Tesco had introduced. 'We could have just said bish bash bosh, let's slash the prices. But we needed to understand why we had come off the rails for the first time in nearly a decade,' said Tim Mason, who worked closely with Leahy during this period.

The answer was to go back to the customer. Ever since Leslie Porter had shifted the outlook of the company from de facto wholesaling to retailing, Tesco had prided itself on being customer- and store-focused. 'MacLaurin would go into a store and come back to head office and say, "I saw something that was all wrong and we need to change it." But JD would go into a store and say, "Why aren't you doing what head office has told you to do?"'

Somehow in the late 1980s Tesco's customers' views had been ignored in the chase after Sainsbury. In 1993 Leahy reported his findings to the board, and recommended a four-pronged strategy. First, stop copying Sainsbury; second, listen to customers; third, build a merchandising offer based on what those customers wanted.

This was to be no Operation Checkout revolution – rather an incremental 'bricks in the wall' response to customer needs.

At Cheshunt, Leahy coined the rather cumbersome slogan 'Tesco: the natural choice for ordinary shoppers' to motivate staff, while for public consumption Tim Mason dreamed up the much more snappy 'Every little helps'. It certainly did.

The Value lines in their distinctive striped packaging promised old-style Tesco value in basic products. The idea was not new to Leahy, who had launched a pilot Value range in a few stores in Scotland in 1981. But during the prosperous 1980s it had never seemed appropriate to extend the concept nationally. Value lines proved a counterpoint to the innovative, but expensive, range of prepared foods. City analysts hated the move, fearing it was taking Tesco back to the pile-it-high, sell-it-cheap days and that it would devalue the company's image. But customers struggling to pay their mortgages welcomed the Value lines and those who were better off appreciated that Tesco was trying to help at a time when money was tight. It all went to show that it was possible to serve different types of customer within one store – it was simply a matter of giving them a choice.

To address the criticisms of poor service Mason came up with the idea of the 'one-in-front' campaign – a promise to shoppers that there would be only one trolley in front of them at any checkout. If there was more than one in front, another checkout would be opened. Cost cutting on staff during the recession had left customers fuming with frustration, imprisoned for up to thirty minutes in a long queue before they could leave the store.

In autumn 1994, two weeks before Tesco planned to launch the 'one-in-front' campaign and when it was in the process of hiring nearly 5,000 new staff, the *Sun* newspaper ran a story that Sainsbury was planning to launch a similar campaign that very weekend.

Tesco's directors held an emergency meeting yet decided that even though Sainsbury would beat them to the starting post, they would keep to the launch date already set. But when David Malpas, who was away on holiday, was contacted for his views he was unequivocal: 'That is pathetic,' he said. 'We must go on Sunday.'

And so the whole business was galvanised into action in order to meet what seemed to be an impossible deadline. Store managers were told to find extra staff – either by hiring or paying overtime; the marketing department twisted arms to take advertising space in the Sunday newspapers. A television advertisement that had already been shot was placed at the eleventh hour on the Sunday night. 'We actually did it from a standing start in about seventy-two hours,' recalled Mason.

Amazingly, Sainsbury backed off from a high-profile campaign, although not without some disdainful comments. A spokeswoman said that Sainsbury had started major customer-service improvements at the end of 1993, and a similar scheme to 'one in front' was already operating in its stores but had not been advertised or given a press launch.

'It's quite ironic,' she went on. 'We identified this problem about checkout queues earlier this year. Tesco obviously got wind of what we were doing and jumped in. But it's not our style to rush out and make claims like they are doing.' Safeway also protested that the 'one-in-front' was of little consequence. 'Our store managers keep an eye on the checkouts and open up others if they see a queue. It's not such a wonderful new idea.'

Nevertheless, Tesco had stolen a march on its rivals with a razzmatazz publicity campaign of which Jack Cohen would have been proud.

David Malpas had recognised the value of prime-mover advantage and had proved his value to the company once again as a clear thinker. The 'one-in-front' campaign pulled in new customers, but more important it improved the throughput of the stores. Even so, strict adherence to the policy did not last much more than a couple of years because prime-mover advantage dissipates as competitors catch up. And the competition had no option but to follow Tesco's lead in shortening checkout queues, which since then have rarely been as long as they were in the late 1980s.

Tesco's next attempt to score prime-mover advantage was with its loyalty card – the Clubcard. This was Leahy's idea. Leahy had an instinct for what customers wanted, even though he always backed up his hunches with research. A working-class boy made good, he was a typical product of the meritocratic Tesco culture. He had worked for more than a decade in the marketing department, initially reporting to Gildersleeve and building a team around him of like-minded young men, notably Tim Mason, who had married one of MacLaurin's daughters, and David Potts. When he became chief executive both joined him on the board. Like him they were sporty, clean-living family men nursing fierce ambition.

As a lad growing up in Liverpool, Leahy had liked the 'divis' his mum used to bring home from the Co-op in lightweight silver 'money'. The Co-op, where he had begun his career, had later experimented with an electronic version and this had fired Leahy's imagination.

He devised Tesco's own electronic 'divi' and called it Clubcard – which was to be Britain's first national store loyalty card. After various pilot schemes, the national launch of Clubcard took place in 1995. It was an instant hit . and customers flocked to sign up. Tesco presented the card with a cynical mixture of humility and gratitude, claiming it was 'a way of saying thank you to our customers'.

And for many customers it did feel like gratitude. There was nothing quite like the warm glow of opening the monthly envelope to find simple vouchers exchangeable for goods up to their face value. Many successors, striving to be different, wound up with systems too complicated to give that hit of satisfaction that comes from receiving what is effectively money in the post. Eventually more than 10m Tesco customers became Clubcard subscribers.

Mason, the marketing director in 2003, who could bore for Britain on the usefulness of Clubcard to Tesco, summed it up: 'The Clubcard makes you do something. When you get the vouchers you have to go to the store to redeem them.' But as Mason also pointed out, the Clubcard gave Tesco access to a wealth of information about its customers, enabling the company to target them for specific products. This could go wrong sometimes, as one elderly lady who used baby shampoo found when vouchers arrived for disposable nappies, but generally it was a triumph.

Tesco had not been the originator of the idea. After the Co-op Safeway piloted a loyalty card in 1995 although it did not go national until well after the launch of Clubcard. But once again, Tesco had placed a big bet on red and won. Inspired by the enthusiasm of Leahy and Mason, Tesco threw the full weight of the organisation behind Clubcard to ensure success.

Sainsbury responded with characteristic disdain by saying loyalty cards were little more than electronic Green Shield Stamps. But the Clubcard proved every bit as popular as Jack Cohen's 'sticky little things' in their heyday, and it had technological knobs on. Clubcard proved a lot more useful to the company than stamps, providing crucial information about customers' buying habits.

Tesco management also trimmed back the number of food lines on offer to make more space for rather more profitable things – clothes, healthcare and electrical equipment. Leslie Porter's Home 'n' Wear concept was re-invented with fresh energy, but without the name.

The fourth prong of attack was Tesco Metro, an aggressive expansion of the fascia back into city centres, but in smaller stores designed for local workers and commuters wanting to top up on their regular big shop. Although most people have access to a car, Tesco was the first of the big four supermarket groups to recognise that people also wanted to shop for food during lunch breaks, or after work in a city centre. Tesco Metro concentrated on ready-meals and easy-to-prepare foods designed for the commuter wanting to pick up a few things for supper before the journey home. By 2004 there were 161 Tesco Metros. Yet again Tesco had seized the initiative and although Sainsbury eventually responded with the Sainsbury Local format, the first one did not open its doors until 1999, seven years after the first Tesco Metro appeared in Covent Garden.

Tesco also recognised that, while it was a good idea to sell petrol in the car parks of its superstores, it was just as good an idea to sell food in petrol station forecourts. So it launched Tesco Express and by 2004 there were 277 outlets. Some were outstandingly successful. The Tesco Express close to Maida Vale tube station in north London quickly attained one of the highest sales per square foot in the group.

Despite this wave of creativity from Leahy and his marketing boys, Tim Mason and David Potts, Tesco would not have achieved market leadership by 1995 if it had not bid for and won William Low, a Scottish supermarket chain, at the end of 1994. The Dundee-based group had only fifty-seven stores in Scotland and the north-east of England, but they were both areas still virtually untouched by Tesco or Sainsbury.

Tesco directors did their research thoroughly and courted the Low directors, explaining what their strategy would be before bidding 225p a share in early August. Sainsbury made a halfhearted counter-bid, which JD later admitted privately should probably have been far more aggressive. Sainsbury directors made virtually no contact with William Low's management, even though they could have made much of the two companies' similar age – William Low was founded in 1868, just a year before Sainsbury. They also let it be known that they would keep only the plum stores and would sell off the rest. Tesco undertook to retain them all – which went down better with the company and the people of Scotland.

Goodwill alone would not have won the day, though, and it took a raised bid of 360p a share, valuing Low at £247m, for Sainsbury to concede defeat. Tesco paid £93m more than its initial valuation. Some analysts congratulated Sainsbury on not over-paying, but Tesco's risk-taking culture served it well; it may have ended up paying double the William Low share price before the bid, but strategically it proved a very shrewd acquisition.

Sainsbury recovered some poise by expanding its American operation but by 1994, its 125th anniversary, things were not going well. To celebrate the anniversary the company published *The Best Butter in the World*, a painstaking glossy history by its archivist Bridget Williams, who, metaphorically at least, sat at JD's feet. Although full of fascinating facts, the impression the book gave was one of serene triumphalism. Nothing, it appeared, ever went wrong at Sainsbury. Throughout the previous century people worked hard, did what they were told and washed their hands a lot. It was just one big happy family. There was certainly no hint of the internal battles being waged.

But by the end of that year JD and his brothers were feeling less than happy, watching their shares continue to fall and their company lose ground to their upstart main rival. It was becoming clear that David Sainsbury and his chief executive Dino Adriano were out of their depth.

The level of antagonism felt towards Tesco emerged in the run-up to Christmas 1994 when all Sainsbury's store managers received instructions from head office to remove a twenty-page Tesco supplement containing money-off vouchers from every copy of the *Radio Times* on their shelves. The resulting fracas left egg all over Sainsbury's corporate face, wasting hundreds of employee hours, infuriating customers and resulting in headlines such as 'Good magazines weigh less at Sainsbury'. MacLaurin wrote to David Sainsbury formally expressing his displeasure and asking for assurances that no similar incident would occur in the future. He got them.

In the scheme of things it was a small scrap, but it highlighted the increasing rivalry between the two groups.

Tesco continued to drive down prices and Sainsbury and Safeway had little option but to follow suit, even if it hit their profit margins. Tesco was so firmly in the ascendant, rolling out one initiative after another, that its rivals were forever on the back foot. David Sainsbury could not believe that the formula that had served his company for so long was faltering.

In 1995 Ian MacLaurin made the decision to retire at 60. The heir apparent was not John Gildersleeve, whom many (including himself) had believed was the rightful successor. Instead the board, guided by MacLaurin, Victor Benjamin and David Malpas, chose Terry Leahy. In February 1997 Leahy became the youngest ever chief executive of a FTSE-100 company at just a week shy of his forty-first birthday.

It was a remarkable appointment. Leahy had been on the main board for less than five years and by big company standards he was extraordinarily young for such a post. But, in Leahy, MacLaurin and his fellow directors saw an almost fanatical hunger to make Tesco not just the market leader, but bigger and better in every way. He combined that with unusual humility and a bloke-next-door type of personality that went down well with customers and shareholders alike. Tesco suppliers and executives, however, found him more ruthless than his predecessor.

In terms of succession planning the choice was close to brilliance and starkly different from the way Sainsbury did things. If one decision, and the way it was made, highlighted the gulf between the two cultures, it was Leahy's appointment as Tesco's chief executive. MacLaurin had been chairman and chief executive but modern corporate governance suggested the roles be split. So the industrialist John Gardiner, already a non-executive director, was made chairman. A former Lex column journalist at the *Financial Times*, Gardiner had made his name at Laird, the electronics group.

What was also remarkable about the appointment was that the two older directors – David Reid and John Gildersleeve – stayed in place to support him. It was well known in the company that Gildersleeve had viewed himself as a prime contender for the top job. Leahy had reported to Gildersleeve for part of his career at Tesco, but the older man rated Leahy highly enough to accept defeat – if not gracefully then pragmatically – and to continue working in the company. A generous pension scheme helped sweeten the pill.

It was unthinkable for any senior manager in Tesco to leave and work for another supermarket group. The culture was too all consuming. After his retirement, MacLaurin was approached to be a non-executive director for another retailer but he felt his loyalty to Tesco ran too deep.

The new chief executive in many ways represented a typical Tesco customer. According to the *Liverpool Post*, Leahy, a working-class grammar school boy, had 'grown up in a pre-fab maisonette on Edbrook Road in the Lee Park council estate in Belle Vale with his three brothers'. He had furthered his career on merit alone and he passionately supported his football team – Everton.

His wife Alison was a doctor in general practice and they had three young children. 'My wife works – that is very typical nowadays,' said Leahy at the time. 'We have children, we live in the suburbs and we are short of time – that's absolutely typical.' The message was clear: his life was not far removed from that of many of Tesco's customers – except of course that he was a lot richer. In 2003 he earned £2.8m including bonuses, more than 100 times the British average wage of £25,000 a year.

Hard working and impenetrable, he focused relentlessly on winning. This, combined with his introvert personality, led observers to dub him the Pete Sampras of retailing after the seven-times Wimbledon champion. 'Put pressure on yourself before somebody else does' was one of his mottoes.

After the flamboyant MacLaurin, Leahy seemed dull and lacking in charisma. When journalists interviewed him they came away baffled that this ordinary bloke, who talked about little else but the customer, had risen to such heights. 'An hour with Leahy is as entertaining as an hour in a supermarket checkout queue,' said one. Another commented shrewdly: 'Everyone should be this dull.'

Leahy's secret ingredient was eternal discontent. 'He was like a bulldog chewing a wasp,' remarked one bemused analyst after a meeting. 'That means everything is going incredibly well,' retorted a Tesco manager.

Ordinary though he seemed, Leahy was not simply running with MacLaurin's torch. It was great to have overtaken Sainsbury, but he knew the position could be reversed. Complacency was never in his vocabulary. 'In this world only the paranoid survive,' he would tell analysts.

He saw all too clearly that the UK food retailing market was overcrowded and relatively small, accounting for about 3 per cent of the gross domestic product (GDP). To stay strong he looked for other markets to exploit. Internet shopping, banking and forays into overseas markets had already begun, but it was under Leahy that they would become big profit earners.

Tesco made one serious mistake abroad with the acquisition in 1992 of the French supermarket group Catteau. It was a useful if painful lesson in how not to do it and in 1997 it quietly sold off the 100 stores at a loss of £8m. Thereafter it avoided the traps retailers traditionally make abroad. Instead of testing the market with small shops and then retiring hurt when they failed to make money, Tesco acquired hypermarkets, quickly becoming a dominant force in the host country. It was a bold strategy that in large part worked only because it used as many local managers and staff as it could.

Although customers everywhere have the same desire for a better life, the way Tesco proceeded in the countries it first entered, such as Hungary, Poland and the Czech Republic, was very different from its UK operation. 'All the products are different, the culture is different and customers respond to different triggers,' said Leahy.

Tesco did not attempt to export the formula of its UK success, opting instead for authentically local stores, run by local managers, but on a grand scale. 'In retailing you have to get in front, to make an impact as we did with our hypermarket in Hungary. Then you might get a chance to shape what Hungarians think retailing should be like.' And despite accusations of destructive globalisation, Tesco claims that, in Hungary, 97 per cent of its products are sourced locally. After Eastern Europe, Leahy looked further east and in 1996 he headed a directors' trawl around Asia. They said yes to Korea,

Thailand, Taiwan and Malaysia and no to Indonesia, China and the Philippines, where the political and economic climate were judged too unstable. Only eight years later did Tesco dip its toe into China with a joint venture.

Yet even after this expansion overseas, by 1997 Tesco had become so dominant in Britain that some of the competition, most notably Asda and Safeway, felt it necessary to draw up plans for evasive action.

CHAPTER EIGHT

STRATEGIC ALLIANCES

*'People of the same trade seldom meet together, even for merriment
and diversion, but the conversation ends in a conspiracy against the
public, or in some contrivance to raise prices.'*

Adam Smith, *The Wealth of Nations*

In March 1997 Alistair Grant retired as chairman of Safeway. His emotional
ties to Scotland were strong and, lured by the offer of a directorship at the
Bank of Scotland, he decided to spend the rest of his life there. His departure
left David Webster, the last and youngest of the three musketeers, alone.

Webster stepped up to be chairman and appointed Colin Smith, a
competent but uninspiring manager, as chief executive. An accountant
by training, Smith knew the company well and was, in Webster's words,
'hugely capable'. But he lacked charisma and leadership abilities. A Mori poll
commissioned by the company in 1998 showed the depth of the problem.
More than 60 per cent of Safeway staff were either neutral about or critical
of the company as an employer, 43 per cent said that downward communication was poor and 72 per cent felt that senior management were inacces-
sible. A climate of fear was evident, 56 per cent believing that any criticism
of company practice would damage their careers.

Webster left Smith to get on with day-to-day operations while he concentrated on the bigger picture. He could see all too clearly that in order to
survive, Safeway had to expand. He recognised that critical mass was vital
when it came to negotiating with suppliers.

But growth prospects had been curtailed when John Gummer was
appointed Secretary of State for the Environment in 1994. The Conserva-

tive minister caught the supermarket industry by surprise when he clamped down unexpectedly on planning permissions for large edge-of-town sites. The move put the brakes on organic expansion for all the big groups. Only Tesco had continued to buy sites during the property slump of the early 1990s and its purchase of William Low had given it superior buying power over its rivals. Tesco could negotiate deals with giants such as Unilever, Mars and Cadbury Schweppes at far better terms than Safeway or Sainsbury could secure. The only way for them to compete with Tesco on price would be to reduce margins in the hope of drastically increasing sales – a difficult and risky manoeuvre.

In 1995 Tesco had become the clear leader with 20 per cent of the market according to Robert Clark, an independent retail market consultant. Sainsbury was down to 18 per cent while both Safeway in the south of the country and Asda in the north remained well behind with about 10 per cent each.

At Asda, Norman and Leighton had also realised the need to make a quantum leap in size. They had breathed life into a dying body and become heroes in the City. In 1997 Asda's profits had risen to £354m from a loss-making position in 1991 and like-for-like sales growth continued to outpace its rivals. But, like Webster at Safeway, they knew they needed a partner. Investors had begun to ask from where the next phase of growth was coming.

Norman and Leighton had re-invented Asda in much the same way that MacLaurin had transformed Tesco. But where Tesco had made Sainsbury its role model for recovery in the 1980s, Norman and Leighton unashamedly copied the American giant Wal-Mart. Founded by Sam Walton in 1962 in Bentonville, Arkansas, where his first store was called Sam Walton's Five and Dime, Wal-Mart grew at a furious pace to become by far the world's largest retailer with sales of $200bn in 2004.

Beneath a folksy, down-home manner, Sam Walton seethed with ruthless passion and he found ways of imbuing it into his entire company, from the humblest floor sweeper upwards. Even though it had been founded only in 1962 Wal-Mart built annual sales to more than double those of its nearest competitor and helped put its main rival Kmart into bankruptcy at one point. A shrunken Kmart later merged with Sears Roebuck.

Vilified by many commentators for its size and what some saw as rapacious expansion across America, Wal-Mart was much admired by rival retailers and most of the business world. John Blundell, head of the Institute of Economic Affairs showed his admiration in a column for the *Scotsman*: 'Wal-Mart is rather more than a chain of shops. It is a force for change. It has vociferous critics but I think it is a force for good,' he wrote after a visit. 'The greatest service it delivers is radically discounted quality goods as its procurement policies are so accomplished. It used to buy only from local US suppliers but Wal-Mart is now an international phenomenon, buying £10 billion in goods from China alone. Can you believe the firm employs 1.4 million staff and serves 100 million customers every week? And serves at a Rolls-Royce level.'

Like Blundell, Leighton was an admirer and enjoyed playing the innocent tourist, visiting the American stores, taking photographs – and sometimes being thrown out by suspicious security men. On one occasion Leighton was snapping away in Orlando's largest Wal-Mart when the store manager came over and told him he was not allowed to take photographs. They fell into conversation about Wal-Mart's stores and no doubt Leighton piled on the flattery. 'Who are you?' the manager asked eventually, intrigued by the tall, affable Englishman who appeared to know far more about retailing than the average tourist.

Leighton confessed he was from Asda, a British supermarket group, and then suggested the store manager contact a director at Wal-Mart's head-quarters in Bentonville to ask for permission for him to carry on snapping. The bemused manager eventually got through to someone in authority and Leighton made his first contact with the Wal-Mart hierarchy over the phone. He was allowed to continue looking round the store but, more important, he secured an open invitation to the company's headquarters.

Archie Norman, then Asda's chief executive, followed up such informal forays with a more traditional approach. 'I rang them up, introduced myself and said we would like to come and see you.' The combination of Norman's courtly English manner and Leighton's brash humour intrigued the Wal-Mart management and the pair were soon invited to make a formal visit to Bentonville. Both Leighton and Norman made several trips, talking to the directors and visiting the stores in one of Wal-Mart's Lear Jets.

Wal-Mart is famed for its cost consciousness – the staff may be called associates but they are lowly paid while directors, in stark contrast to their equivalents in most large corporations, travel economy class on scheduled airlines. They stay in three-star hotels and, even more surprising, share rooms.

A thorough review of the stores is undertaken each week. In the early days Sam Walton, a licensed pilot, would fly his little bi-plane around the country to conduct his inspections. Later the company bought a small fleet of Lear Jets and every Friday the directors would set off in different directions to visit the stores and report back at a Saturday-morning board meeting.

All this Norman and Leighton found fascinating and relevant. Although Wal-Mart was predominantly a non-food retailer whereas Asda sold mainly food, Norman and Leighton believed that Wal-Mart had the most creative and interesting retailing philosophy on the planet. Not only that, the Americans' ideas chimed with what they were attempting to do at Asda and could be used to great effect. Much of the motivational razzmatazz Leighton introduced at Asda was based on the way Wal-Mart did things.

'At that point we made Asda a single-status company,' recalled Norman. 'All the car-parking spaces, all the individual offices – everything went. Staff became colleagues [after Wal-Mart's 'associates'] and although we could not pay everyone the same we decided that anyone who stayed for a year would get share options.'

In the words of one observer, 'They did everything a management could to mirror and match the way Wal-Mart did things.' Even so, there were certain aspects Asda did not adopt, for example conducting the company's annual meeting like a fundamentalist religious event starting and ending with their own version of the Wal-Mart chant: 'Give me a W, give me an A ...'

As the relationship progressed, the Wal-Mart chairman Rob Walton, Sam's eldest son, took to visiting Asda's Leeds headquarters and taking a look round the stores. On one occasion, after the duo had unapologetically copied a Wal-Mart price-cutting campaign known as 'Rollback', Walton was astonished at the similarity. 'Your shops look more like Wal-Mart than our shops do,' he exclaimed, adding with a laugh. 'And actually, I think you're doing it better.'

Leighton and Norman had something else on their agenda apart from making the American giant Asda's role model. They were also metaphorically trailing their petticoats with their eye on marriage. Both men had seen turning round Asda as a huge challenge, but they had little interest in merely minding the shop once it was ticking along smoothly. They knew that if they left for other challenges the Asda share price would collapse, so their plan was to find a corporate parent for their baby.

The culture at Wal-Mart had traditionally been one of organic growth rather than acquisition but the new generation of directors were finally looking at expanding outside America. Wal-Mart's tough attitude towards suppliers and the creation of a nuclear winter for small stores in towns where it set up were beginning to stir up a backlash in the press and local government.

Britain was a tiny market in US terms and Walton and his team were more interested in getting a toe-hold in continental Europe, but they failed to appreciate the difficulties under which business labours in highly regulated countries such as Italy, France and Germany. In 1997 Wal-Mart spent about $2bn buying two German companies, WertKauf and InterSpar – a move that turned out to be a costly mistake – and resisted making a play for Asda.

Meanwhile, at Safeway, Webster had been eyeing Asda's progress and saw his opportunity to become a leading force in the supermarket game. In the summer of 1997 he and his chief executive Colin Smith invited Norman and Leighton to dinner. To show the seriousness of their intent, they travelled to Leeds and took them to a restaurant in Asda's home town. They put forward a proposal that the two companies should merge in a £9bn deal that would put the combined market share at more than 20 per cent once necessary disposals had been made, just behind Tesco, which by then had progressed to 22 per cent.

The two groups had little overlap. Safeway's strongholds were in the south and in Scotland while Asda's portfolio was dominant in the north of England. Norman and Leighton were immediately interested and saw the logic of merging the two geographically disparate groups.

Various discussions followed but, as so often happens in takeover talks, egos got in the way. Asda at the time was slightly smaller in terms of stock-market value and there was much discussion about what the combined company should be called and where it would be based. According to Webster, the understanding they came to was that such decisions should be deferred until after the deal was completed. His concern, apparently shared by Norman and Leighton, was that the name of whichever brand was jettisoned would be tarnished if the deal failed to go through.

The talks grew serious and together they worked secretly on a submission to the Office of Fair Trading in order to obtain confidential guidance on the deal. Safeway's traditional adviser, Rupert Faure-Walker of Samuel Montagu, was bolstered by investment boutique Wasserstein Perella, formed by three Americans, Bruce Wasserstein, Joseph Perella and Geoffrey Rosen. Their relationship with Webster went back to Argyll's bid for the UK arm of Safeway. Other members of the team were Geoffrey Cohen, a retail analyst, and Howard Covington, an ambitious young banker and maths genius who had left SG Warburg to join them.

Asda employed Bob Wrigley of Merrill Lynch as its main investment banker and retained David Mayhew, the redoubtable de-facto head of Cazenove, as its corporate stockbroker – to bolster Asda's influence with shareholders.

They thrashed out the makings of a deal. But both sides realised there was little point in attempting a merger if the new Labour government was going to block it. Webster knew from bitter experience that these matters were by no means cut and dried and it was futile attempting to read the minds of the mandarins. But when the two companies sent their submission to the Office of Fair Trading in July it did not stay confidential. Its recommendations were on the point of being passed to Margaret Beckett at the Department of Trade and Industry when news of the proposed deal leaked.

In September 1997 the *Sunday Telegraph* broke the story that Safeway and Asda were in merger discussions. But to Webster's anger, the journalist 'revealed' that the name of the combined group was to be Asda. In the days that followed, the Asda version of events emerged in the City pages. Webster and Norman would have been joint chairmen while Leighton would have been chief executive. Webster and his public relations director Kevin Hawkins held firmly to their view that decisions on the name and board structure had not yet been made.

Norman appeared to want something more glamorous for his revived company than to be subsumed by the Safeway brand and the fiercely ambitious Leighton wanted to oversee the integration of the two groups and could, understandably, not contemplate playing second fiddle to Colin Smith. What Webster later described as 'a sharp interchange' took place. The deal was off.

Archie Norman had become a Tory MP in the election of 1997 and, despite the collapse in the talks, he decided to reduce the time he spent at Asda in order to give more energy to politics. In February 1998 he took over the role of non-executive chairman from Sir Patrick Gillam, and Leighton stepped up to become chief executive.

Leighton saw that the revitalisation of Asda had gone as far as it could and that further significant growth would be difficult against the forces of Tesco in the south and Morrison in the north. He decided to make one last attempt at restarting the talks with Safeway and rang Webster. They arranged to talk at a hotel near Heathrow and appeared to have a meeting of minds. They spent another three months negotiating and identified some £230m of synergies. They agreed that Webster would be chairman, Leighton would be chief executive and Colin Smith would be in the top operational role. Faure-Walker and Wrigley actually shook hands on the deal, so solid did they believe it to be, and began working on drafting the press announcement. Then, at the last minute, Norman, intervened, declaring that the merger could not go ahead unless the company was to be called Asda and based in Leeds. Leighton may have been furious but he felt he had to abide by his chairman's decision, non-executive or not.

A furious Webster pulled stumps again – this time for good. His next approach was to Sir Richard Greenbury, then chairman of Marks & Spencer, known best as Britain's premier mid-market clothing retailer but also with a superior food business that had about 3 per cent of the market. For many years Marks & Spencer led the food market when it came to innovation. Not only was Marks & Spencer the first company to air-freight tomatoes and other vegetables from warmer climes, it also taught British farmers how to grow more exotic produce such as crisp-heart lettuces from California. It was Marks & Spencer, working with a small company called Alveston Kitchens, that launched chicken Kiev as a chilled meal in the mid 1970s. The runaway success spawned a range of chilled ready-meals that the supermarket chains, headed by Sainsbury, set out to copy. By the mid 1990s food accounted for 40 per cent of Marks & Spencer's total sales.

By 1997 Greenbury could already see his clothing business heading for trouble and was intrigued by Webster's approach. Webster's idea was simple – Marks & Spencer would buy Safeway and convert all the stores to the Marks & Spencer brand – selling off those surplus to requirements. It would have given Marks & Spencer's food business a huge leap forward and transformed the group from a clothing company that also sold food to the exact opposite. The larger ex-Safeway stores would sell both clothes and food while the smaller sites would sell food only.

Sadly it was far too bold a move for Greenbury to contemplate seriously. Marks & Spencer simply did not do takeovers and mergers, any more than it recruited senior people from outside the company. Greenbury, who had joined Marks & Spencer at 17 years old, had been steeped in the clothing tradition and did not relish the idea of food becoming the dominant product range. The two men met twice in Safeway's Mayfair office close to Park Lane, but once discussions widened to include the Marks & Spencer board, the proposed deal was soon toast. Safeway became even more vulnerable, but a bruised Webster took the view that to allow the company to drift would be a disservice to his shareholders.

Norman and Leighton were becoming impatient, if not desperate, for a deal. Norman's once warm relations with his old boss Geoff Mulcahy at Kingfisher had cooled to Arctic levels when Norman had left. But in the spring of 1998 Norman bit the bullet and picked up the phone to discuss a merger with Mulcahy. Those first icy conversations had come to nothing. Then, in early 1999, Norman re-opened negotiations. He and Mulcahy had together done much of the transformation of the old Woolworth chain into a retailing conglomerate including B&Q, the electrical store group Comet and the high-street chain Superdrug. Mulcahy needed more retail space to take his company forward and Asda's 40,000-square-foot sheds looked tempting. The two men at least shared similar business values.

Ever pragmatic, Mulcahy this time embraced the opportunity and in June 1999 Kingfisher launched an all-share offer for Asda, valuing the group at £5.8bn. The deal had mixed reviews, with some analysts complaining that the price should have been higher. Yet initially, at least, it looked like the perfect solution for both Norman's and Mulcahy's problems. The combined group would have sales of £19bn, giving it both the buying and marketing clout to expand globally. But once the top teams of Asda and Kingfisher began the detailed thrashing out of how the 'merger' might work, particularly which director was going to do what, and whose services might become redundant, underlying problems began to surface.

Mulcahy had two characteristics that unsettled his potential new colleagues at Asda. He liked to control everything down to the last detail, yet at the same time he found making decisions difficult. One analyst had dubbed Kingfisher 'the brains trust of retailing' because Mulcahy and his team spent so many hours sitting round a table batting ideas back and forth without coming to conclusions. 'Geoff was forever changing his mind,' recalled one insider at the time.

The code governing takeovers and mergers in Britain gave companies sixty days after the formal publication of the details of a bid to win shareholder support – it was enough time for Norman and Leighton to feel they were making a mistake. Relations between the two management teams soon soured. Stock-market investors picked up the negative vibrations and the

Kingfisher share price began to slide amid fears that the deal would be called off. The clash of personalities must surely have been severe to precipitate what then took place.

Wasserstein Perella, though still retained by David Webster for Safeway, saw an opportunity. The partners felt that Wal-Mart would be a far superior and more logical owner of Asda than Kingfisher – and of course, if they put the deal together they would earn a large fee. From their experience with Safeway they had gained an intimate knowledge of Asda's business. Historically, the American bank Goldman Sachs had advised Wal-Mart, but its young Turks had opted to work for Kingfisher. They believed they had cleared the matter with their largest client – and did not expect Wal-Mart to counter-bid. Thus the field was clear for Wasserstein Perella's Geoffrey Rosen and Howard Covington to visit Wal-Mart's group treasurer Jay Fitzsimmons to try to interest him in bidding for Asda. They had all the facts at their fingertips thanks to the work they had undertaken for the Department of Trade on the proposed Safeway/Asda merger.

Fitzsimmons, who, like Wal-Mart's chief executive Lee Scott and chairman Rob Walton, had got to know Asda through Norman and Leighton, still believed that the UK market was too tiny to bother with. Besides, the problems he had encountered in tightly regulated Germany had dampened his enthusiasm for acquisitions. Even so, like true salesmen, Howard Covington and his retail strategist partner Geoff Cohen rang Fitzsimmons at 5 a.m. Bentonville time in June 1999 soon after Kingfisher and Asda announced their deal. They suggested that unless Wal-Mart wanted to let Asda slip through its fingers Fitzsimmons should urge his chief executive Lee Scott to launch a contested bid at a higher price. But Scott was wary of breaking up an agreed deal where both sides appeared in accord and he also expressed concern that if Wal-Mart waded in with a hostile bid they would lose Asda's top team, for whom he had the highest regard.

Covington, Cohen and Rosen – an Anglophile American whose role was link-man between London and Bruce Wasserstein – kept the Wal-Mart directors informed, ringing them almost every day, and also gained permission to tell Norman and Leighton that Wal-Mart might be interested in bidding if there was some indication the move would be welcome. In New York, Bruce Wasserstein was also in touch with Wal-Mart.

Covington and Cohen went to take tea with Norman at the House of Commons bearing the news that 'Wal-Mart would be interested if Asda was interested'. Norman's response was worthy of a Jane Austen heroine under siege from a suitor. He said that he would be doing his shareholders a disservice if he refused to consider another bid – and if Wal-Mart wanted to come up with an offer it should do so. But he was careful not to commit himself in any way. However, as the days ticked by and the Kingfisher share price continued to fall, so lowering the amount it would be paying for Asda, Norman and Leighton made a decision.

Just ten days before the deal with Kingfisher was due to close, Leighton put in a call to Rob Walton in Bentonville. The two men had struck up a good friendship and Leighton had no qualms about being straightforward. He told Walton of the problems with Kingfisher. 'If you want to buy our business, which you should,' he told him. 'You have nine days to do it.' He also mentioned that he would be 'passing through' Bentonville in the next few days and could drop by and discuss it. His timing hit the spot and within hours Leighton was booked on Concorde, armed with a detailed presentation for Wal-Mart's directors.

Speed was the essence, yet so was secrecy. On Concorde, Leighton's fellow travellers consisted of top investment bankers and key executives of major companies. The last thing Leighton wanted was to be recognised and enticed into conversation by inquisitive bankers, so he sat uncharacteristically quietly at the back of the plane wearing dark glasses.

All went according to plan until they landed in New York, when a call was put out over the aircraft's speaker system: 'Would Mr Allan Leighton meeting the Wal-Mart plane come to the front exit.' A Wal-Mart Lear Jet was on the tarmac just yards away and an embarrassed Leighton walked down the steps of the supersonic jetliner and into the emblazoned Wal-Mart plane. Miraculously, the event went unreported in the press.

At Bentonville, Leighton was met by Walton in his trademark pick-up van and whisked to the boardroom. He spent two and a half hours giving his presentation to a group of directors including Walton, David Glass, Jay Fitzsimmons and Lee Scott. When he had done his best to answer every question, they told him to 'go over the road and have a hamburger for half an hour'.

When he returned they were clearly enthusiastic. 'We think we would like to do it, but we need to come to England and take a look round – tomorrow.' A team headed by Glass arrived in Leeds and were ushered round the local Asda stores. 'I introduced them as my American friends,' recalled Leighton, who was concerned that the staff might guess who the visitors were and why they were there. If anyone did, they stayed away from the press.

By Friday the Wal-Mart team were back in Bentonville, where they held a board meeting the following morning. That afternoon Rob Walton rang Leighton and said, 'Allan, it is 115p cash and we are yours'. Somehow, Leighton pushed them up another 5p to 120p a share, which valued the company at £6.7bn.

When Norman had first arrived in Leeds on that rainy December morning in 1991, Asda's stock-market value had been £500m. Less than ten years later it was being sold for thirteen times that. To long-term investors – and for many of the staff and management who had shares – he and Leighton were heroes.

Geoff Mulcahy felt somewhat differently when he answered his phone at 7.35 on the following Monday morning. He had been trying to get hold of Norman or Leighton for most of the previous week and from past experience he knew that unanswered calls in the middle of a deal almost certainly spelt trouble. Norman sat with Leighton as he dialled Mulcahy's home number. 'Hello, Geoff,' said Leighton. 'I have some bad news. We have sold the business to Wal-Mart for 120p cash. It will be coming over the wires soon.'

There was a short pause before Mulcahy said, 'I'll get back to you.' But by 2004 the two men had still not spoken.

The events of the previous nine days had been kept secret from the world. Such was Wal-Mart's confidence in its fund-raising ability that nobody had spoken to the company's bankers about financing the deal. The only proviso from Wal-Mart was that Mulcahy should not be informed until after 7.30 a.m., when the stock market opened because the intention was to buy up 15 per cent of the Asda shares.

Wasserstein Perella were keen that the Wal-Mart directors should be well rested when they arrived at the Monday-morning press conference in London at which the deal was to be announced, and insisted on upgrading them to business class – much against the parsimonious ethos of the Wal-Mart culture. Not only that, they were booked into the five-star Browns Hotel in Mayfair and allocated a room each instead of sharing.

On the Sunday morning Leighton met Covington, Rosen and Asda's own astounded investment banker Bob Wrigley from Merrill Lynch plus lawyers from both sides. Together they thrashed out the finer details of the deal.

150

On the previous Friday Covington had rung David Bick, an old ally from the world of public relations, and warned him that he might be needed over the weekend to handle a top-secret announcement. Bick was duly summoned on the Sunday afternoon to organise the announcement and a press conference the following day. Bruce Wasserstein flew down from New York to attend.

While helping to draft the press release, Bick asked why there was no mention of how the biggest cash transaction in the history of the London stock market was to be funded. 'Oh, we will deal with that tomorrow,' said group treasurer Jay Fitzsimmons. True to his word Fitzsimmons picked up the phone on Monday morning in the offices of Wasserstein Perella and with a few calls raised $10bn within fifteen minutes at advantageous rates. 'It was one of the most impressive scenes I have ever witnessed,' an awestruck Covington told his colleagues later.

By Monday afternoon Kingfisher had put out an announcement that it was withdrawing from the fray.

Financially the Wal-Mart takeover handed every Asda staff member who had served for more than two years an average £1,500. For Norman, the sale of his shares netted him more than enough to concentrate on politics full time. Leighton, for the time being, decided to stay and work with Wal-Mart.

For the other supermarket operators, Wal-Mart's sudden presence in their midst struck terror into their managements' hearts. Food manufacturers, farmers and other suppliers shuddered at what they feared lay ahead. The only suppliers who could rise above the fear were the big brands – Mars, Cadbury, Coca-Cola. Procter & Gamble and Unilever, with their wide range of branded goods and huge sales already established with Wal-Mart, were also in a better position than many others (Wal-Mart accounts for 17 per cent of Procter & Gamble's turnover).

Shortly after the takeover was announced Tesco called an all-day 'war cabinet' meeting to discuss how they would deal with the American invader. Terry Leahy returned from the Far East post haste to chair it. 'We decided,' he said later, 'that instead of waiting to see what they would do and respond, we at Tesco would set the agenda for Wal-Mart.' The stakes had been upped yet again, and this time the game would be about price and square footage.

When octogenarian Bill Quinn's book *How Wal-Mart is Destroying America (and the World)* was published in 2000, it became mandatory reading for British supermarket executives. And if they had not already done so, they also read Sam Walton's folksy autobiography *Made in America*.

Mulcahy was not the only man to feel betrayed. Over in Safeway's Hayes headquarters, David Webster had been less than pleased to discover that Wasserstein Perella, his adviser during the talks with Asda, had acted for Wal-Mart, benefiting from the information it had gained while working for him. His solution was simple. He fired the firm.

High on the euphoria of pulling off one deal, Cohen and Covington suggested to Wal-Mart that a follow-up bid for Safeway would now make a lot of sense. They could see clearly that, because of the far higher cost of land compared with the United States and the planning constraints introduced by the previous Tory government, Wal-Mart in Britain would soon find its expansion plans constrained. It seems unlikely, with hindsight, that the Competition Commission would have countenanced such a move, but in any case Wal-Mart decided Safeway was not worth its 180p share price at the time.

Webster knew nothing of this, but he decided to fight fire with fire. He hired everyone's favourite headhunter, Anna Mann, to find him a new chief executive. True to her reputation she came up with a tall, charming Argentinian called Carlos Criado-Perez, who beguiled journalists and staff alike with his love of dancing the tango, making his own bread and reading Homer.

Carlos, as everyone called him, had spent most of his career running supermarkets in various parts of South-East Asia for the privately owned cash-and-carry chain Makro. In 1996 he had taken a senior executive role at Wal-Mart. Something of a free spirit, he clashed with the regimented ethos at Bentonville. He never quite fitted in and, according to one Wal-Mart insider, the executives viewed him with suspicion because he read the works of left-wing philosophers such as Bertrand Russell.

An extrovert with a talent for indiscretion, in sharp contrast to his chairman, he soon made his mark at Safeway, where he abolished plastic packaging wherever possible and piled the fresh fruit and vegetables high like a Mediterranean market place. 'Lettuces,' he told one bemused visitor who watched him rearrange a display, 'should not be squashed, they should look happy.'

He created what he called 'New Safeway' – a tongue-in-cheek dig at 'New Labour', jazzing up the interiors of the stores, increasing the range of fresh food and vastly expanding the 'ready-to-go' food range, including a scintillating range of Indian meals. Pizza-spinning chefs, extensive fresh-fish counters and hot woks were all part of the retail theatre he brought into stores, later dubbed 'retailtainment'. He opened several new superstores of 60,000 square feet in which he experimented with florists, patisseries, dry cleaning and photo-developing, of which some were more successful than others. He also dumped the loyalty card, claiming he could use the £2m a year it cost to administer in more lucrative ways.

Analysts warmed to him. Robert Clark, the retail consultant, praised his energy and creativity: 'Carlos has brought something new to UK retail by upping the innovation in stores.'

Unlike his predecessor, Colin Smith, Carlos was a people person and set about picking the brains of everyone he could. 'Carlos was in listening mode for the first two months,' said one director. 'And he was very receptive to ideas during that time.'

One of the people whose brains he picked was Kevin Hawkins, the head of corporate affairs, who went on to head the British Retail Consortium in 2004. Intriguingly, much of what Carlos implemented could be found in a Safeway internal memorandum put together by Hawkins. Hawkins had observed the way Smith had operated and come to some interesting conclusions. The memorandum from Hawkins to Carlos, marked 'private & personal' and headed 'What the business should do', was evidently in response to an instruction from the new chief executive to put his thoughts into writing.

He did not mince his words: 'We urgently need a step change in our price perception, our availability, our freshness and quality to stop the current erosion of our customer base,' he wrote. He then suggested a plan of action. 'Do fewer but deeper promotions – shouted much more loudly in store and through the advertising media.' This idea became the lynchpin of Criado-Perez's new strategy and resulted in what he called the 'Gonzalez offers', where the prices of some items were slashed by as much as 50 per cent to lure customers into the stores. It was loss leaders with a twist. In order to prevent rivals simply matching the cuts he would target a group of stores in one area, print promotional leaflets in secret and deliver them to the surrounding households on the eve of a campaign, each of which would run only for a couple of weeks. He operated on what is known in supermarket-speak as the WIGIG principle – when it's gone, it's gone. The effect on Safeway's profits and share price was dramatic. Sales volumes of some products shot up by 400 per cent.

Hawkins also criticised the culture of fear and the inherent 'us and them' mentality between staff and management. Hawkins urged better communication. 'Get all directors to hold impromptu mini town hall or "soap box" meetings with their teams, so they can listen as well as communicate.' He also advised Criado-Perez to visit managers in key stores and discuss in depth their ideas to improve store performance. Such advice fell on receptive ears and within months of Criado-Perez arriving the shares were rising. They continued to do so for the next two years. Overnight, it seemed, Webster became relaxed and smiling – and never short of praise for his chief executive. Profits rose from £236m in 1999/2000 to £355m in 2001/2.

But the gloss eventually began to fade. As Criado-Perez remarked during an interview in 2003, when a company tries a new successful tactic it takes roughly three years for the competition to catch up and start copying it. After that the advantage is lost.

During 2002 Safeway's share price began to slide back. This was partly due to the savage bear market in equities around the world that had followed the bursting of the dot-com bubble in spring 2000. It had been prolonged by the September 11 terror attacks and the uncertainties in the run-up to the invasion of Iraq on 20 March 2003.

Even so, Safeway shares underperformed relative to the rest of the food-retailing sector as profits growth slowed and investors realised that although Criado-Perez had revitalised the company, and talked bravely of taking on Tesco by building twenty-five new hypermarkets, Safeway just did not have the buying power of its bigger competitors.

The more you buy from suppliers, the better price they will give – in the trade this is known as a volume discount. Hence by 2003 Webster reckoned that in general Tesco could buy 5 per cent cheaper than Safeway while Wal-Mart's advantage was as much as 10 per cent.

Either Safeway passed this price disadvantage on to customers by charging them more, or took the hit on its own profit margins. The Gonzalez strategy was to slash prices on a selected few products and charge more for the rest. But too many customers wised up and adopted a strategy of 'guerrilla shopping', grabbing the deep discounts and doing their main shop elsewhere.

Sainsbury and others also went down the special-deals route, favouring the BOGOF model – Buy One Get One Free – although many customers complained that they did not want two of the same item, just one that was keenly priced.

By autumn 2003 Webster could again see the writing on the wall. It had been obscured for a while by Criado-Perez's sales-boosting tactics, which had produced sparkling sales and profit growth for a couple of years, but Webster knew that the growth was not sustainable.

It was time once more for him to 'show a pretty ankle'. In the past he and Ken Morrison had met regularly at trade events and had talked merger possibilities from time to time. This time, when they crossed paths and the subject of Safeway's future came up, Webster responded by suggesting they meet for a discreet tête-à-tête.

At Sainsbury, the new chief executive Peter Davis found himself in an even worse position. He had the Sainsbury family with more than a third of the shares looking on expectantly, waiting for profits magically to increase. Davis had been delighted to be asked to return to his former company in 1999, but when he arrived in 2000 nothing had prepared him for what he found both inside and outside. Beneath the surface the company was in disarray with outdated depots, IT systems and shabby stores. Bureaucracy was even more entrenched than he remembered.

In 1999 Davis had been on the point of moving up from chief executive to non-executive chairman of the Prudential, a company once synonymous with personal pensions and insurance. Under his four-year leadership the Pru had been modernised to become a provider of a wide range of financial services to both individuals and institutions.

He told acquaintances that he was looking forward to a portfolio career. He had sat on the board of Boots since 1991 and talked of picking up a few other non-executive director posts mixed with work on government quangos and enjoying his time at the Royal Opera House, of which he was a board member. He had, in fact, told both Dominic Cadbury at Cadbury Schweppes and his old friend James Blyth at Boots that he would take on the non-executive chairmanships of their companies, although news of neither had leaked into the public domain. Life would be more relaxed; there would be time for him to go sailing on his ocean-going yacht, watch his wife's race-horses and enjoy being with his grandchildren.

All that changed after the Pru's chairman Martin Jacomb, a City grandee, spent a weekend with his old friend John Sainsbury at his country residence in Preston Candover. They fell to talking about the future of the company now that David Sainsbury had finally bowed to shareholder pressure and resigned in order to become Labour's science minister and to devote more time to his charitable trust, the Gatsby Foundation.

Jacomb suggested that JD should try to persuade Davis to return to Sainsbury as chief executive. Jacomb had watched Davis operate at the Pru and much admired the way he had transformed the business. He also believed from the passion and authority with which Davis spoke that he really understood the nitty-gritty of grocery retailing.

A few days later Davis took a call from the Sainsbury chairman, George Bull, an amiable old campaigner who in 1998 had arrived from Diageo (the company formed by the merger of Guinness and Grand Metropolitan) as chairman. Bull asked to see him as soon as possible.

Intrigued, Davis probed him on what topic could be so urgent. Bull replied that he needed to talk to him about the Marketing Council, of which they were both members. 'And what is so urgent about that?' asked Davis. There was a pause. 'Can I come round?' Bull replied. Davis found a hole in his brimming diary and when Bull arrived he asked Davis if he would consider returning to Sainsbury to 'sort it out'.

It was what Davis had dreamed of ever since his departure in 1986, but he gave little sign of his enthusiasm. Instead he said he would think about it and talk it over with his wife, Sue. When he told her Bull had asked him to return to Sainsbury as chief executive to sort it out, her response, as a customer, was a heartfelt, 'Well, somebody needs to'.

Just as in 1986 she had backed his decision to leave after it became clear that he would not be allowed to run the company, now she backed his return, even though it would mean disappointing Dominic Cadbury and James Blyth. But before he made a final decision, he asked to meet the current board and be reintroduced to 'the family'.

The challenge was tempting. Running Sainsbury had always been his ambition as a younger man and if he pulled off a strong recovery he would be proving JD wrong in his original judgement. Just as compelling, he saw it as his last chance to make some serious money, and even possibly secure a peerage.

With Sainsbury in such dire need of strong leadership, Davis was able to negotiate a generous pay package including share options at eight times his salary. This would secure him, he believed, a few million pounds of capital as a financial cushion with which eventually to retire. Davis had always been well paid – he had earned £689,000 in his last year at the Pru – but he also enjoyed an expensive lifestyle, running four houses and two yachts as well as financing his wife's racehorses. He had no wish to give up any of these trappings of wealth when he retired. He also mixed with men who, like him, had started with little but had become very rich.

He and James Blyth had worked together in their early careers at General Foods and there had always been friendly rivalry between the two. Blyth had been awarded a peerage while Davis remained a mere knight. Blyth had also made more money. Colleagues who observed Davis's lavish way of living could see his motivation for taking the job quite clearly. 'Peter wanted to go round one more time,' said one. 'He could not resist the idea of making some serious money.'

Davis weighed the matter carefully. He dreaded interference from his old boss at Sainsbury, however, and he needed a couple of assurances before he would sign up. First, he requested an audience with JD and an undertaking from him that he would not interfere in the running of the company in any way. Second, he insisted that all family shareholders should issue a statement of unequivocal support when his appointment was announced. The family was in a weak position: Sainsbury shares had fallen from 411p to 319p over the previous five years and they had underperformed the food-retailing sector by a staggering 43 per cent.

That Christmas he made two difficult telephone calls, one to Cadbury, who was understandably furious at being let down, and one to Blyth, who was enjoying a family skiing holiday in Courcheval in the French Alps.

Friends who were with Blyth recalled his anger at hearing the news and how he demanded that Davis immediately tender his resignation from the board of Boots. Davis's change of heart meant Blyth's succession plans had to be recast. It also meant that the new chairman of Sainsbury was privy to all Boots' strategic planning at board meetings for the past eight years. Sainsbury and Boots might not have been direct competitors but there was considerable overlap in health, baby-care and beauty products.

On 14 January 2000 Sainsbury announced Davis's return to the fold as chief executive to replace Dino Adriano. Despite an accompanying profit warning, the shares jumped 5 per cent on the news, which was greeted with enthusiasm by most City analysts. They had monitored Davis's successes at Reed International, where he had created real shareholder value through rigorous rationalisation and a series of takeovers including the fellow publisher Elsevier. At the Pru he knocked the business into shape by selling its reinsurance business, buying M&G, the fund management group, and launching Egg, the online bank, which subsequently floated.

Some analysts remembered him from when he had been JD's right-hand man at the time that Sainsbury fought back so successfully against Tesco in 1978 with its Discount 78 campaign.

Investors had seen at Asda how new management could turn round a retailer's fortunes – and if Marks & Spencer was still struggling that was partly because they had not found the right man for the job. In fact Davis had been approached by Marks & Spencer as well – thanks also to Martin Jacomb, who was one of their senior non-executive directors. But the Marks & Spencer directors dithered over the decision and Davis made it for them. Analysts welcomed his return to Sainsbury. 'You don't appoint someone like Peter Davis to trade your way out of trouble,' said one. 'You appoint someone like that to kick a business into shape.'

Dino Adriano left Sainsbury after two lacklustre years at the helm, no doubt with a sigh of relief, and then devoted himself to working mainly for well-known charities such as the WRVS and Oxfam.

When Davis arrived in March 2000 morale throughout the company was low. There was, he believed, everything to gain and by October he had confidently presented a three-and-a-half year recovery programme to investors. He had been shocked, however, at the state of his old firm. Davis had not appreciated the impact of years of underinvestment in the company's infrastructure, nor had he fully taken on board the increased competitiveness of the industry. His first inkling came when Safeway's chairman David Webster rang him and told him he was a fool for going back. 'Why are you coming back now?' Webster asked. 'It is much worse than when you left.'

Davis had returned to his old company full of optimism that he could save the day at the dawn of the new millennium. A naturally gregarious character, Davis rang the heads of the other supermarket groups to re-establish contact. While at the Pru he had met Terry Leahy several times to talk about helping Tesco set up its financial services arm – a job that ultimately went to the Bank of Scotland – and the two men had got on well. Yet when Davis left messages for Leahy there was no response. On the third try Tim Mason, Tesco's marketing director, returned the call. It appeared that cosy chats between the major protagonists had become as much a part of the past as custom-sliced bacon.

Despite these omens, Davis hit the ground running and for the first year hardly a week passed without some new announcement from Sainsbury. Buying and selling companies was his forte and he set about paring Sainsbury back to its core as a retailer of predominantly quality food. For-sale signs were put up over Homebase, the DIY chain, which had never been able to compete with B&Q, and over the embryonic Egyptian operation, which had attracted attacks from Muslim terrorists, who believed Sainsbury to be a Jewish company.

Urged on by his marketing director, Sara Weller, Davis addressed the middle-aged image of the group by hiring Jamie Oliver, a young blokeish celebrity chef, to make a new television advertising campaign to replace a disastrous series of ads starring John Cleese. After all, in his first incarnation at the company, the TV cook Delia Smith had done wonders for sales. Finally Davis went shopping for a new headquarters.

At the Pru, he had witnessed how moving from the original headquarters in Holborn Bars had transformed attitudes inside the group. The same magic, he felt, would work if Sainsbury could move away from the historical site at Stamford Street, which could then be sold to release £100m of capital.

As luck would have it, Paul Hamlyn, the publishing tycoon, was working on redeveloping the old *Daily Mirror* site at Holborn circus with Roger Seelig, a property specialist and former investment banker. Hamlyn and Seelig had bought the site for about £40m from Victor Blank, who had just taken over as chairman of Mirror Group, publisher of the *Sunday Mirror*, the *Daily Mirror*, the *People* and some regional newspapers. The old building had been Robert Maxwell's headquarters and came complete with a helicopter landing pad on the roof. A few years before, the *Mirror* had wanted to make a fresh start well away from the taint of 'Captain Bob' and had taken space in Canary Wharf along with its sister papers, following the lead of the *Telegraph* and the *Independent*.

The new building, a gleaming glass-and-steel cylinder, became available just as Davis was in the market for his new headquarters. Its central position, imposing architecture and modern technology looked ideal as a new beginning and by October 2001 more than 2,600 head-office staff had moved from nine separate old-fashioned buildings in south London. The glitzy new building had a vast entrance hall and a free café in which visitors could sip a cappuccino and nibble a pastry while they waited for their hosts to collect them. The rent was at the top end of the scale at more than £57 per square foot per annum. It may have helped generate a different mindset, but to outside observers it smacked of folie de grandeur, particularly compared with the 1960s industrial estate in Cheshunt where Tesco's directors resided, or Safeway's main offices in Hayes.

Davis addressed e-commerce by appointing two new directors to review Sainsbury's internet strategy and revamped the board, bringing in heavyweights such as Peter Levene, later to become the chairman of the Lloyds' of London insurance market, and Jamie Dundas, the chief executive of the property group MEPC. Bridget Macaskill, who had overlapped with Davis at the Pru, joined in 2002. Davis promised investment on stores and depots as well as cost savings.

By May 2001, Sainsbury shares had shot up by 32 per cent to 421p and sales and profits had slowly begun to rise. More than a hundred stores had received makeovers and the number of customers was up by 6 per cent.

Good news continued to flow from Holborn Circus and Davis was looking increasingly happy and sounding upbeat, whether at the Royal Opera House or socialising with the country's leaders. If Wal-Mart could cultivate Tony and Cherie Blair, why should not Davis? He bought in Jan Shawe, his former head of public relations at Reed and the Pru (and at Sainsbury during the early 1980s), to handle the media. But, always slightly insecure, he failed to bring in talented executives from outside who might challenge his own ideas.

By January 2002 it looked as though Sainsbury's sales growth had edged ahead of Tesco for the first time in six years. Tesco announced sales for the seven weeks over Christmas up by 6.2 per cent on a like-for-like basis while Sainsbury's had risen by 6.4 per cent. Davis claimed that Sainsbury was, at last, winning back customers from Tesco, a claim instantly denied by Leahy and his boys, who maintained that to keep driving down prices was the only way to boost sales.

On this Davis still demurred. A committed 'foodie' and wine connoisseur, he believed that if Sainsbury concentrated on quality and providing a wide choice of lines, it would win through. He refused to cut prices in the main Sainsbury stores to compete with Tesco and Asda except in SavaCentres deliberately aimed at the less well-off customer.

Davis was stuck with two problems about which he could do nothing – the size and the number of Sainsbury's stores. The company's 463 outlets were mainly in better locations than Tesco's 729, but Tesco, with 19m square feet, could boast nearly 30 per cent more floor space. Davis initiated a programme of extending existing stores – for which planning consent was much easier to gain – but Tesco and both Safeway and Asda had been playing that game too and were too far ahead to catch.

In order to get all its esoteric food lines on display, the Sainsbury aisles had to be narrower than its competitors' and the gondolas higher. Sainsbury became a more confusing and claustrophobic place to shop than Tesco or Asda and no one seemed to have a real grip on the store management. Shoppers began complaining and some changed allegiance. 'We buy organic,' one young mother told a Sainsbury staff member. 'But at Sainsbury it is all over the shop. At Tesco, the organic stuff is all in one place and much easier to find.' Complaints began to grow about out-of-stock items and ill-informed, unhelpful staff.

Davis had joined in March 2000, aged 59. Eighteen months later, his energy began to flag. Colleagues who had worked with him in the 1980s found he lacked enthusiasm for mundane trading issues. 'In the 1980s he used to be a hard-nosed retailer, passionate about the detail of stores,' said one. 'But when he came back he did not seem that interested in the day-to-day operations and he would brush over questions in meetings. He always seemed in a hurry.'

Davis had worked out that it was impossible to trade his way out of trouble and instead focused his attention on the prospect of buying another company. 'Peter was in love with mergers and acquisitions,' said one colleague, 'but pulling off a big deal proved a lot harder than he had anticipated.'

Doing company-transforming deals was something at which Davis was good. They had worked for him before and he needed one to work now. He kept Sainsbury's advisers at UBS Warburg and Goldman Sachs busy putting together hypothetical transactions. He even had several meetings with James Blyth about bidding for Boots but instead settled for a joint venture in 2001 by which Boots took over the health and beauty aisles in some larger Sainsbury stores. The idea failed and was scrapped less than two years later.

Seeing Asda's and Tesco's success at selling clothes, Davis ran the numbers on Marks & Spencer. In many ways, two old adversaries merging their world-famous brands could have been a dream ticket. They could have sold a full range of food with Marks & Spencer specialities at the top of the range and plenty of space for clothes. It had the potential to be a stunningly successful merger, but Davis pulled back. Eventually his eye fell on the fourth player in the supermarket hierarchy, Safeway.

He found David Webster's door open and had several private meetings with him about a straightforward Sainsbury bid for Safeway. But they both suspected that the competition authorities would never allow Sainsbury to make a successful takeover bid because there was too much overlap of stores in the south of England.

But what if a northern-based company could be persuaded to join Sainsbury in a bid and subsequently divide up the spoils? From his position at the Pru Davis had watched Asda's abortive attempts to merge with Safeway and had understood the logic. Now that Asda was owned by Wal-Mart, he felt it was at least worth talking to Tony de Nunzio, one of the original turn-round team, who had become chief executive when Leighton left the company.

The idea of a joint bid appealed to de Nunzio but he found it impossible to elicit interest in the idea from Lee Scott and David Glass in Bentonville and the talks lacked momentum. Then in early 2002 Scott began to show some enthusiasm, but that brought other problems. Originally Davis had been proposing a 50–50 split of Safeway stores between the two predators, but once Bentonville became interested it moved to 60–40 in Asda's favour and eventually went to 70–30. It also became clear that both Asda and Sainsbury wanted many of the same stores. At that point Davis retreated – it would have been too much like playing Robin to Wal-Mart's Batman.

Then on 7 September 2002 Lucy Farndon, retail correspondent of the *Daily Mail*, sent Safeway shares soaring with one of the best scoops of her career. Wal-Mart had been secretly sounding out the Office of Fair Trading to see whether Asda would be allowed to make a £2.8bn takeover bid for Safeway. The story was written with the kind of authority and detail that made the stock market believe it and Safeway shares leapt 15p to 221p on the day as 48 million shares were traded, ten times the normal volume. Even though Safeway issued a statement saying it 'was not in discussions with a third party', the announcement from Wal-Mart that 'we do not comment on market speculation' provided sufficient confirmation for most seasoned City observers. There could be no doubt about it; Safeway was in play.

SUPPLIERS – FRIEND OR FOE?

'Blaming supermarkets is the easiest excuse for commercial failure there is.'

Kevin Hawkins, Director General of the British Retail Consortium

Few relationships arouse more passion in commercial life than those between retailers and their suppliers. In essence that passion is about power – whoever controls the consumer's heart receives the lion's share of the profits. Manufacturers of 'must-have' brands such as Kellogg's, Mars or Persil command a greater share of the available profit pot than a small sheep farmer whose lamb chops are indistinguishable from those of hundreds of other small sheep farmers. The balance of power has now moved so far in the supermarkets' direction that many suppliers accuse them of behaving like old-fashioned highwaymen: 'Stand and deliver – your money, or a delist'. Even global companies such as the mighty Unilever, whose rock-solid brands include Persil, Dove and Walls, have had to rationalise their ranges in response to the emergence of fewer, larger customers.

Power corrupts, but in reality there are as many types of buyer–supplier relationships as there are buyers and suppliers. Individuals count. Forty years ago the manufacturers of major brands held the pistol to the small retailers' heads, aided and abetted by post-war price controls. Back then the food and drink manufacturers were accused of bullying and indulging in uncompetitive practices, particularly in commodities such as bread and beer. 'We were steeped in corruption,' admitted one retired executive.

Until the 1960s small grocers bought much of their wares through wholesalers. But as retailers became larger and more powerful, middlemen disappeared, leaving buyers and sellers to negotiate directly – a recipe not only for lower prices as the wholesaler's profit disappeared but also for friction.

This friction permeates all types of retailing. In 1984 the *Sunday Telegraph* hosted a luncheon on the top floor of the old Telegraph Group building in Fleet Street, since occupied by Goldman Sachs. The principal guests were Stanley Kalms, founder and at the time chairman of the electrical-goods chain Dixons, and Harry Solomon, then chief executive of Hillsdown Holdings, a major food supplier to Marks & Spencer and the supermarkets. Halfway through the main course Solomon remarked that the relationship between retailers and their suppliers was becoming more like a partnership. 'Absolute rubbish,' growled Kalms, thumping the table. 'It is war – that's what I tell my buyers. It is their job to get the lowest possible price.'

The argument continued fast and furious amid a lot of laughter for most of the lunch, as Kalms and Solomon squared up to each other. Yet, underneath the jollity, they were deadly serious. For some years Solomon and other private-label suppliers such as Chris Haskins Northern Foods were treated almost as partners by Marks & Spencer and Sainsbury. They had a good dialogue with their counterparts, invested millions of pounds in dedicated factories for one customer on a handshake, and could rely on the orders to keep on coming.

During good times some suppliers became complacent and were shocked to discover that when unexpected problems arose, the relationship reverted sharply to one of master and servant. Even Solomon was on one occasion summoned back from his holiday in France to face a painful dressing down from his opposite number at Marks & Spencer.

Kalms's warlike attitude stemmed partly from his own personality, but also from the nature of electrical retailing, where prices are constantly falling and there is a wide choice of suppliers from around the world.

For Kalms you could substitute Jack Cohen in his heyday, or John Sainsbury, who by all accounts took a brutal if professional attitude towards the big branded Sainsbury suppliers while nurturing innovative smaller suppliers who provided 'private-label' items.

Hillsdown was one of them. Solomon and his team built a lucrative business in the 1980s producing sandwiches, smoked salmon and chilled dishes for Marks & Spencer, expanding to supply Tesco and Sainsbury with similar products. The relationship was symbiotic, Marks & Spencer providing the retail intelligence while Hillsdown had the technical expertise.

There was an element of mutual trust. Kalms, on the other hand, was at the time attempting to deal with Alan Sugar of Amstrad, whose early personal computers were flying off Dixons' shelves, sparking regular rows between the two men about margins and availability.

Whether it is computers or food, the rule is the same. The more consumers want a specific brand and are prepared to inconvenience themselves to get it, the more profits will go to the maker of that brand. In the early 1960s food manufacturers such as Rowntree, Cadbury, United Biscuits and Rank Hovis McDougall called the tune and their customers – a plethora of independent shops and small multiple grocers – danced to it. But two key events completely changed the balance of power.

The first and most cataclysmic for suppliers was the abolition of resale price maintenance – effectively price fixing by manufacturers – by Ted Heath when he was President of the Board of Trade in 1964. The second was the development, first by Sainsbury and soon afterwards by all the major supermarket groups, of own-label products that competed with well-known, established brands at a lower price. After resale price maintenance was abolished, manufacturers fought a losing battle against increasingly competitive retailers.

Each retailer has a different way of dealing with its suppliers. In the early 1990s one ready-meal manufacturer had this lighthearted comment to make about his customers. 'Marks & Spencer want their suppliers to make a profit, Sainsbury doesn't want them to make a profit, Tesco doesn't care whether their suppliers make a profit and Asda doesn't know if their suppliers make a profit.' It is a fine balance. Supermarket managements need to allow their suppliers to make enough profit to keep the goods coming consistently – but not so much that they become complacent.

As an outsider coming into the food industry, John Nott, the former Tory minister, who took over the chairmanship of Hillsdown Holdings from Harry Solomon in 1993, was shocked by what he saw as 'the thuggish behaviour of the supermarkets'. Nott had spent most of his life in politics and farming. In his memoir, *Here Today, Gone Tomorrow,* he complained bitterly that 'We had only one problem in Hillsdown – our customers!' In the food business, Hillsdown's significant customers were Sainsbury, Tesco, Safeway, Asda and Marks & Spencer. 'Together they represented a complex monopoly, using their overwhelming buying power to squeeze their suppliers, most of them in the farming industry,' wrote Nott.

He was particularly outraged by the actions of Sainsbury: 'At its most ruthless stood Sainsbury. On several occasions I visited its headquarters to see the Purchasing Director. The atmosphere ... was poisonous: apparently miserable staff and an arrogance towards suppliers, consistent with the bullying approach of a third-rate corporal in a bad regiment.'

Chief culprit at Sainsbury was Tom Vyner, whom many suppliers despised, although they were pleasant to his face. 'Tom was a charming man to have dinner with, but in negotiations he was an animal,' said one. 'He was also under John Sainsbury's thumb.'

Vyner had the reputation of being quicker than other retailers to threaten to delist products or drastically reduce their shelf space if the supplier did not lower the price or stump up money for a promotion.

At Tesco, Daisy Hyams's successor as buying director, John Gildersleeve, enjoyed more autonomy than Vyner. Buying was his empire and Ian MacLaurin and Terry Leahy trusted his judgement. He and his team were tough, but significantly more pleasant to do business with than their main competitor. 'Sainsbury buyers were hateful to deal with,' one former supplier recalled, 'far nastier than Tesco or the others. When Tesco overtook Sainsbury, we all cheered.'

But a number of smaller, long-standing suppliers such as the chicken breeder Lloyd Maunder and the Indian recipe-dish maker Noon Products felt more warmly about their biggest customer. 'We have always had mutual respect,' declared Gulam Noon. 'If they are going through a choppy situation, we will support them. Loyalty is a two-way traffic – they have been a loyal customer so I should be a loyal supplier as well.'

In 2002, struggling to turn its fortunes round and fighting hard to win back market share, Sainsbury introduced the PICO (Price In, Cost Out) 'open-book' system. In order to keep Sainsbury's custom, suppliers had to open their accounts to Sainsbury buyers, who would then try to find ways to eliminate more costs. Suppliers complained that this eroded trust as well as profit as they suffered cuts in their prices, often at the last moment or even retrospectively.

Recently, however, Tesco has emerged as the master of what Paul Wilkinson of RHM dubbed the 'stand-and-deliver' form of negotiation. Tesco directors may take their counterparts at their suppliers to exotic locations to play golf and whisper sweet nothings about partnership, but down the line Tesco buyers grant them no quarter on pricing. After Wal-Mart took over Asda in

1999, Terry Leahy and his team at Tesco went on the offensive, determined to drive down prices. Once Tesco had more than a quarter of the UK market, even the biggest suppliers felt the heat. Stories of Tesco buyers renegotiating prices retrospectively began to surface; some suppliers complained of a bullying arrogance that did not previously exist.

'If you are a small supplier, you slog all the way to Cheshunt to see a buyer,' said one. 'They routinely keep you waiting in that horrible reception area for an hour to two hours and when they eventually appear they ask what you are doing there, or say that the meeting is not in their diary. Sometimes they just tell you they have no time to see you. Then they grudgingly agree to give you five minutes so you are at a complete psychological disadvantage when the negotiation begins. They do it so you will be glad to come away with an order for any quantity at any price.'

Tesco buyers, however, argued that their job was to get the best possible deal and that a degree of psychological warfare went with the territory.

In Yorkshire, Ken Morrison rated highly with suppliers, despite the low prices charged in his stores. 'Nobody ever complained about doing business with Ken,' said Chris Haskins after his retirement from Northern Foods. 'He is tough but fair.' In the past, that was due to Morrison's smaller size and proportionately reduced buying clout. Whether Morrison buyers would take a harsher approach once Safeway had been fully integrated into the group remained to be seen.

Perhaps surprisingly, in view of its rapacious reputation in America, Asda under Wal-Mart reportedly treated UK suppliers with more humanity than when Archie Norman and Allan Leighton ran things. The great banana fiasco in 2003, when Wal-Mart struck a deal with Del-Monte, the world's third largest banana supplier, which operates in Costa Rica and Cameroon, and severely undercut the price of Caribbean bananas, the traditional mainstay of UK supermarkets, sparked off a wave of unfavourable publicity. The coverage was stirred up mainly by rivals such as Sainsbury, which reportedly lost £12m as it dropped its own prices in response. Altogether, the rest of the UK supermarket industry was estimated to have lost £30m. The issue became intensely political and ministers from the Windward Islands spoke movingly on BBC Radio of how Caribbean producers would go out of business at those prices – which were achievable only because South American bananas are more intensively grown – and have no option but to resort to growing drug-producing crops instead.

After that Wal-Mart worked hard on improving its reputation in the UK, courting local communities, the press and the City. Asda said that whenever it introduced a new product it would look first for local supplies. It also initiated a policy of encouraging small food producers, for example simplifying communication procedures by allowing farmers to communicate by fax rather than email. Meanwhile, the management was quietly extending existing Asda stores and buying land where it could.

Asda regularly received industry accolades for having the best-run stores and delivering what it promised to suppliers who paid millions of pounds a year to promote their brands in-store. Asda traditionally had been more supportive of brands because it had not promoted own-label as aggressively as Sainsbury, Waitrose and Tesco.

'Asda is the best date in town,' said one supplier in 2004. 'If they take money from you for promotions, those promotions go into every store and you can expect a sales uplift of up to a third.' That was in stark contrast to Sainsbury, about which the same supplier grumbled that paid-for promotions rarely reached more than half the stores.

When Wal-Mart won control of Asda in 1999, most retail watchers expected the Wal-Mart name to appear prominently above the stores. But although the phrase 'part of the Wal-Mart group' began to appear above some store entrances, the wholesale rebranding forecast by many had yet to take place five years after the takeover.

Wal-Mart was bruised by the anti-capitalist backlash in the United States, which focused on the reputation of the company as never before. Here is what Bill Quinn said in *How Wal-Mart is Destroying America (and the World)* about the way Wal-Mart treated US suppliers: 'Because Wal-Mart is so big, it can (and does!) demand just about anything it wants from its vendors, anything from deeper-than-usual discounts to downright disadvantageous shipping policies to enforced returns on slow-moving merchandise. Some manufacturers are getting to the point where they just say "no" to doing business with Wal-Mart: the huge sale is not worth the even huger headache.'

The result of such adverse publicity was that Asda's relationship with traditional suppliers in the UK did, on the whole, improve after the Wal-Mart takeover, although cutting its milk suppliers from three to one in the summer of 2004 sent a ripple of fear through the food industry.

Wal-Mart's global buying power in non-food is mighty, but 80 per cent of its fresh-food products are still bought regionally. Among the global companies, even multinational Unilever operates on a regional basis and Wal-Mart has made an effort to source locally in the UK – at least for some products. Whether attitudes would change if Asda were to grow significantly – its market share was already up from 13 per cent to 15 per cent by 2004 – is open to debate.

Quinn might have captured the imagination of the consumer lobby but those in the business world saw things differently. 'The thing about Wal-Mart is you are either in or out – the policy is to use as few suppliers as possible but if you are one of them, the guaranteed volumes mean you make money. They are good, reliable payers,' said one large supplier. Wal-Mart also works extremely closely with its major suppliers, sharing information and coordinating marketing. Unilever, which sells 6 per cent of its output to Wal-Mart, has seventy full-time staff working in Wal-Mart's Bentonville headquarters. 'Wal-Mart creates a climate that is win–win for both of you,' said one Unilever executive. 'And Tesco has learned a lot from that model.'

The idea that the relationship between suppliers and their major customers could ever be totally harmonious is naïve. If it became too cosy, it would be no time at all before a consumer watchdog would accuse them of price fixing in a plot to rip off the customer. It is an economic imperative for the supplier to negotiate the highest price for his goods and the retailer's job to get the lowest, so at the very least there must be constructive tension between suppliers and their retail customers. Inevitably, this means that some brands do better than others as they jostle for position on the crowded shelves.

In the media, suppliers are often portrayed as oppressed underdogs, victims of the will of power-mad supermarkets that suck out all their profit and make impossible demands. Suppliers, too, tend to blame their customers for the low prices they receive, even though price levels are basically governed by the laws of supply and demand. Inevitably the least efficient are the first to suffer when buyers decide to make economies of scale – and they unsurprisingly complain the loudest. The most noise of all is usually heard from the UK fresh-produce suppliers – the farmers.

Milk supply, where there is huge excess capacity, is a classic example. Asda, using the Wal-Mart model, precipitated a rationalisation in the milk market in May 2004 by deciding to cut back from three suppliers to just one. Arla, which bought Express Dairies in 2003, was the lucky winner, although judging by the initial drop in the share price, investors were not so sure about the lucky part. Asda and Arla would be working more closely and it would be easier to trace where each carton of milk came from, we were told, as Arla duly lowered the price paid for milk to farmers by 0.4p a litre.

Robert Wiseman Dairies a Scottish milk producer, and Dairy Crest lost Asda's business. But when Tesco and Sainsbury cut their suppliers from three to two soon afterwards, Wiseman recouped its loss by securing new contracts with both. Sainsbury dropped Arla and Tesco ended its contract with Dairy Crest, which emerged as the net loser. In the marketplace, uncertainty is the only certainty.

Yet success as a supplier is about more than price alone. The milk wars are, in part at least, about continuity of supply. The bigger the supermarkets become, the more 'resupply' becomes a burning issue. Consumers demand consistency and stores cannot afford to be out of stock of regular lines, as Sainsbury found to its cost in 2004 when customers, infuriated by bare shelves, went elsewhere.

Supermarkets need suppliers with computer systems that can interface with theirs. They need to know their suppliers enforce the strictest hygiene codes. And, if the product is of high quality and also a speciality, they do not want them to supply another customer who is willing to pay more.

Their counterparts on the other side – producers and manufacturers – also desire continuity. They need 'quality of earnings', which is why they commonly invest £20m to £40m of their own money in building dedicated factories to serve just one customer. Partnership, albeit an often unequal one, has become a necessity in the modern world.

Partners are also prepared to experiment. Using the retailer's market intelligence, manufacturers will experiment with new products, knowing that if they fail – and according to the statistics nine out of every ten new products fail within two years – they have the comfort of a long-standing customer for other products.

Sometimes a customer does find an alternative supplier at short notice and a manufacturer may have to lay off staff – although shrewd suppliers will soon find another customer to take the output. For example in the 1990s Hillsdown started making low-calorie sandwiches for Marks & Spencer in addition to their mainstream products. Customers snapped them up and turnover grew to be a third of all the sandwiches they made. But one lunchtime, Derek Rayner, then Marks & Spencer's chairman and something of a bon viveur, tasted one and thought it so unpalatable that he demanded they be delisted immediately. An embarrassed buyer had to break the bad news, but Hillsdown managers gritted their teeth and soon procured an order from Boots, which marketed the low-calorie sandwiches under the name 'Shapers'. As Francis Bacon once put it: 'Adversity doth best discover virtue'.

Suppliers, however valued, are always the junior partners. As supermarkets have grown, manufacturers have discovered that over-dependence on one customer puts them in a vulnerable position. What may look like a licence to print money one year may turn into a factory-closure notice the next. It is a risk they have to take. Fashions and markets change; new competitors appear. The most canny suppliers, even those with long-standing relationships, arrange their business to ensure they are not too dependent on any one customer.

Gulam Noon's company Noon Products makes all Sainsbury's chilled Indian food while another of his companies provides the pickle and chutney. Noon began making chilled recipe dishes for the group in 1989, when Tom Vyner decided to give him a chance, and he had built the turnover to more than £90m by 2004. Sainsbury remains his biggest customer and he formed a close relationship with David Sainsbury who, like Noon, was a major financial contributor to the Labour party. Noon also counted Peter Davis, when he was chief executive, as a friend.

But from the early years Noon Products also sold to Waitrose and soon included Safeway, now Morrison, as a customer. The recipes for his different customers vary slightly and he has one 148,000-square-foot factory manufacturing exclusively for Sainsbury and other units making dishes for Waitrose and Morrison, although not Tesco or Asda.

But even in 2004, Sainsbury accounted for 60 per cent of Noon's business, which, as a result, has captured 29 per cent of the UK chilled Indian food market. By producing food that Sainsbury customers loved – and that no one else could match – he had a more equal relationship with the company. Unsurprisingly his views on Sainsbury differed sharply from many of those of the bigger groups selling branded goods, or those supplying fresh commodities such as fruit, vegetables, meat and fish.

'I think I could write a book about the relationship,' said Noon fondly. 'I would not say they have been arrogant or difficult. I have seen many directors and buyers, and we have always had an incredible relationship.'

Noon experienced an example of loyalty in a crisis when fire tore through one of his factories in 1994. 'David Sainsbury rang me umpteen times and said they would not buy a single pack of Indian food from anyone else. They put up a sign in the stores saying "due to a fire at our supplier this range of products is temporarily suspended". His relationship with Sainsbury made him a multi-millionaire and helped earn him an OBE and a knighthood.

Noon is an exception among the ranks of browbeaten Sainsbury suppliers simply because he runs an exceptional company making 'authentic Indian food' of a quality that others struggle to meet. A passionate entrepreneur who adores Britain, he has refused to compromise his principles: 'We are a chef-driven company because you cannot stick to formulas if you are using fresh ingredients. I am the biggest user of fresh coriander in the UK.' Noon uses three-quarters of a tonne of fresh coriander a day, the same amount of fresh garlic and half a tonne of fresh ginger. He said he would never contemplate using powdered versions.

The relationship has not been entirely without friction. In the early days Noon had to educate the Sainsbury executives, who wanted him to put sultanas and apple in his dishes. 'I told them I would not make Colonial bastardised curries. My philosophy was to manufacture authentic Indian food and by doing this I have been successful.' When he suggested widening the range to regional dishes in the mid 1990s he took several Sainsbury directors on a buying trip to India, making them taste everything from street food to the cuisine of the best hotels. 'Nobody got sick and they all had a jolly good time,' declared Noon.

Over the years Noon has had to lower his profit margins, but he has been handsomely rewarded for his sacrifice. His margins in 2004 were only half what they were ten years previously, but his turnover with Sainsbury had quintupled. Suppliers sometimes complain of being 'imprisoned' by the supermarkets but the bars can be gilded, as Noon and several other food entrepreneurs have discovered.

Dr Philip Beresford, the compiler of the *Sunday Times* Rich List, put Noon's personal fortune at more than £50m. He was one of sixty-nine people in the 2004 List's food and drink sector; others included the Warburton bread family with £230m, the meat supplier David Samworth with £190m, Alan Wiseman of Robert Wiseman Dairies with £108m and the turkey farmer Bernard Matthews with £168m.

At the other end of the scale are the small farmers who turned up at Tesco's annual general meeting in 2004 to claim that more than 4,000 of their number a year were going out of business because of the low prices paid to them by the supermarkets. The National Union of Farmers blamed much of the misery on a six-year farming recession aggravated by the knock-on effects of the foot-and-mouth epidemic of 2002 and the strength of sterling, which made imports effectively cheaper. But the NFU also pointed to 'the decreasing share farmers receive of the retail price of what they produce'. By 2002 the proportion farmers received had dropped to a quarter of what their products sold for in the shops.

Farmers, like most producers of commodities, are in a weak position because they are relatively small. Whether they produce beef, lamb, apples or tomatoes, the competition is international, and the strength of the pound has helped importers and made it more difficult to sell abroad.

What most concerns small producers and their champions in the food lobbies is the sheer scale of the buying power of the supermarkets. During 2002–3, there was much coverage of alleged bullying by supermarkets of small sheep farmers living on the edge of the poverty line. Yet despite the howls of protest from the Welsh hills, the lamb chops kept arriving.

The price of lamb at market is determined, like anything else, by supply and demand. In 2002 whole lambs were fetching as little as £12 a head, but by spring 2004 they had jumped to £40 a head after the least efficient shepherds pulled out of the market, so reducing supply and boosting the price to remaining farmers. In other sectors of farming, profits were also rising. Figures from the Department of Environment, Food and Rural Affairs showed total farming income dropping from more than £6bn in 1995 to £1bn in 2003, while annual income per person fell from £25,000 to nearer £15,000 over the same period.

Britain's shrinking band of small farmers have seized what some see as the moral high ground and moved into the emotional soft spot in the nation's psyche that was previously reserved for coal miners. Of course, no one should under-estimate the depths of individual suffering, yet there is nothing inherently moral about growing food or rearing and slaughtering animals – any more than there is anything particularly noble about the dangerous and dirty job of hacking coal from an underground pit. Farming is an industry and, like any other factory, if a farm does not make a profit, it will go out of business. Whatever the faults of the supermarkets, few farmers ever voluntarily give up their contracts with them – high-volume, low-margin pickings are better than low-volume, high-margin ones if the sales are big enough. And, according to Defra, farmers have proved surprisingly reluctant to retire.

One response to low profits has been the growth of farmers' markets, which allow smaller growers and meat producers to sell direct to the customer. All goods displayed must be the produce of the stallholder. Since 2000 the number of markets has grown to more than 400 and turnover in 2004 was £166m. Stallholders on average earn £8,500 a year from farmers' markets, although at the top end they can earn £20,000. So far the supermarkets have not felt threatened. Sainsbury even paid for the utilities in the farmers' market that takes place in its own car park in Finchley Road in north London.

Free-marketeers believe that our food would be cheaper if farmers were not subsidised by the Common Agricultural Policy. They believe that farmers should be treated no differently from metal bashers, textile workers or miners. Much of the world's poverty could be eradicated if developing countries were allowed to grow the food best suited to their climates and export it to Europe. The economist Roger Bootle wrote in his book *Money for Nothing*: '… the EU operates an outrageously protectionist agricultural system that directly harms European consumers, taxpayers and the peoples of many other countries, including poor farmers in Africa and aspirant EU members in Eastern Europe. It spends $40bn a year subsidising the production and export of huge surpluses of cereals, sugar and dairy products.'

John Blundell of the Institute of Economic Affairs believes that the cost of food in the UK is 'at least 25 per cent higher than it need be' because of the European Union. He argues that, 'If the Commission lowered its tariff barriers, vast acres of land on other continents would come back under husbandry and prices would fall further.'

Some reform of the CAP is underway, leading to calls from the NFU for farmers to work together and form co-operatives.

Although farmers are the most vocal of supermarket suppliers, many others are dissatisfied with their lot. Of the branded manufacturers, the ones that have been most squeezed in the past ten years own the second-tier brands. Yet in Britain's competitive business climate, few will complain publicly or officially because their continuation in business so often depends on the goodwill of their customers. According to one former head of a bakery company, 'Nobody ever tells the real story to the competition authorities; they have too much to lose.'

When a big-brand company refuses to cut prices as much as its customer would like, the penalty is a reduction of orders. Campbell's soup, for example, has far less UK shelf space today than it did twenty years ago, partly because Campbell's has refused to cut its margins as much as its customers would like it to. Campbell's, like many other big brand owners, plays on an international stage, and some of what it loses in UK sales is recouped from sales overseas, where price competition is less ferocious.

A typical punch-up between a manufacturer protecting its brand and an aggressive retailer took place in the late 1990s when Asda decided to sell a look-alike own-label version of the Penguin chocolate-biscuit bar made by United Biscuits. Displaying scant subtlety, Asda called its product 'Puffin'. The Puffin's size, shape and wrapping were almost indistinguishable from Penguin's and Asda displayed it at a lower price close to the genuine article.

United Biscuits executives were furious and asked Archie Norman and Allan Leighton to stop producing it. They refused. United Biscuits threatened to sue Asda, on the grounds that the bar was a direct copy, but Leighton retorted that he would take away £60m of orders if they went to court. In the event United Biscuits proceeded and won the case. The revenge was not quite so severe as had been threatened, but United Biscuits still lost many millions of pounds' worth of business from Asda that year.

Some suppliers are more pragmatic than others. Harry Solomon, who chaired Hillsdown in the 1980s up until 1993, built a largely non-branded food company that had 20 per cent of the British poultry and egg market and a canning business second only to Heinz. In contrast with John Nott, his successor, he worked on the principle that it was his job to find a way of serving the supermarkets. 'I enjoyed dealing with them. They were tough cookies but that is the way of business.'

Solomon retired at the time of the price war that successfully curtailed the growth of the discounters such as Lidl, Netto and CostCo. The resulting pressure on manufacturing profits prompted consolidation of the food-manufacturing industry. Nott put it this way. 'They were squeezed to death when the supermarkets went to war with the discounters, cutting food producers' margins into shreds. The Stock Market was no longer willing to finance the UK food industry – only the international brands managed to survive in their original form.'

They were tough times, but the reality was that most of the factories survived under new ownership. Those companies that in Nott's words had 'gone down the plughole' were taken over either by bigger companies or by private equity groups in the early 1990s – but they did not cease to exist.

RHM, the former Ranks Hovis McDougall, was taken over by the Tomkins group in 1992. Tomkins already owned Smith & Wesson, the US pistol maker, and the RHM deal earned it the soubriquet 'guns to buns group'. In 2000 RHM was sold to Doughty Hanson, a private equity firm. Hillsdown went to the American private equity house Hicks, Muse, Tate & Furst, while United Biscuits was taken over by another financial bidder. Unigate sold off part of its business and was restructured and renamed Uniq – and it is still quoted on the London Stock Exchange.

What comes around, goes around. With the return of 'animal spirits' to the stock market in early 2004 and a new trend towards branded goods in supermarkets, food companies began reappearing in the quoted sector. In May 2004 Hicks, Muse, Tate & Furst announced the flotation of Premier Foods, a company looking remarkably similar to Premier Brands, one of the Hillsdown subsidiaries, but with a few additions and subtractions. Premier Foods included Hartley's jam, Branston pickle and Typhoo tea when it floated in July 2004. The chief executive, Robert Schofield, came from United Biscuits. Even so, the shares soon fell below the flotation price as the stock market judged that the going would stay tough although no one could have foreseen the Sudan 1 food scare in early 2005.

The British food industry was forced to adapt to changed circumstances, to become the modern, efficient suppliers its customers required. Having re-invented itself, it prepared to slog it out. Unilever declared that in Europe trading would be 'as tough as you like for as long as you like'.

Supermarket customer opinion has now swung back in favour of branded products; shoppers are willing to pay a little more for the assured quality of a well-known brand in preference to a cheaper own-label product that is possibly inferior. For example, in 1996 own-label bread accounted for 50 per cent of supermarket bread sales. By 2004 that was down to a mere 30 per cent after bakers such as the family-run Warburtons and RHM, which makes Hovis, actively pushed their brands and consumers responded. Differentiation is the name of the game that produces higher profits for both retailer and supplier. In the summer of 2004 Hovis launched the first branded full-sized loaf to be sold part-baked, giving bread lovers the satisfaction of a 'home-baked loaf' without the hassle of making it.

Asda under Wal-Mart has been at the forefront of the movement back towards branded goods – partly because Asda never had a strong own-label brand in food and partly because it can make more money from selling them.

Without the modern supermarket there would be no year-round grapes or strawberries, no asparagus in May, no lamb in winter and far less organic or 'fair-trade' produce sold. Marks & Spencer, Sainsbury and Waitrose were the pioneers, urging their suppliers to improve the standard and range of fresh food available to the British customer. Avocado pears, papayas, mangoes and many other fruits and vegetables that were difficult to find twenty years ago are now commonplace.

British supermarkets, with Marks & Spencer in the van, have also nurtured food manufacturers in demanding standards of hygiene more rigorous than anywhere else in the world. The popularity of chilled ready-meals when they were first developed by Marks & Spencer posed huge potential health risks if they were prepared in a way that was not micro-biologically safe. Food poisoning is bad for business. Led by Marks & Spencer, whose chief food technician, Nate Goldberg, set uncompromising standards regarded as ridiculously stringent by the rest of the industry at the time, retailers demanded increasing levels of cleanliness and efficiency from their suppliers.

The supermarkets, responding to the desires of their increasingly sophisticated, health-conscious and environmentally aware customers, have driven most of the changes in what we have eaten over the last thirty years. Yet their sheer size leads to distrust. In response to the 'foodies' lobby's calls for better-tasting food, supermarkets, again led by Marks & Spencer in conjunction with Waitrose, have concentrated on the taste and what the trade calls the 'eating quality' of its food.

Better eating quality usually means a higher fat content, but an outbreak of 'silly season' reporting in the summer of 2004 resulted in the newspapers accusing supermarkets of putting 'stealth fats' in their food, despite the fact that the sugar, carbohydrate and fat content were all clearly stated on the packaging. One article also contained a table comparing obviously heavily loaded products with so called 'home-made' ones, although whose home they had been made in was not made clear. One example was Jordan's Country Crisp breakfast cereal, which contained more fat than its home-made muesli. If the newspaper had compared its version to Jordan's Natural

Muesli it would have found there was hardly any difference in fat content – but that would have spoiled the story.

Tesco's response was simple. 'People do enjoy eating some products that are less good for their diet than others, so what we do is to make it easy for them to buy a healthy alternative.'

Customers have a choice about what they buy. If they want a delicious bread enriched with olive oil they can have it. Or they can instead take home a much cheaper standard white loaf with minimal fat. You pays your money and you takes your choice.

So powerful have supermarkets become that when there is a food scare, the supermarkets rather than the manufacturers come under fire. Suppliers are now regarded as the underdog, with good reason. When the Competition Commission investigated the industry in 2000, it sent teams of investigators to interview representatives of twenty-four grocery chains having more than ten grocery outlets. They also interviewed their suppliers. Understandably, the main focus was on the big four groups plus Marks & Spencer, Waitrose and Somerfield.

When the investigators talked to suppliers they found 'a climate of apprehension' among them in relationship to 'the main parties', and although most of them complained privately about aspects of their treatment by the big supermarkets, they refused to do so officially or, in some cases, even to name the supermarket in question. Many refused to give evidence unless the commissioners would guarantee confidentiality; others were too scared to give evidence at all. Every supplier feared reprisals – orders cancelled or reduced in price or the delisting of peripheral brands.

In their frustration, the investigators gathered all the unattributable allegations together – a staggering fifty-two in all – and confronted executives from the main supermarkets with them, asking which of the unpopular practices they had indulged in during the previous five years. The supermarkets owned up surprisingly readily. 'We found the majority of these practices were carried out by many of the main parties,' said the report.

The most common 'offences' included asking for discounts or non-cost-related payments, sometimes retrospectively, making sudden changes to contractual arrangements or imposing new charges without warning and unreasonably transferring risks from the main party to the supplier, such as expecting a buyer's expenses to be paid on a visit to a factory or farm. The investigators made it clear that a 'request' from a big customer with major buying power was tantamount to an order.

Despite such unpalatable practices, more than 50 per cent of suppliers considered that their relationship with their major customers was good or excellent; 11 per cent put it as excellent and 35 per cent put it as acceptable. Only 5 per cent deemed their relationship as 'fairly poor', but that does not necessarily paint a true picture because of 'survivorship bias'. In other words, the Competition Commission failed to interview suppliers who had already been dropped by their customers or pulled out themselves because their relationship had become so unsatisfactory.

The findings showed that, although they might complain, most suppliers understood the nature of commerce and were prepared to adopt a 'swings-and-roundabouts' approach along the way. 'It is all fairly standard stuff,' remarked one wearily. What did emerge clearly from that 2000 report, however, was that all suppliers, even the biggest such as Unilever and Procter & Gamble, believed the balance of power was tilting firmly towards the big supermarket groups. In the event of a dispute over quality or price, less than a third of large suppliers said they had an adequate negotiating position, while for small suppliers this dropped to 15 per cent.

The Commission inspectors concluded that the various supermarket practices did, in fact, adversely affect the competitiveness of some of suppliers and distort competition in the supplier market – and in some cases in the retail market. 'We find these practices give rise to a second complex monopoly situation.'

This was serious stuff and they continued in the same vein, stating that, as a result, 'suppliers are likely to invest less and spend less on new product development and innovation, leading to lower quality and less consumer choice'. Of the situation faced by the smaller food retailers they said: 'Certain of the practices give the major buyers substantial advantages over other smaller retailers, whose competitiveness is likely to suffer as a result, again leading to a reduction in consumer choice.'

The Commission recommended that the government introduce a code of practice to address these issues. A code was duly drawn up and put into effect in February 2001. The idea was that if supermarkets broke the code, suppliers should complain to the OFT, who would take up their complaints while seeking 'to maintain confidentiality, although this could not be guaranteed'.

By June 2004 the OFT had received no complaints whatsoever from suppliers – presumably because it could not guarantee confidentiality. And, as one official admitted, in certain cases it would be all too obvious which supplier was complaining. Not to be outdone, the OFT decided to conduct a compliance audit of the supermarkets, which it subcontracted to an accountancy firm, PKF.

During the following nine months the auditors endured intense lobbying from various pressure groups. Such unlikely bedfellows as the Women's Institute and Friends of the Earth joined forces in a group called Breaking the Armlock and there was a steady stream of 'anti-supermarket' stories in the press.

In other words, it was business as usual.

CHAPTER TEN

THE BATTLE FOR SAFEWAY

'Individual initiative will only be adequate when reasonable calculation is supplemented and supported by animal spirits, so that the thought of ultimate loss which often overtakes pioneers ... is put aside as a healthy man puts aside the expectation of death.'

John Maynard Keynes

Few retail observers doubted Lucy Farndon's revelations of Asda's predatory intentions in the *Daily Mail* in September 2002, but during the weeks that followed the speculation over a bid for Safeway gradually subsided. Perhaps Asda had decided against it, analysts reasoned, or maybe the 'boys from Bentonville' had deemed it a takeover too far.

But Safeway's chairman, David Webster, knew the story to be all too true and he set about taking evasive action that autumn. He and Peter Davis had talked several times about merging Safeway and Sainsbury. The two companies had similar cultures and in an ideal world Webster would have preferred to do a deal with Sainsbury, even though there would have been considerable geographical overlap and a good number of stores would have had to close.

Davis saw it as his dream ticket and got as far as making a detailed bid proposition, which Webster considered carefully. But the Safeway lawyers told Webster that because both companies operated in the south of England and often had stores in the same town, the merger would almost certainly be referred to the Competition Commission. Davis took independent legal advice and was told that the Office of Fair Trading could be mollified by commitments to sell some overlapping stores – but as he was not prepared to make a hostile bid, he had to accept the Safeway view. Reluctantly both men put the proposal on ice.

Once Webster felt the hot breath of Wal-Mart, however, he went into action. He had no wish for his company to be subsumed by the American giant – particularly as Asda before its takeover had played cat and mouse with him a few years earlier. Webster had seen Ken Morrison at an industry dinner that autumn and they had talked around the subject. Now he took the next, possibly the only, logical step and rang him. The two men had long had a cordial relationship and had often 'taken tea' together. Webster's predecessor, Alistair Grant, had first discussed merging Safeway with Morrison in the 1980s. Morrison had said at the time that if he ever did a deal with another supermarket, it would be Safeway because he could see the similarities in the culture.

Morrison had long wanted to make the move south but Tesco and Asda had grown too big for his company to bid for, while the Sainsbury clan still controlled the destiny of their family business. Morrison was not the least interested in selling the company his father started. He saw himself as predator, not prey. At one time he had had held discussions with the John Lewis Partnership with a view to buying Waitrose, but it soon became clear that there was no chance of the parent body parting with its upmarket food arm.

Yet for Morrison, at 71, to bid for another public company was a huge leap. He had built his company slowly through organic growth and had only ever made one small acquisition other than buying suppliers. He had built a company with 5 per cent of the market, a concentration of stores in the north-east and a reputation for outstanding value and fairness in every aspect of its dealings. In a rare interview, he once said that if he had any regrets it was that perhaps he was overcautious. It seems unlikely he would have thought seriously about bidding for Safeway if Webster had not made the first approach.

At an age when most founder chairmen step up to be life president or are at least thinking about retirement, Morrison might have been expected to settle for a deal where he could hand on the management of his group to Safeway – almost a reverse takeover. But that was not Morrison's idea at all. He wanted Safeway's sites – but his belief that his way was the best way never faltered. He wanted none of Safeway's southern-style management or systems.

Morrison and Webster arranged to meet for a preliminary conversation

– what is known in the trade as a 'conversation that never happened'. Over lunch at Nuthurst Grange, a discreet venue perfect for clandestine meetings, they talked the matter through, sizing each other up. After several hours' discussion, the two men left the hotel convinced that they could do a deal – that Morrison's view of what he could pay was not far removed from what Safeway's shareholders would accept.

A more formal meeting took place in mid-November, also at Nuthurst Grange, at which investment bankers were present. By all accounts that meeting was warm and friendly with everyone getting along well. 'We had a straight talking, very tight negotiation with Ken,' said one Safeway adviser. 'The relationship between us all was very close and warm.'

But Christmas trading had begun and Morrison needed some time to work out the details of how his management, who were used to running 119 stores, could swallow the much bigger Safeway with its 479 locations.

At Sainsbury, time was running out for Davis, who had abandoned hopes of doing a joint bid for Safeway with Asda. Once Wal-Mart's American management had focused on the acquisition, they had moved the goalposts. What had started out as joint deal splitting the Safeway assets 50–50 with Sainsbury had gradually changed to 70–30 in Asda's favour. Despite this, Davis still clung to the idea that Sainsbury on its own might be allowed to take over Safeway if it agreed to sell their overlapping stores. His relationship with Webster remained cordial and they continued to talk from time to time. Blissfully unaware of how events were developing between Webster and Morrison, Davis still believed a bid from Sainsbury would be well received and he prepared the documentation for a formal offer, aided by UBS Warburg and Goldman Sachs.

During the four weeks before Christmas, money cascades into supermarket tills. Takings rocket by 50 per cent compared with normal trading as householders stash away provisions for the festival. Even though, in recent years, supermarkets close only on Christmas Day and Boxing Day, rather than shutting down for four or five days as they used to, British shoppers retain their siege mentality about the holiday. Cost consciousness flies out of the window with the impending arrival of in-laws, aunts, uncles and cousins and £1.6bn is spent on food and drink, including, according to the British Retail Consortium, 10 million turkeys, 25 million Christmas puddings, 35 million bottles of wine and 10 million satsumas. The figure for indigestion remedies is unavailable.

Behind this smokescreen of frenzied activity Morrison and Webster beavered away with their advisers, preparing their case. They thought it was a good one, the two groups possessing only a few overlapping stores, which could easily be sold. Both men worked towards a deal that Safeway could recommend to its shareholders, sometimes working weekends to thrash out the details.

They had a final due diligence meeting on Sunday, 8 December, at the Hilton Hotel in Nottingham, with by then a full entourage of bankers, brokers, lawyers and auditors present.

That meeting was as cordial as the others, although Webster and his team felt some sadness that, after the takeover, Morrison planned to sweep away everything connected with the Safeway culture. Even the sophisticated computer systems would go, although the technology was vastly superior to anything Morrison had.

Ken Morrison wanted to 'Morrisonise' the whole shebang and to dismantle Safeway's Hayes headquarters as soon as possible. Only those who were willing to move to Yorkshire would keep their jobs. It may have seemed harsh but, as ever, Morrison and his team spelt out their plans clearly.

Both sets of investment bankers believed the chances of a competition referral were remote, although Webster knew from bitter experience about the vagaries of regulators. He also suspected, given his conversations with Davis, that a counter-bid from Sainsbury was almost inevitable. Indeed, Webster had told Morrison about his talks with Sainsbury – it had strengthened his bargaining position – and he also revealed that Safeway had had an approach from Kohlberg Kravis Roberts, the American private equity house headed by the legendary Henry Kravis. KKR had been immortalised in *Barbarians at the Gate,* a book by two American journalists, Bryan Burrough and John Helyar, which described how the firm launched a buy out for RJR Nabisco. Since 1986, when Argyll had bought Safeway's UK chain from KKR, Webster had kept the contact alive.

KKR specialised in taking public companies private with a view to refloating them eventually or selling them on, but KKR executives said they would need to spend months raking over the files doing due diligence before they could make a decision. In contrast, Ken Morrison was a Yorkshireman who had already made up his mind. Shrewdly, though, he negotiated a £29.2m break fee payable to Morrison to cover his costs if the bid lapsed or was withdrawn because Safeway accepted a rival offer. All was set for an announcement on Wednesday, 18 December, but other factors intervened and Morrison decided to hold fire.

Christmas and New Year came and went with the usual lack of financial news. Then, just as overfed children were returning to school for the spring term on Thursday, 9 January 2003, Morrison launched its £2.9bn all-share bid for Safeway, valuing its shares at 278p against a market price of 213p the previous Friday.

To market traders who had all but forgotten about the previous autumn's speculation, this was a bombshell. Safeway and Morrison had kept the deal top secret and the market was caught unawares. Safeway shares were chased up to 256p on hopes of a counter-bid – and Morrison shares sank to 238p, reducing the value of the bid to £2.5bn. Stock-market dealers marked Sainsbury and Tesco lower on fears of fiercer competition from the new force. Morrison predicted the combined group would have sales of more than £12.6bn and a market share of 16.1 per cent – still lagging Sainsbury, which at the time had more than 17 per cent.

Morrison's bid acted like cannon fire signalling the start of a new battle. Safeway, the lacklustre third player whose shares had been drifting downwards, underperforming the market, suddenly became the most coveted prize in the sector. On its own, neither Tesco, Sainsbury nor Asda had regarded Safeway as a threat, but for it to be in the hands of someone else was a different matter entirely. Renowned for its ruthlessly efficient operation, Morrison in possession of the Safeway store portfolio and the superior buying power that would accompany it would threaten even Tesco.

A shocked Davis, who had thought Wal-Mart would bid first, cancelled all his social plans and worked over the weekend with his advisers to produce an indicative counter-bid the following Monday. In cash and shares it was worth substantially more than the Morrison bid at £3.2bn. In the midst of the preparation Davis had realised there was no need to make a formal offer with all the attendant costs of underwriting for the transaction to be examined by the competition authorities. It was enough, his advisers said, simply to announce his intention of bidding to the world. Davis was first out of the traps on the Monday morning, but the rest of the sector lined up close behind him, armed with their own indicative bids.

'Feeding Frenzy', roared the headlines, and by Monday afternoon Safeway's shares had risen by 42 per cent in three trading days. The following morning Wal-Mart announced its great desire to make a bid.

They were bitter-sweet times for Webster. He had the unenviable task of addressing 2,000 staff at the Hayes headquarters and telling them that, if the bid from Morrison was successful, the office would be closed. Only 800 of their jobs would remain – and they would be in Bradford.

Wednesday passed relatively quietly but on the morning of Thursday, 16 January, came the news that CSFB First Boston, which had been the stock-broker to Safeway since 1995, had resigned so that it might advise KKR on a potential bid. Webster and his team were not only incensed at the disloyalty, but thought CSFB's decision to give up a certain fee for an uncertain one rather strange. 'Credit Suisse First Boston has set pulses racing again by resigning as broker to Safeway, a client for eight years, to work on a tentative but potentially much more lucrative proposal from Kohlberg Kravis Roberts, the renowned Wall Street investment firm,' reported the *Sunday Times*.

That morning Neil Richardson, a senior executive in KKR's London office, called Webster to give him the details of the third 'indicative offer'. Within the week, Safeway had been transformed from a Cinderella with little hope of going to the ball into the prettiest girl on the dance floor, besieged by suitors. Ken Morrison had taken on the unlikely role of Prince Charming.

The following weekend brought little reprieve, the Sunday newspapers speculating frantically about which company might be next to enter the fray. 'Behind the scenes bankers, venture capitalists and other retailers are hatching ever more audacious plans to bag Safeway,' wrote Matthew Goodman and Paul Durman in the *Sunday Times*. One particular player from outside the food-retailing industry was doing his sums. Philip Green, the one-time maverick who had so successfully taken over the clothing retailers Bhs and Arcadia, had decided to join the party. The *Sunday Times* had been well-briefed by sources close to Green: 'It seems that for Green, already one of the biggest names in retailing through his ownership of Bhs and Arcadia, the pull of the most heated takeover battle in years is impossible to resist,' they wrote. 'But while Green has [Allan] Leighton as his chairman at Bhs, the former Asda boss will not be spearheading Safeway if Green succeeds. He has lined up Stuart Rose, previously Arcadia's chief executive, to run the supermarket group.'

As predicted, Green came out with the fourth indicative offer the following morning, leaving Morrison's bid as the only formal one on the table, albeit one mired in the mud. 'Safeway is a one-off opportunity,' said Green, going to the heart of the matter. 'It is never going to be available again.'

Sensing at the very least a long haul and the growing likelihood of a Competition Commission referral and inquiry, stock-market dealers marked down Morrison's shares, lowering the value of the offer still further.

Just as the City thought every bid in the woodwork that could come out had come out, Tesco's chief executive Terry Leahy astonished everyone by announcing that he, too, planned to throw his hat into the ring. 'We are prepared to make an offer that would be compelling to Safeway shareholders in a mix of cash and shares.'

Steely Leahy, as the *Daily Mail* dubbed him, declared that the Safeway bid frenzy signalled a restructuring of the industry, which was why he wished to put Tesco's case. 'I say in competition terms our case is at least as good as Wal-Mart and Sainsbury, and in consumer terms we think it is much better'.

Leahy knew full well the Competition Commission would never allow a company with already more than a quarter of the market in its sector to bid for another in the same line of business, but he had another agenda. He knew that by bidding Tesco would, under Rule 20 of the Takeover Code, be allowed access to the confidential information about Safeway's trading accounts and balance sheet that had been given to Morrison. And if the regulators had not quite decided whether to refer some of the bidders, then Tesco's entry would help them make up their minds. A referral would mean a minimum of three months during which all bids would be put on ice, weakening Safeway and taking up management time in rival companies. It was a period that Leahy and his young lions would use to their advantage.

Webster had been prepared for Sainsbury and KKR to counter-bid, but he had not expected Wal-Mart to enter the fray and he had certainly not countenanced the idea of a bid from Tesco with its already large market share. As the Morrison share price slid, so did the value of its bid. By the end of January the bid price had fallen to below 230p a share and Webster reluctantly withdrew his recommendation. If another firm was prepared to offer more to shareholders and the OFT allowed it to bid, he could not stand in the way.

The grand total of six bidders in the battle for Safeway involved twelve investment banks – every London-based bank of note. For sheer numbers of would-be bidders, it had become the most extraordinary takeover war ever witnessed on the London Stock Exchange.

Marks & Spencer contemplated joining in – but in the end its chief executive, Roger Holmes, erred wisely on the side of caution. He made it clear he would be happy to pick up any stores that might be for sale, but he had enough to do without becoming embroiled in a tooth-and-nail auction.

Philip Green had other ideas. Always an optimist, he believed that because both Bhs and Arcadia – whose brands included Top Shop, Burton Menswear, Miss Selfridge and Dorothy Perkins – sold clothes rather than food, his request to put in a bid would be waved through by the OFT. An entrepreneur with a record of successful trading behind him, he styled himself a 'hit-and-run merchant'. When he bought Sears, the retailing conglomerate, he soon broke it up and sold off most of the component parts at huge profit. Many believe his strategy with Safeway would have been to sell off the stores to the rest of the sector. Although Morrison's bid valued the group at around £2.5bn, a cleverly timed revaluation of the store portfolio put Safeway's property assets at £4bn. It was clear there was money to be made. He formed an investment vehicle called Trackdean to bid for Safeway.

By the end of January, his hopes of quick approval had vanished. Green announced he would be making a formal submission for clearance to bid – but further announcements should not be expected for 'several weeks'. In other words, he would have to stand in the queue, the same as all the other bidders. 'So it was goodbye to the quickie, farewell to the mouth-watering prospect of a rapid cash offer for Safeway from entrepreneur Philip Green,' as Martin Dickson wrote in the *Financial Times*. Never one to keep his feelings to himself Green complained that in the clothing industry rival shops 'open next to each other all the time. There seem to be different rules in this industry.'

Speculation raged as to the various permutations. Why should not Sainsbury and Morrison get together and divide the spoils between them? Why did not KKR bid for Morrison and then Safeway and refloat them three years later at a profit?

Behind the scenes each group lobbied its case. The spectre of Wal-Mart hung over the rest of the industry like a dementor in J. K. Rowling's Harry Potter books, sucking the happiness out of everyone. The outcome that struck terror into the hearts of Tesco and Sainsbury executives was that of the giant Wal-Mart, valued at £150bn, getting its hands on Safeway. Wal-Mart's new-store openings in America in 2002 were equivalent to the whole of Tesco's square footage.

Peter Davis told colleagues that if Wal-Mart were to acquire Safeway,

Sainsbury would be 'dead in the water'. Even Tesco would struggle against its global buying might. Wal-Mart's chief executive Lee Scott paid one of his visits to Downing Street to put his case and Leahy and Davis made their submissions to the OFT.

In February the OFT officials were still deliberating about how to proceed and Morrison and Green remained optimistic that their bids would receive clearance to proceed while the other four would be referred. In the Safeway team, both Robert Swannell and Rupert Faure-Walker were confident that the Morrison bid did not justify a referral. They reckoned without the emotion and political sensitivity that surrounds supermarkets.

At the time of the Competition Commission report in 2000, the conclusion had been that four into three should not go – so how could Tesco, Sainsbury or Asda even think they would be allowed to bid? Time dragged on and KKR, having done some more homework on the intensely competitive nature of British supermarkets, withdrew from the fray.

In early March the OFT passed its recommendations to Patricia Hewitt, the Secretary of State for Trade and Industry. All parties held their breath for firm news.

Finally, on 19 March, the OFT dropped its bombshell. The Morrison bid and the other three bids from rival supermarket groups were all to be referred to the Competition Commission. Only one bidder received clearance to continue – Philip Green. David Webster and Ken Morrison were as devastated as Green was elated.

Competition lawyers claimed to be astounded and astonished. Alastair Gorrie, a competition partner at Coudert Brothers, was quoted saying, 'The Morrison bid is so obviously a pro-competition deal that it is counter-intuitive to have referred it. It really is surprising.'

Penny Boys, the OFT deputy director general, said that 'undertakings in lieu of a reference would not be appropriate because of the difficulties in identifying and addressing the local areas of concern'. In other words, the OFT could not work out which Safeway stores Morrison would have to sell for there to be no competition issues in local markets. It all looked so strange. Many believed it was only because Tesco and Sainsbury had lobbied so hard that Morrison's bid had been referred. 'They have left that business in limbo,' remarked one analyst about Safeway. 'Asda and Tesco are going to trash it by putting it under more and more pressure with price wars.'

So less than three years after the 2000 Competition Report in response to the

'Rip-Off Britain' campaign waged in the press, the supermarkets were back in the dock, showing once again the intensely political nature of food retailing.

Despite his robust, confident manner in the weeks that followed, Peter Davis knew that his plans to revive Sainsbury could not succeed if Wal-Mart acquired Safeway. He thought that was unlikely, however, and used his contacts to discover the lie of the land. But he also knew something it took the stock market rather longer to work out: that for Sainsbury, merging Safeway's enviable store portfolio with Morrison's ruthless efficiency would be almost as bad.

For a while Sainsbury appeared to carry on serenely, but if a strong fourth player the same size as Asda were to be created, the company's future and Davis's career prospects were bleak.

There was little hint of this in the interviews he gave. 'The Shrewsbury-educated public schoolboy is not cowed by the big beasts of the retail jungle,' wrote one commentator. 'His career at the highest levels of British business has been preparation for this role.'

Nine months earlier in mid 2002, however, Sainsbury's recovery had already begun to lose momentum. Davis realised that modernising the distribution network and upgrading the depots would take more money than he had calculated. He remained adamant that he would not drive prices down until his modernisation programme was complete, but the stock market began to have its doubts.

Aged 61, Davis also found that rising at dawn to travel the country visiting stores, suppliers and depots had lost its charm. Much of his work was hard and grinding, far less agreeable than lunching with investment bankers or politicians. After eighteen months he had had enough and in November 2002, during a five-hour journey back from a store visit in Bolton, he composed a letter to his chairman, George Bull, saying that he wanted to begin the process of appointing a successor. Davis said he would stay until March 2004, but that he would be perfectly happy to go in 2003 if the board found a new chief executive to succeed him.

Bull took the matter to a board meeting, clearly worried about having a change of executive leadership after only two or three years. Most of the directors shared his concern. It was then, at their moment of need, that Davis was able to negotiate a new pay package that included a hefty 864,000 shares and a special bonus if he succeeded in finding a suitable new chairman when the time came.

Meanwhile the directors decided to appoint a managing director to handle some of the day-to-day operational matters that Davis had found so irksome. The best internal candidate was Stuart Mitchell and, after Morrison launched its bid for Safeway, Davis delegated most of the mundane duties to Mitchell while he got on with the more stimulating business of attempting to do deals. Sara Weller was also promoted to the board, setting her and Mitchell in direct competition for the top job.

At Safeway, Webster was falling out with his charismatic chief executive Carlos Criado-Perez, who had not taken kindly to his chairman attempting to sell the company to Morrison. On 9 January, when Morrison announced its move, Criado-Perez had been able to reveal that Safeway had enjoyed its best Christmas trading ever with like-for-like sales up by 4.2 per cent. Robert Clark of the Retail Knowledge Bank rated the Argentinian highly: 'Safeway is a more saleable asset than it was. Carlos, in his reign, has tied the package with a nice bow rather than the old piece of string that would have been there beforehand.' Criado-Perez, however, had not intended that his revival of Safeway should simply make it more attractive to a buyer. He had, in common with many others in the company, hoped for an independent future and the sweet smell of success turned to ordure when Webster and the board recommended Morrison's offer. It soon became apparent that there would be no job for him in Bradford or anywhere else in the Morrison firmament. He would collect more than £1m as compensation, but it was no secret within the company that he would have preferred to go on running an independent Safeway.

Webster reaped the whirlwind of the Argentinian's disappointment. A weary Webster told friends in his understated way, 'managing Carlos through all this is quite demanding'. The two men mended their fences after a few weeks, but Criado-Perez made no attempt to conceal the difficulties of running Safeway through the Competition Commission reference period, which in the event lasted far longer than anyone thought it would. Even so, Criado-Perez continued to do his best, supported by the board and in particular by Kevin Hawkins, then Safeway's corporate affairs director, whose strategic vision for the company had been so remarkably close to the Argentinian's.

Criado-Perez launched a charm offensive against Safeway suppliers who had turned tough on prices, seeing little point in currying favour with a management that would not be in place much longer. He visited all the big

Safeway stores and gave pep talks to managers and he held a series of morale-boosting meetings at Hayes for the group's store managers and staff. For stores in parts of the land remote from Hayes he staged video conferences.

Safeway also put in place retention bonuses for senior staff and reviewed the terms of the annual bonuses paid to all staff. The combination of Criado-Perez's leadership and enhanced financial incentives meant that, far from the predicted mass defection of staff, not one store manager or senior executive had left by the summer. Neither was there any evidence of the petty pilfering that sometimes occurs when the staff of a company under siege become disillusioned and believe that their prospects are bleak.

The essential difference between Webster and Criado-Perez was that Webster, an old City hand, had the interests of his shareholders closest to his heart. Reluctantly he had concluded that Safeway could not deliver value for shareholders if it remained independent; the buying power of Tesco and Wal-Mart was simply too great for Safeway to compete on price. His chief executive could not afford to take such an objective view and he was, by nature, imbued with what John Maynard Keynes called 'animal spirits'. Understandably he put the stores, the staff and the customers first and hoped for survival.

Directors and managers from all the bidders spent much time preparing and presenting their cases to the Competition Commission, which was chaired by Sir Derek Morris. Safeway told the Commission that its relatively poor operating performance was due to structural rather than managerial problems. Despite capital expenditure of more than £4bn in the previous decade there had been only modest improvements in operating profit because its network lacked scale to match the prices of operators such as Tesco and Asda.

Safeway's competitors did not mince their words. Asda told the Commissioners that Safeway was not 'an effective constraining competitor' and there was little prospect of this changing. Asda's analysis suggested that Safeway was 'a high-price operator with weak consumer appeal, attracting customers largely because of the convenient location of its stores, rather than any reason relating to the retail offer'.

Sainsbury took the view that Safeway was not viable in its present state for the medium term; it had the infrastructure costs of a national operator but with smaller sales volume than its competitors.

Tesco criticised Criado-Perez's Gonzales strategy and said that too much of Safeway's activity had been focused on tactical ploys to stimulate short-term business, so undermining sustainable profits.

Intriguingly, unlike Sainsbury and Asda, Tesco told the Commissioners it believed Safeway could recover on its own. Executives pointed out that Asda had nearly gone bankrupt in the early 1990s and that Tesco's image in the past had been so poor that consultants had recommended changing its name. Tesco thought that the fundamentals of the Safeway business were sound, given that it had a substantial, broad-based store portfolio that it was continuing to expand.

Unsurprisingly, the Morrison evidence was the most complimentary, although not entirely free of barbs. Safeway was a sizeable national player that exerted a national competitive constraint on the larger national retailers, it said. But it suffered from a lack of strategic direction and weak brand positioning.

Even though KKR had withdrawn in late February, executives still gave evidence. They believed that Safeway could improve its operating performance by 'adjusting its product offering to include more competitive, fresh and private-label offerings and by altering its pricing strategy, but this would involve significant implementation risks'.

Philip Green's investment vehicle, Trackdean, said that Safeway's profitability could be improved 'by focusing on operational efficiencies, product quality, supply chain opportunities and central overhead costs'. In other words Green would cut costs wherever he could, just as he had done at Bhs.

The big challenge for every potential bidder would be how to increase sales densities – sales per square foot of retail space – at Safeway. Historically, they were lower than at the three main rivals, all of whom believed this could be corrected by reducing prices. Morrison hoped for additional profits from increased throughput in its food processing and packing subsidiaries. It also cited its success in increasing sales in a number of stores it had bought from Somerfield as evidence that it would be able to do the same in the relatively better-performing Safeway stores.

The Commissioners invited submissions from interested parties, placing advertisements in relevant local and trade papers as they had done in the course of preparing their 2000 report. No stone, it seemed, was to be left unturned as the employees of Safeway carried on saying hello to each customer at the check-out and trying to look cheerful. The views of the Consumers' Association and the National Consumer Council were placed at the front of the 'evidence' within the eventual report, but the Commissioners also spent the summer canvassing the views of many small suppliers, some of them anonymous but others happy to be named – R. L. Clapp & Sons (Cheesemakers) Ltd, Thumbs Up (Bury) Ltd, the Windward Islands Banana Development & Exporting company – as well lobby groups such as Friends of the Earth, the Countryside Alliance and political groups such as the Green Party. Charities such as Crisis had a say along with the Association of Town Centre Management, the Institute of Asian Businesses and the Transport and General Workers' Union. Not surprisingly, most of these organisations were against any further contraction in the number of supermarket players.

Support came from unlikely places. The National Association of Clubs for Young People, for example, said it had worked in partnership with Sainsbury and Homebase 'who had generously donated gifts in kind over the years'. It was a nice tribute, although whether it influenced the Commissioners is unclear.

The nub of the Consumers' Association's concern was local choice. How many different stores would there be within easy reach of customers? It declared that, 'whilst three fascias could work effectively, it was more likely that four would be better, both in terms of choice and the effectiveness of competition'.

This was absolutely in line with the Competition Commission's 2000 report.

A close second to the issue of choice was pricing. Morrison and Asda set their product prices nationally. At Morrison, a pound of Braeburn apples costs the same in Bradford as it does in Kent. The same is true of Asda. But Tesco, Safeway and Sainsbury practice 'price flexing' and adjust their prices to local markets, taking a view on what they will bear. The Consumers' Association said, 'Account should be taken that the Sainsbury and Tesco bids would exacerbate local price-flexing problems.' It then appeared to contradict itself by going on to say that the national pricing policies of Morrison and Asda were against the public interest, presumably because it considered those in the poorer regions of the country to be subsidising those in more prosperous areas.

In other words, the supermarket groups were damned if they did and damned if they didn't.

Despite the distractions of launching the bid, Morrison, which has its year end in January, kicked off the results season on 17 March when it reported a healthy 16 per cent rise in pre-tax profits to £283m on turnover up by 10 per cent at £4.3bn. The holy grail of like-for-like sales were up by 5.4 per cent. Ken Morrison said the publicity around the bid had increased customer numbers visiting his stores by 2.3 per cent, although Morrison shares flickered up only 1p to 168p against the 210p just before the January announcement of the bid for Safeway.

Tesco was next to report its results. They were good, although not spectacular. Pre-tax profits had risen by 13 per cent to £1.4bn on sales up by 11.5 per cent to £28.6bn.

At Sainsbury, Peter Davis's cost-cutting appeared to have paid off and 2003 pre-tax profits came in 17 per cent ahead of the previous year at £667m, though sales were up by only 3 per cent, which worried analysts. Even so, the results were good enough for Davis to don a chef's hat and apron and be photographed tasting one of the celebrity chef Jamie Oliver's concoctions. But Davis did warn of tougher times ahead, and he made it clear yet again to anyone who might be listening that he would be happy to co-operate with another bidder to get his hands on at least some of the Safeway stores.

The strain of living under a takeover referral was beginning to show at Safeway. In early June the company reported a 20 per cent slump in pre-tax profits to £270m for the year ending March 2003, although earnings per share fell only 8 per cent and sales were holding up. Higher prices paid to suppliers cost £20m, fees to advisers had already eaten up £17m and the company had paid £5.5m in bonuses to keep the services of its key executives – all this came straight off the bottom line.

The waiting game continued. In June there was growing excitement at the prospect of a 'remedies letter' from the Competition Commission that would indicate to each company what it might have to do in terms of selling stores, in order that its bid might be approved. When the much-anticipated long and complex statement appeared on 24 June, its conclusions were on the murky side, although most observers concluded that Morrison had reason to be optimistic, while Tesco, Sainsbury and Asda did not.

After a lot of huffing and puffing about what was a supermarket and what was not, the Commissioners seemed to have come up with the definition of a store offering one-stop shopping in premises of more than 1,400 square metres. They were slowly and painstakingly coming to the obvious conclusion that Morrison and Safeway together created a fourth strong player and that this would be better for competition than any other combination, or even the status quo.

Philip Green sat on his hands while the Commission deliberated, preferring to see 'how low the apple hung from the tree'. Green had never even bothered to undertake serious due diligence and cancelled the one scheduled meeting he had made with the Safeway board claiming illness. He shrewdly realised that Sainsbury's future was in jeopardy whichever of the industry bidders won Safeway. He decided to proposition the aristocrat of the sector. He had talked to Peter Davis a year before with a view to supplying Sainsbury with clothing, and had received a courteous though negative response.

Green viewed the remedies letter with dismay. He saw that his prospects for buying Safeway and parcelling up the stores to sell to the other supermarket groups at a tidy profit were bleak.

Bored, but still interested in food retailing despite advice from those who told him it was far more difficult than clothes retailing, he paid another visit to Sir Peter Davis in his glittering headquarters, this time armed with a banker's letter proposing a cash offer for Sainsbury of 330p a share, which was almost a third more than Sainsbury's 250p share price at the time. Davis, an open-minded man, discussed the matter with one or two colleagues but refused to take it to a formal board meeting. He simply could not see the aristocratic Sainsbury family agreeing to sell out for £6.4bn to Philip Green.

Unlike the board of Marks & Spencer, Davis did not go public with Green's approach and, for once, Green retreated gracefully to await the Commission's findings on who might bid for Safeway and in what circumstances.

On the morning of Friday, 26 September, all parties were watching the Stock Exchange screen with added interest. Ken Morrison, who was preparing for his daughter Eleanor's wedding on the following day, sent his joint managing director Bob Stott to London to be with Nigel Turner and other advisers at the investment bank ABN Amro's Bishopsgate offices when the news was announced. Bang on schedule at 11 a.m., up flashed the statement on the screen. Morrison's bid for Safeway had got the go-ahead. Even better for Morrison, none of the other groups were to be allowed to bid. As a sop to them, Morrison would be compelled to sell fifty-three designated stores.

Wal-Mart executives, who had hoped they had a direct line to Downing Street and thus to the Commission, were disappointed. A few days before the report was published Wal-Mart had put forward a plan under which it would bid for Safeway with a proviso that a large chunk of stores would be sold to Morrison. Lee Scott personally visited the Commission in London to put his case. If the head of the largest retailer in the world took the trouble to fly the Atlantic, surely he should have some influence. But his arguments fell on deaf ears. Wal-Mart had also put together a back-up plan to form a joint company with a private equity firm, or even Philip Green, to buy part of the company. But despite all their executives' efforts, Wal-Mart, Tesco and Sainsbury were left having to negotiate with Morrison for some of the stores that had to be sold.

How Scott and his colleagues must have regretted turning down Wasserstein Perella's suggestion to follow up their purchase of Asda with a bid for Safeway back in 1999 when the price was 180p. Back then, though, the Americans had no concept of how tight planning regulations were in the UK compared with those in the USA, nor how expensive the land – the key factors holding back Asda's growth under Wal-Mart's ownership.

For Webster and Criado-Perez the news of Morrison's victory was bittersweet. The risk of being swallowed by Wal-Mart had gone, but so had any hopes that the price of Safeway would rise as rival bidders competed for it. Webster had believed, even after the remedies statement, that there would be some leeway for the others to bid providing they sold a certain number of stores.

A key aspect of the report was that the big four could not trade stores among themselves without obtaining the Commission's permission, a restriction that extinguished any remaining spark of Philip Green's interest.

Ken Morrison had Safeway over a barrel. He could claim quite justifiably that it was now weaker than when he first made his offer, and drop his price accordingly. At the same time, Morrison's shares had risen strongly over the summer and he now had some highly valued paper to use.

Morrison spent the next few weeks haggling over the details of the store disposals with the OFT, taking an unduly long time according to some critics. Once that was complete, Morrison had twenty-one days to put in another formal bid for Safeway. At ABN Amro Nigel Turner and Nigel Mills went to work redrafting the documents.

Morrison and his team could not resist attempting to buy Safeway more cheaply. At one point, negotiations between the two sides became so tense that Webster told his advisers to start preparing the defence for a hostile bid. Meanwhile, he made it clear to Morrison that if the new offer was below the previous one he would be unable to recommend it to his shareholders. In other words, to get Safeway cheaper Morrison would have to make a hostile bid against which Webster would mount a spirited defence. It would be expensive and would take yet more time – and Ken Morrison was not getting any younger.

Webster also mentioned that he had been approached by a private equity house that was interested in making an all-cash offer for the business. Quite how much the mystery bidder was prepared to pay never emerged, but it all helped to concentrate Morrison's mind.

Ever cool under fire, Webster held his nerve. On 2 December the same four men who had initiated the bid thirteen months earlier gathered again for a 'crunch meeting' – this time at the five-star Mandarin Oriental Hotel in Knightsbridge. Once again it was Webster and Swannell for Safeway, and Ken Morrison and Nigel Turner for Morrison. In the event, Morrison decided not to risk making a hostile bid. He kept his reputation for Yorkshire fairness intact and even improved the new offer a fraction on the previous one, adding some cash.

On 15 December Morrison finally announced his new bid terms amid sighs of relief from Safeway shareholders. Worth £3bn, the new deal was one Morrison share plus 60p in cash for every Safeway share. It added up to 289p per Safeway share. That stood up well next to the value of the original all share bid, which may have started at nearly 300p but at one time, as the Morrison's shares cratered, had sunk to less than 230p.

The *Financial Times* headlined the influential Lex column on 15 December 'Groundhog Day', after the film of that name, giving credit both to Webster's negotiating skills and to Morrison's pragmatism: 'He knows he is getting a good deal. The 53 Safeway stores he is required to sell will fetch a strong price. By offering a cash component he, personally, also retains a bigger equity stake in the combined business.'

Eleven months and six days after Morrison made his first bid Webster could hold his head up to shareholders while he walked off into the sunset with a pay-off of £2m plus pension pot of nearly £9m. Criado-Perez received £1.4m and the former finance director Simon Lattin £948,000.

Yorkshire thrift did, however, push Morrison into making one error of judgement. In order to save his company £15m in the stamp duty payable at 0.5 per cent on a traditional takeover offer, the deal was formulated as a scheme of arrangement. This delayed Morrison's management taking control by five weeks and left the Safeway staff and management in limbo during

February and early March, a time of year when many negotiations with suppliers on rebates take place. As a result, analysts believe that Morrison lost much more than the £15m stamp duty it had saved.

On the day after the deal, the Lex column concluded with some prescience: 'Morrison is already taking a huge risk by spending £3bn on a group twice its size. It will need all the cooperation it can get from Safeway management to give the complex integration a reasonable chance of success.'

After the announcement, however, Morrison's shares roared triumphantly ahead. By Christmas 2003 they had reached 229p and the takeover met with almost universal approval. At 72, Ken Morrison had become a City hero, and on the last Sunday of the year the *Sunday Times* awarded him its 'Business Person of the Year' title – dubbing him 'Britain's own Sam Walton'. The differences between Sam Walton and Ken Morrison are greater than their similarities, but it is true that each man started with one outlet and developed a business with a reputation for outstanding value.

The drama of the takeover and Morrison's age swayed the *Sunday Times* judges in his favour as well as the classic rags-to-riches tale of the boy who started with one market stall and created a FTSE-100 company with thirty-six years of unbroken profits growth and £13bn of sales. Paul Durman, the journalist who wrote the piece accompanying the award, summed up the reasons for bestowing it: 'For making such a well-judged move on Safeway, for seeing off his supermarket rivals, for keeping Morrisons growing all the while, for giving us something interesting to write about – and all this at the age of 72.'

Morrison remained unimpressed, refusing to be interviewed for the tribute and once again demonstrating his shrewdness – newspaper accolades are all too often followed by downfall. And, as Morrison was well aware, the hard work was only just beginning. Unforeseen problems had begun to surface.

Even so, he refused help from the management of his new acquisition. When the final bid had been made, Morrison had agreed that Safeway's Lawrence Christensen, the logistics director, and Jack Sinclair, a man with much trading expertise, should become part of the enlarged Morrison group. When the time came, however, he decided he did not want them after all. It was a sign of the arrogant behaviour that was to come. But before that there were a few details to finalise, such as shareholder meetings to obtain formal approval for the deal.

Even the normally restrained David Webster could not prevent his emotions showing at the final shareholders' meeting of Safeway as an independent company. It was held at the Thistle Tower Hotel on the banks of the Thames in the shadow of Tower Bridge on 11 February, Webster's fifty-ninth birthday. Shareholders witnessed their usually sanguine chairman close to tears as Peter Foy, a non-executive director, said that shareholders owed Webster 'a profound debt of gratitude'. Indeed, anyone who had in 1977 bought shares in Louis C. Edwards which became part of Argyll would have made 200 times their money.

Not all of the shareholders agreed. One complained that Morrison was 'getting Safeway on the cheap' and that Safeway had played Santa Claus to him. Webster responded with some sympathy. 'The outcome of the competition process placed Safeway in a straitjacket', he said, giving vent to heartfelt criticism of his old adversaries. 'If there has been an ogre in the corner of my corporate career, it has been the regulators,' he told his audience.

Another shareholder speculated that James Gulliver 'must be turning in his grave'. Webster avoided responding, but reminded his audience that the late Sir Alistair Grant had always been open to a merger with Morrison. Despite some grumbling, shareholders gave their overwhelming approval for the bid.

Then, after thirty years with the company in its various guises, Webster, the last survivor of the three musketeers, bid them farewell for the final time to the strains of Frank Sinatra singing 'My Way'.

However emotional Webster felt, he at least had a financially secure future and what appeared to be an enviable new job as part-time chairman of InterContinental Hotels. For many of the lower-ranking Safeway staff, particularly the 1,700 at the Hayes office, most of whom would lose their jobs, it was a lot sadder.

In sharp contrast to the subdued and nostalgic atmosphere in London, there was optimism in the air that morning in the Bradford hotel where Ken Morrison formally asked Morrison shareholders to approve the bid.

He declared to his adoring audience, many of them lifelong shareholders, that just because the deal would more than double the size of the company to 552 stores, he had no plans to stray from its tried and trusted recipe for success. He also made a pledge that the company would stay based in his birthplace Bradford, still one of the more depressed Yorkshire towns. A new, modern, more luxurious head office for 1,200 people would be ready to move into in 2006.

'We prefer to be in Yorkshire, not because it is cheaper but because it is better,' Morrison said. He also revealed that, despite his well-known views on the irrelevance of non-executive directors, he had bowed to the government-commissioned Higgs Report on corporate governance. He was close to appointing the two non-executives required of FTSE 100 Index companies and they would, at the very least, have strong Yorkshire connections.

The new Morrison would, according to retail market research house Taylor Nelson Sofres, have a market share of 15.3 per cent compared with Sainsbury's 16.5 per cent and Asda's 17.1 per cent. There was then a huge leap to the market leader Tesco, which had 27.2 per cent of the UK supermarket sector at the time. After all the deliberations by the Competition Commission Tesco still dominated. The UK shopper was left not with four strong players but with Tesco and three medium-sized competitors.

Three weeks later, on 8 March, Morrison took control of Safeway. Up until that moment there had barely been a critical word said or written about either Ken Morrison, or his company. The Morrison way had provided nearly four decades of unbroken profit growth, significant employment in depressed areas, and stores where customers enjoyed shopping and relished the low prices. Fellow directors and staff revered him. The few analysts who knew Morrison rated him highly. Rivals admired him. Even his suppliers said good things about him.

Any tentative speculation that attempting to integrate Safeway with no help from the previous management might be folly was brushed aside. By March, most people believed that Morrison would somehow pull it off in his inimitable way. City analysts seemed to think that he was as close to being able to walk on water as any mortal gets.

Morrison blithely disposed of Safeway's sophisticated satellite-linked computer systems as well as those of its top management who had wanted to stay on and assist in the integration. He announced it would take three years to Morrisonise all Safeway stores but he had ordered price cuts on 7,500 lines throughout the group, abandoning Criado-Perez's Gonzalez high/low strategy and thirteen separate regional pricing structures. 'It was a very complex business,' he said. 'Far too clever for us.'

After their steep rise over the preceding few months Morrison's shares drifted back at the beginning of May to 240p. This was possibly a result of profit-taking, but analysts began to take a deeper look at the Morrison operation and, despite their reputation for never leaving London, took the train up north.

Morrison converted four Safeway stores to its own format in the first month. Citigroup's David McCarthy visited the Chester store and produced a 'buy' recommendation headed 'Early conversions suggest spectacular results'. The market-street concept had been introduced, he wrote, with the family butcher, the fishmonger, grocery provisions and bakery all in evidence. He noted, however, that there was no pie shop or the usual hanging display of bananas. The cake shop had been hidden at the back of the store. 'It was a "Market Street-Lite" concept in our view, but impressive nonetheless.'

McCarthy visited the store on a Tuesday evening and discovered low prices and shelves stripped bare by happy shoppers, indicating that Morrison had been surprised by the volume of customers. But on the following morning he reported a swift replenishment of stock. 'The importance of this recovery should not be under estimated … it shows that the stores have safely made the transition from Safeway systems and procedures to Morrison's and that Morrison's systems and logistics work very effectively.' He even judged that they worked 'a lot better than Sainsbury's new systems'.

Three-month sales figures, however, showed how Safeway had been suffering. In the twelve weeks to 1 February sales had fallen by 4 per cent in contrast to those of its new owner which had risen by 15 per cent. Tesco sales had surged by 11 per cent and Asda's 9 per cent. Poor old Sainsbury had managed a sales rise of just 2 per cent. But those figures masked how Tesco had been growing at a faster rate every month for the previous six, and was comfortably outpacing Asda. Leahy's vow to set the agenda for Wal-Mart, rather than the other way round, was paying off.

On 20 May Morrison held its first annual shareholders' meeting since the takeover. By 11 a.m. there was standing room only in the upstairs conference room at Bradford's Hanover International – a slightly down-at-heel conference hotel. One long-term shareholder looked around the full hall in amazement. 'There used only to be a few of us,' he remarked.

Ken Morrison took the stage flanked by his two joint managing directors, Marie Melynk and Bob Stott. He smiled beneficently at his audience and then whipped through the resolutions, asking for questions on only two of them. Sales at the early Safeway conversions had soared by 40 per cent. But the news on the un-Morrisonised Safeway stores was not so great: customer numbers had fallen by 7 per cent since the takeover and sales were down by 7.3 per cent, excluding petrol.

Despite the mixed news he was upbeat about the future. 'We're trying to get customers to change the way they shop, so they shop the whole shop. It's a long job,' he said. 'Although there remains much work to be done on the integration of the Safeway business, I view the future with optimism.'

In the front row sat his two new non-executive directors. David Jones, the chairman of Next, the clothing retailer, was one of them. Jones had built up Next after the departure of George Davies in the 1980s to become a serious threat to Marks & Spencer in mid-market fashion. Although from the Midlands, Jones had recently become chairman of the Yorkshire County Cricket Club. The other non-executive director was Duncan Davidson, the founder and chairman of the York-based housebuilder Persimmon. The two men stood up as Morrison introduced them.

A shareholder rose to pay tribute to the chairman, declaring him to be a typical Yorkshireman. 'He sees all, hears all, says nowt. That is Ken's way,' he said to a ripple of appreciative laughter.

As if to prove the point, Morrison then thanked everyone for attending and declared the meeting closed. He invited his audience to stay for coffee afterwards and mingle with the directors. A couple of shareholders delayed the refreshments by insisting on asking questions, the normal form at most FTSE 100 annual meetings. Although slightly taken aback, Morrison answered them courteously and then closed the meeting for a second time.

As analysts, journalists and City shareholders buzzed around Morrison afterwards, he kept his counsel. On the stock market, Morrison shares began to fall.

CHAPTER ELEVEN

SAINSBURY IN RETREAT

*'Distribution is like a sewage system. When it works, nobody knows
it is there. When it doesn't, there is a terrible stink.'*

John Harvey, former chairman of Tibbett & Britten

Peter Davis had run out of time. The Competition Commission had denied him the kind of company-transforming deal that had helped make him a hero at Reed Elsevier and the Prudential. Without taking over one of his competitors, or at least being able to buy a big chunk of their stores, he was dished and he knew it. Even if he could match the other strengths of Sainsbury's competitors – cheaper prices, wider ranges, consistent availability – he could do nothing about the fact that Tesco had nearly 1,900 UK outlets compared with Sainsbury's 721. Those site acquisitions that had looked so overpriced to the competition in the early 1990s had provided the foundation for Tesco's success. More stores meant higher turnover, hence more buying clout and lower prices. Tesco could keep its margins at a consistent 6 per cent while Sainsbury's had slipped from 8 per cent in the glory days of John Sainsbury's reign in the 1980s to less than 4 per cent.

True, Davis bought fourteen of the Safeway stores Morrison had to sell, but the increasingly aggressive Waitrose had nabbed the best nineteen of them, spending £300m and giving the group a power base in the north of England, a long-held ambition of the chief executive, Steven Esom. With its emphasis on organic and fair-trade products, Waitrose had become the supermarket du jour among the chattering classes, the only one in which its members would happily admit to shopping. Waitrose was the new Sainsbury.

By the spring of 2004 Tesco had one and a half times the square footage of Sainsbury and a market share of 28 per cent compared with Sainsbury's 16 per cent. Sainsbury also lagged Tesco in tapping into the convenience-store market, which was growing at more than 7 per cent compared with only 3 per cent for all food retailers. In November 2002 Tesco had increased its stake in this market to nearly 5 per cent of the outlets by buying 1,200 T&S convenience stores and following that up with forty-five Cullens, Europa Foods and Harts shops in London. Sainsbury, by comparison, bought fifty-four Bells stores soon after and eighteen months later acquired the 114-strong Jacksons chain in the Midlands for conversion into 'Sainsbury at Jacksons', though only after meeting some resistance from the Office of Fair Trading.

Smaller rivals such as Budgen, Iceland and Somerfield had called for a Competition Commission referral, but the OFT apparently decided that supermarkets and convenience stores were two separate markets, even though sales from the 54,000 convenience stores in Britain accounted for about 20 per cent of the £115bn grocery market in 2004.

Overseas Tesco romped ahead and for the first time had more retail space abroad than at home. In contrast Sainsbury had drawn in its horns, selling its only overseas operation, the American subsidiary Shaws. 'Shaws was profitable but it was going nowhere. And Wal-Mart was coming in that region,' said one director.

Even on the internet, Tesco had grabbed market leadership, breaking through the £500m sales barrier and producing profits of £12m in 2003. 'You shop, we drop' adorned the delivery vans. Sainsbury online – Sainsbury to you – continued to struggle and only just broke even while Ocado, the Waitrose online joint venture started by former Marks & Spencer and Goldman Sachs executives, was coming up fast with its compelling slogan 'devoted to your shopping'.

In every aspect of trading, Sainsbury had become the poor relation. Even the Sainsbury bank continued to lose money. It may have been more socially responsible, coming first in Business in the Community's Corporate Responsibility Index, but that was no solace to shareholders.

What would have been unthinkable just a decade earlier had come to pass: Davis's dreams of returning Sainsbury to its former glory, of proving to John Sainsbury that he should have been made chief executive back in 1986, of enhancing the family's fortunes and making his own, all lay in tatters.

In the autumn of 2003 Sainsbury and Asda were neck and neck. Asda had pushed Sainsbury into third place according to figures from Taylor Nelson

Sofres, although Robert Clark, the independent retail consultant, still ranked Sainsbury second. (Sainsbury was still clearly ahead of Asda in food but the product mix of the two companies was so different that comparisons were tricky.)

For eighteen months the non-executive directors had increasingly been doubting Davis's promises of a sustainable recovery and wondering if his commitment was wavering. They thought he spent too much time outside the business and delegated too much of the everyday running of it to Stuart Mitchell and Sara Weller. 'Actually it was more like abdication,' said one non-executive.

In the summer of 2003 Davis had still been predicting that all would be well, the benefits of the new capital spending would come through and then the company could commence a price-cutting campaign. But it would be folly, he told his directors, to launch a price war before the teething problems with the distribution system had been overcome. His statement in the July 2003 annual report had been as upbeat as ever: 'We have continued to deliver on our promises during the past year despite increasingly tougher market conditions. We are reporting a second consecutive year of double-digit growth in underlying group profit before tax at 10.8 per cent and an underlying operating profit growth for Sainsbury's supermarkets of 13.3 per cent.'

Even retail analysts were impressed by Davis's briefings: 'Peter sounded so confident the strategy would work when he briefed us, but we gradually realised he had little idea of what was going on in the stores,' said one. 'From the start he had the attitude of a chairman rather than a chief executive.'

Lord Levene of Portsoken was the senior non-executive director, a role that involved keeping in touch with large shareholders. A frequent traveller to the Far East, Levene sometimes dozed through the more tedious parts of board meetings to the amused disapproval of his colleagues. When awake, he spent time checking his emails on his Blackberry organiser and asking the occasional acerbic question. He never pretended to have read all the mountains of paperwork sent to directors. But if his colleagues thought he was not paying attention, they were mistaken. Once it became evident the recovery plan had failed, he roused himself from apparent slumber to campaign for Davis's removal. And like a lion awakening, he was formidable.

Levene was the heavyweight non-executive from central casting. He had joined Sainsbury in May 2001, a year after Davis, bringing with him his reputation as a bruiser – a corporate politician who could move effortlessly between the money men of the City of London and the ministers and mandarins of Whitehall. A former defence industrialist, he was appointed chief of defence procurement at the Ministry of Defence, where he took on the legendary Arnold Weinstock over cost over-runs at GEC. From there he went on to advise John Major's Conservative government on improving Whitehall efficiency and then became Lord Mayor of London. In November 2002 he took on the chairmanship of the Lloyd's of London insurance market during its crucial recovery period.

At 62 he was the same age as Davis and, as his track record showed, if there was a coup to be organised, he was the man to lead it.

Levene had been a thorn in Davis's side more or less from the point he joined Sainsbury. He was staggered by what he found at a company that was seen by outsiders as one of the great establishment icons of corporate Britain. Friends reported that he thought the culture rather peculiar. When he arrived Sainsbury had just stopped rewarding its customers with Air Miles as a loyalty bonus, a decision recommended by Sara Weller in her role as marketing director. Just how bad a decision it was quickly became clear. 'The impact on the business was immediate,' said one former director. Tesco instantly took over the Air Miles contract, scoring a huge publicity coup in the process.

George Bull, who had celebrated his 65th birthday in 2001, had his heart set on retirement but the last thing Davis wanted was a new chairman who would need to be played in and who might be less in tune with his plans. If Bull left, Davis wished to be both chairman and chief executive while he took his corporate plan to fruition. The Higgs Report had not then been published but the separation of the chairman and chief executive roles that it would later recommend had become accepted as good practice under previous corporate governance codes. When, in early 2003, Bull and Davis had put the idea to the non-executive directors that Davis should do both jobs, Levene and most of the others could barely believe their ears. 'We were horrified,' said one. 'The gist of their argument seemed to be that because Sainsbury was such a national institution they could flout the guidelines.'

Before making any decision the non-executives insisted that Bull and Davis sound out Sainsbury's big City investors. When they did, they met with almost total hostility and returned, 'with their tails between their legs', admitting that the Square Mile's big guns were appalled at the idea. But the intransigent Davis made his position crystal clear: 'I am not going to work for another chairman,' he said.

The board feared that the stability of the company depended on keeping Davis happy, so they lobbied Bull to stay on as chairman, which he reluctantly agreed to do. The board did what it could to buttress Davis, backing his promotion of both Weller and Mitchell to the board of the supermarket subsidiary, Mitchell as managing director and Weller as his deputy. But this partial solution to the problem failed to address the all-important question of who would eventually replace Davis. Weller and Mitchell saw themselves as competing for the top job but the non-executives had other ideas from the start. One remarked, 'Sara is a very bright and cerebral woman but she is not chief executive material. Stuart is a solid and reliable lieutenant.'

Then Davis bowled the board another googly. His original pay package on joining Sainsbury had included share options worth eight times his salary if the share price rose to a particular level, but in the long bear market Sainsbury's share price had fallen to below 230p, far less than the 340p at which it had stood when he joined in March 2000.

Davis, an old hand at boardroom battles, insisted that if he was to continue as chief executive he must have a new, performance-related salary package and made it clear he was on the brink of quitting if the board did not agree. 'We were halfway through a recovery plan; we were between a rock and a hard place,' recalled one board member. Sainsbury's long-serving personnel director, John Adshead, designed just the package Davis wanted.

And so in March 2003 Davis's new deal that was to cause so much outrage among shareholders just fifteen months later was agreed. On top of his salary he would be paid a bonus related to meeting various targets on the distribution side and for recruiting a suitable successor. As long as pre-tax profits were 70 per cent of the previous year, his bonus would be assured. Bridget Macaskill, a non-executive director who had overlapped with Davis at the Pru and was a former chairman of Oppenheimer Funds, had grave misgivings and made sure they were minuted. But like Levene and the others she eventually gave her approval.

While the Competition Commission laboriously probed and deliberated throughout 2003, Levene kept in touch with the major shareholders, although only Davis and Bull communicated with the Sainsbury family. Among the City institutions Levene found nothing but mounting anger towards Davis. He must have realised, however, that any attempt to oust Davis at such a delicate stage would cause more problems than it would solve. He needed a replacement chief executive in place first.

In January 2004 George Bull announced post-Christmas like-for-like sales up by only 2 per cent in the four weeks to the beginning of January compared with a blistering 10.2 per cent rise by Morrison and a 7.5 per cent increase from Tesco. The disappointing performance triggered a wave of profit down-grades by City analysts. Dave McCarthy at Citigroup cut his profit estimate by 20 per cent and most analysts trimmed their profit forecasts for 2004 to around £710m – just a fraction up on the 2003 figure. The press comment was scathing. 'Even with all the stops pulled out, Sainsbury is losing sight of the leaders,' reported the *Financial Times*'s Lex column.

As if to rub salt into the wound, the day after Sainsbury's lacklustre trading performance was announced, Tesco displayed its muscle by raising £1.5bn of new money through a placing of 315 million new shares. A similar amount of money would also be raised by property sales, Terry Leahy told the City. Tesco shares fell briefly as investors began to fear a big overseas purchase, but Leahy assured analysts that a major acquisition was not planned. He was merely building a war chest. It was chilling news for competitors.

'We are gearing up our business. The UK non-food market is worth £100bn and we have only got a 5 per cent share. We want to get more space into Extra,' he said, referring to the 100,000-plus square-foot hypermarkets where food and non-food shared sales equally. Tesco had eighty Extras by January 2004 but was known to be aiming for 400. Although many of those would be created by extending existing stores, Leahy wanted to ensure there was enough money to buy sites when the opportunity arose. He and his fellow retailers had been lobbying the government for years to relax the Gummer planning regulations on out-of-town expansion – he had reason to think their efforts would soon pay off and he was well prepared for when they did.

While Leahy wooed the City, Davis found himself under renewed sniping from disillusioned analysts and investors who sensed that, although as chief executive he was still technically steering the ship, there was in fact nobody on the bridge. Neither Stuart Mitchell nor Sara Weller were felt to be a leader strong enough to succeed him as chief executive and the board decided to search for both a new dynamo to head Sainsbury and a chairman-in-waiting to serve as a deputy to Davis, who would have a short spell as chairman.

It was time once more to call on the services of Anna Mann at Whitehead Mann. During her glittering career in retail headhunting she had put together the winning team of Archie Norman and Allan Leighton at Asda in 1991, found Carlos Criado-Perez for Safeway and come up with the olive-oil pressing Luc Vandevelde from Belgium to be chairman of Marks & Spencer, where he had overseen the short-lived recovery with Roger Holmes. Mann had also suggested Justin King, one of Allan Leighton's Young Turks at Asda during the recovery years, to run the Marks & Spencer food business. Although in theory a conflict of interest should have prevented her from putting forward anyone from Marks & Spencer, someone there had made the error of bringing in one of Mann's rivals, so she had no qualms about including Justin King on her shortlist of people to replace Davis as chief executive.

Fast-talking and likeable, the 42-year-old King had moved to Marks & Spencer only two years before. He had helped roll out most of the 119 smaller Simply Food stores but he had made little impact on the business, which even after Marks & Spencer's problems remained at the forefront of excellence. Towards the end of his watch, growth slowed slightly but the Sainsbury non-executives thought he should be their man. 'It was a difficult choice between Justin and one other candidate,' said one. 'They were both first class.'

Although he admired the rigorous quality controls at Marks & Spencer King found the slow-moving hierarchical culture constraining. After the open-plan, open-door style at Asda, he was metaphorically in need of oxygen and the challenge of revitalising the once-mighty Sainsbury with 16 per cent of the market was appealing. King could also see the parallels between Sainsbury in 2004 and Asda in 1990, although he did not realise how bad things were until he arrived.

King was still in touch with his old mentors Norman, who by early 2004 had become deeply disillusioned with politics, and the voluble Leighton, who was not enjoying chairing Royal Mail. They both urged him on and showered him with advice. Unlike the many commentators who believed Sainsbury was between the rock of Tesco and the hard place of Waitrose, they both felt Sainsbury could be turned round given a clear strategy, strong leadership to motivate the 'colleagues' (as the staff would soon be called, à la

Asda), and huge amounts of energy. The gist of their advice went something like this:

Focus on making Sainsbury a proper supermarket like it used to be. Simplify the offer: there is no need to have five different types of hummus or six varieties of mince pies. Concentrate on high-quality fresh produce and revitalise the private label – once the powerhouse of Sainsbury profits. Forget non-food apart from essentials such as stationery and health and beauty; there is not enough floor-space. Replace Jamie Oliver as the face of Sainsbury: he distracts from the main message. As for a marketing slogan, 'Making life taste better' is dreadfully weak. Nobody has ever come up with anything to beat JD's 'Good food costs less at Sainsbury's, although much work is needed to make it true again.

Leighton and Norman were clearly two men itching to have a go at Sainsbury themselves, but for the moment they could only offer advice to their erstwhile junior. Leighton was a non-executive director of Loblaw, the Canadian supermarket group owned by the Weston family, whose Associated British Foods company had once run Fine Fare and also owned Fortnum & Mason, the exclusive emporium on London's Piccadilly. He arranged for King to visit Loblaw before he took up his position at Sainsbury 'to see how they do it'.

To lure King, Sainsbury paid up handsomely – £675,000 a year salary plus £685,000 to compensate him for losing his M&S share options and bonus scheme – although significantly less than the £850,000 Peter Davis received as chief executive.

When King's appointment was announced Sainsbury shares moved up and John Sainsbury said he and his brothers 'fully supported' King's appointment. Judith Portrait, trustee for David Sainsbury's 24 per cent, declared herself 'very pleased'.

While King was educating himself about Sainsbury during his five months' 'gardening leave' imposed by Marks & Spencer under the terms of his contract, Davis got on with the task of working with Anna Mann to find a replacement chairman. For this Davis would be paid a special bonus. Davis accepted a reduced salary of £500,000 in his new role as chairman when King joined at the end of March 2004, but he kept the rest of the package he had negotiated in March 2003 intact. All the non-executives approved it, something they would later regret. Davis said that, despite other offers, he would not take another job until March 2005. 'I have been approached about two senior chairmanships, but I have turned them down,' he declared.

Although the Higgs Report into corporate governance published in July 2003 had recommended that a chief executive should not become chairman of the same company, Davis was going to hold the job for only a year or so and the board backed him, convinced he was necessary for the company's stability.

Ironically, back in 2002 Davis had been tempted by an approach to chair the government's corporate governance review. He had been eager – such a task would have almost certainly have elevated him to a peerage – but when he had asked the non-executive directors for their opinion they were horrified. 'We thought he was insane even to contemplate such a time-consuming job when Sainsbury so clearly needed all his efforts,' said one. 'Peter had to be restrained from taking it on, although he later thanked us for stopping him.' Now he was openly ignoring the recommendations of the committee he had been so keen to lead. After all, Derek Higgs had been junior to Davis when they were both at the Pru, so who was he to dictate his ex-boss's actions?

Shareholders dared to hope once more when Sainsbury announced King's appointment in early December 2003 and Davis declared that the two of them were at one on strategy. 'We are determined to extend our lead on quality and then drive down price,' said Davis. 'Justin is in full agreement.' But there were still some months to go before their new chief executive could begin work. Until then George Bull remained chairman and Peter Davis chief executive. They were to be crucial months.

With the share price sliding against a backdrop of negative stockbrokers' circulars, Davis and Anna Mann had to find someone brave enough to chair the company. For once in her stellar career, Mann misjudged the tide of sentiment in the City. She put forward Ian Prosser to be chairman. Prosser had been the head of Bass, the brewing company, which had changed its name to Six Continents after Prosser decided to focus on its Holiday Inns and InterContinental hotel chains. Billed as one of the 'great and the good' and a man 'who could hold his claret', he had sat on the Boots board with Davis and often mingled with Bull and other Sainsbury directors at grand business functions. Like Mann, the directors overlooked his reputation as an autocrat and the fact that he had been one of the last company bosses in the FTSE 100 to split the roles of chairman and chief executive.

Prosser's buying spree of expensive hotel acquisitions at the top of the cycle had sent his company's shares tumbling to the fury of City investors, a fact that Mann and the Sainsbury directors either ignored or were unaware of. Nor did any of the non-executives seem to know that shareholders had protested when Prosser had been proposed as chairman of Standard Chartered in late 2002. When accused of not doing their homework, they claimed nobody at Sainsbury or Whitehead Mann had bothered to tell them: 'Whitehead Mann said he was a good chap. Peter and George said he was a good chap. They did not mention that the institutions hated him,' said one.

Bull and Davis pressed their case for Prosser with the board. Bull convinced his colleagues that enough time had elapsed since Prosser's departure from Six Continents – even though he had left only in late 2003 – for any ill feeling among the institutions to have dissipated. But City investors had not forgotten the pain of their losses and could not comprehend why a bunch of heavyweight non-executives failed to object. When Sainsbury announced the appointment on 10 February 2004, the press was incredulous. 'For head-hunters to offer him up showed a strange lack of judgement,' wrote Patience Wheatcroft, business editor of *The Times*. 'But for the company to have accepted the idea was crazy, lazy or desperate.'

The board was certainly desperate – and there was a shortage of suitable, willing candidates. The directors had also been lulled into compliance by Sainsbury's investment bankers, who had sounded out major shareholders behind the scenes. 'Only about half the people we talked to were against his appointment,' said one banker. 'The older generation were quite positive.'

What had swung Prosser's appointment was the approval of the Sainsbury family, who held more than a third of the shares. John, his brothers and David Sainsbury all had good relations with Bull. They had no first-hand knowledge of Six Continents and did not share the ire of those who had suffered from the fall in the share price during the later years of Prosser's chairmanship. The day the discontent surfaced in the press, Tim Sainsbury told one journalist over tea in his elegant town house that he was mystified as to the reason for the fuss.

But fund managers had few doubts. How could a man whom they believed to have lost them significant sums of money be about to take such an important job as chairman of Sainsbury when the company was in crisis? 'He was regarded as an autocrat whose interests were not always aligned with those of shareholders,' said one.

Emboldened by recent activist triumphs such as the removal of Michael Green as the chairman of Carlton Communications, the media company he founded, the shareholders voiced their displeasure. Uproar ensued, rising to a crescendo when it emerged that Davis stood to gain an extra £844,500 through a bonus dependent on his finding a suitable successor.

Just a week after his appointment had been announced, Prosser did the sensible thing and agreed to stand down. 'It was a mistake,' said one former director, 'but Ian Prosser behaved with distinction. He said, "I am going and I don't want any money." He behaved like a perfect gentleman.'

But there were angry recriminations. The non-executives berated Davis and Bull for not telling them about the Standard Chartered incident. Davis and Bull said, 'We thought you knew.' Judith Portrait is understood to have told colleagues she felt the directors should have researched the matter more thoroughly. The embarrassment all round was palpable.

Whoever was to blame, Sainsbury needed to come up with a plan B to recruit a chairman-in-waiting and it fell to Levene to produce it. His first step was unceremoniously to dump Anna Mann. His second was to hold a beauty parade to find a replacement headhunter; the winner was the firm of Egon Zhender.

For Justin King, waiting in the wings, the whole fiasco showed him how far the breakdown in relations with the City and press had gone. 'There was no goodwill left,' he said. He could hardly have felt confident about his decision to quit one ailing retailer for another.

When he finally arrived on 28 March he found the boardroom riven with conflict and distrust, although most directors still hoped that Davis's prophesies of success would materialise. 'They were still clinging to the hope that they might yet arrive at the end of the rainbow and there would be the pot of gold,' said King. During his 'gardening leave', in addition to visiting Loblaw he had also visited fourteen retail chains in the United States and had unofficially visited many of Sainsbury's most important stores – so he hit the ground running.

His impressions of Sainsbury stores from his incognito visits had not been favourable, but when he made his first critical Wednesday presentation of his views the reaction of the board directors was hostile. 'They were so disconnected from what was happening in the business, they found it hard to believe me,' King said later.

Instantly nicknamed Tigger by the staff, King initiated a thorough review of the business by bringing in a team of consultants from McKinsey. It was headed by its retail guru Michael Mire, at a reported cost of £1m a month – although the team stayed no longer than one month. Mire was an old friend of Norman and had advised Asda during its time of crisis.

Within weeks King began putting into practice the price-cutting campaign that had been largely developed by Davis and Mitchell, although he got the credit. 'Sainsbury cut prices by over 2 per cent last weekend,' wrote JP Morgan's analysts on 5 May in a circular headlined, 'Goodbye Profit, Hello Pain'. 'This price cut is the first sign of Justin King's impact on strategy, and in our view confirms his serious commitment to tackling Sainsbury's core pricing problem.' The broker went on to opine, however, that Sainsbury was still at least 5 per cent more expensive than Tesco and that Asda and Tesco could be expected to respond. Hopes of the price cuts resulting in extra sales and higher profit looked ill founded.

The revolving door at Sainsbury began to circle more swiftly. Stuart Mitchell, who took the blame for the ill-functioning distribution systems, left in May closely followed by his ambitious deputy, Sara Weller, who, like him, had once hoped to step into Davis's shoes. She had started her career at Mars with King. 'She is a ferocious lady and was furious that Justin got the top job,' remarked one colleague. 'She quit as soon as she could.' She left to become managing director of Argos, which calls itself 'the UK's leading general merchandise retailer'. Keith Evans, the director in charge of non-food, and John Adshead, the personnel director, also left.

On 19 May after seven weeks in the job, King made his first public statement announcing full-year profits down from £667m to £610m. Sales rose by only a tiny 2.2 per cent to £15.3bn while the all-important like-for-like sales dropped by 0.2 per cent. But he gave a robust, steady-as-she-goes type of statement, saying that the previous strategy was not fundamentally flawed but its execution had been poor. 'It is not a strategic problem, it is an executional problem,' he summed up. But what really grabbed investors' attention was that Davis, who stepped up to be chairman as King joined, was to receive 80 per cent of his performance-related shares despite his failure to revitalise the company.

The details revealed that under the agreement of the previous March Davis could receive up to a million shares as a 2004 bonus for meeting various lowly set targets, for recruiting a new chief executive and a new deputy chairman (which he had failed to do), and that 700,000 shares would be awarded if

Sainsbury made just 90 per cent of undisclosed budgeted profits. He had lost 75,000 shares for the Prosser fiasco, but was still entitled to 864,000 shares, worth more than £2.4m.

Martin Dickson in the Lombard column of the *Financial Times* was scathing: 'If you want to get a sense of what is wrong with J. Sainsbury, and why there is such cynicism in Britain about fat-cat pay, look no further than the grotesque £2.4m bonus awarded this week to Davis.'

King continued to bounce his way round the business like a Tigger should. One of his first initiatives was to invite a select band of Sainsbury suppliers to a brainstorming meeting to canvass their views of what was going wrong. Adopting an unusually casual mode of dress for a Sainsbury director, he arrived at the meeting in an open-neck shirt to find seven men attired in suits and ties.

They may have been more formally dressed than him but they did not mince their words. 'Sainsbury is in crisis,' they told him. 'Your management is operationally inept.' They accused Sainsbury executives of spending too much time at head office. 'They are so lazy, they just sit in this glass tower all day,' said one, referring to the Holborn Circus headquarters, 'and never go near the stores.'

If King was shocked he did not show it but he painstakingly wrote down their comments. 'I cannot turn it round immediately,' he said, 'and I need your help.' He then asked them for promotional investment support to help Sainsbury claw back some market share. They retorted that they would not help King until he could improve store efficiency so that promotions boosted sales enough to recover the cost.

After the suppliers came the analysts. Towards the end of May King held a series of 'get-to-know-you' meetings with retail analysts, who were impressed with his personality but thought him lacking in startling insights: 'In the land of the blind, the one-eyed man is King,' reported Cazenove in its summary of the meeting.

The briefings that King gave to his board were more informative and the news from the front line was shocking. King talked to more than a hundred store managers as well as operational executives, uncovering huge discrepancies between what Davis and the directors believed and the reality.

Behind the scenes the trust between Davis and Levene, his senior non-executive director, had collapsed. In board meetings there was an atmosphere of growing suspicion and paranoia. Levene began lobbying King for

Davis's early departure. Davis later told friends that he viewed Levene as two-faced and double-dealing. But such is the inevitable behaviour of a corporate assassin.

Levene had become convinced from his private conversations with shareholders that Davis had lost all credibility with the City and the sooner he went the better. Even when he was travelling overseas Levene kept up his campaign. During one meeting with Davis, King was summoned from the room by his secretary to take an 'urgent call' from Levene who was in Tokyo. His message was stark: Davis must go soon.

None of this intrigue slowed Davis in his relentless networking or attendance at grand occasions. On 9 June he was out hobnobbing with the cream of business society from both sides of the Atlantic at the centenary concert of the London Symphony Orchestra attended by the Queen and Prince Philip. Tickets for the event, to raise money for the LSO, cost £2,000 apiece.

On the surface Davis appeared to be his normal affable self but those trying to engage him in conversation about Sainsbury found him decidedly jumpy. 'Peter just couldn't wait to get away from me,' said one.

The McKinsey team confirmed King's own research in concluding that profits in the financial year were going to be a long way below what even the most pessimistic analyst had forecast. The reaction from shareholders would be one of horror.

King told his dwindling band of directors that the company needed to issue a second, more severe, profit warning. After that, the full board fell into line behind Levene and decided Davis had to go. Nor could he possibly merit the bonus they had all approved less than three months before. The challenge would be to persuade Davis to relinquish his job without a public fight.

Davis was no stranger to negotiating controversial pay-offs. After his success at Reed, where he had slashed sales but greatly increased profits, Davis had fallen out with the Dutch directors following the merger with Elsevier in 1994. He walked away that time with a pay-off worth £2.02m, enraging some institutional shareholders.

At Sainsbury, it was clear that Davis's failures were far more serious than a bodged attempt to recruit a successor. The expensive new network of distribution depots was not just having a few teething problems, it was in chaos. One critic claimed that some of the new 'fulfilment factories' did not even take standard-sized pallets for transporting goods, although the reality was that some suppliers were exceeding the prescribed height to which goods should have been packed. Suppliers also found instructions on labelling confusing and their wrongly labelled goods were rejected by the warehouse's electronic scanning equipment.

In his travels, King had found store managers suffering from a 'victim mentality' – the new distribution methods meant that they could not even order goods for their own stores to keep their shelves filled. The resulting shortages of standard items such as trimmed green beans and oranges became a source of great irritation to regular shoppers, and according to McCarthy, it takes only one shopper in 200 to change supermarket allegiance to open up a 5 per cent difference between the profits of the two chains.

With hindsight it was clear that Davis had been over-ambitious when it came to spending shareholders' money. He had arrived to find 800 full-time staff working in IT plus 200 from various contractors. 'Every night, 200 staff had to be on duty to sort out problems because the system was so old,' he told analysts. 'We needed to do seven years' upgrading in three.'

He contracted out the upgrading of the computer and distribution systems to Accenture, the renamed Andersen Consulting, which he had successfully used at the Prudential. He was not, however, content to choose new systems comparable with those used by Waitrose and Marks & Spencer; he wanted something at the cutting edge of retail technology. He signed up for the next generation of systems. 'Peter wanted to leapfrog the competition, and leap-frogging is a risky business,' said one adviser.

One example was a software system called Market Max. 'It was like giving the buyers a Ferrari when they were used to a Fiesta,' Davis admitted later. Davis had splashed out more than £3bn on new stores, the new systems and the distribution network. But although profit margins had improved for a while, sales failed to respond and the problems with distribution were widely reported in the press. New self-scanning tills being tested in selected stores also proved problematical – customers could not work out how to use them.

While Davis was spending billions on distribution and IT, he put a block on all but essential spending in other areas in a desperate effort to boost Sainsbury's bottom line. When one supplier rang a senior buyer at Sainsbury to ask if he could present a new store-display product he was told: 'Do not even think about coming to the meeting unless buying your product will save us money.' Training and staff levels in the stores were cut, leaving those who remained often demoralised and lacking in expertise.

Davis is a talented, clever, man, good-hearted in many ways, but he loved the trappings of wealth too well. Not only had he bought an expensive new boat, he had also bought a grand house in Gloucestershire to live out his retirement in style. He still had his old boat and owned two other houses. A Bentley Continental sat in the Gloucester garage, and then there were his wife's racehorses to finance.

Davis enjoyed public life – rubbing shoulders with the rich and powerful in business, politics and the arts. He relished travelling abroad on behalf of the company, especially when it was to upmarket suppliers where he could indulge his appetite for good food and wine. Tours of the grand châteaux of France were a highlight. Davis also hated to turn down invitations – whether it was to a City dinner, the opera, or to sit on a government quango. At the stockbroker Seymour Pierce, Richard Ratner, the firm's analyst, waggishly likened Sainsbury to George Orwell's *Animal Farm* and cast Davis in the role of Napoleon – the pig who was 'more equal than others'.

A director of UBS in Switzerland, Davis joined the board of the Royal Opera House in 1999 and his links with various charities took up considerable time. He cosied up to the Prince of Wales by chairing Business in the Community until December 2001, and he also sat on the Policy Commission on the future of farming and food. From December 2002 he was a board member of the government's Implementation Group for sustainable food and farming strategy.

Even as late as May 2003, when the wellspring of criticism against his leadership of Sainsbury had already begun, he accepted the government's invitation to chair the Employer Task Force on Pensions. In a remark that would within the year hold heavy strains of irony, Andrew Smith, the pensions secretary, said: 'Sir Peter's extensive business experience will be a valuable asset in helping to make a success of future pension provision.'

It was hardly surprising when critics complained that he spread himself too thin. 'You don't see Terry Leahy out and about at all these events,' remarked an observer pointedly. 'He doesn't even play golf like the rest of the directors.' Even Davis's friends could see the dangers ahead. 'I'm afraid Peter got seduced by the grand life that goes with being chairman of Sainsbury,' said one.

By the summer of 2004, all he could hope for was to retire gracefully, although his friends warned him he should think about giving some of his bonus back. 'I told him he should take a severe haircut,' said one City veteran, 'but he could not afford to. He needed the money too badly.' Another said: 'If it had happened to me I would have said I didn't want the money.'

As the shares continued to fall, anger over his bonus mounted. It was not only shareholders who were cross. The staff had endured a miserable couple of years. Many of the junior and middle management had suffered a pay freeze and been forced to re-apply for their own jobs – sometimes twice. The previous Christmas, most of the staff had found their normal bonuses either trimmed or non-existent. Even the traditional staff Christmas gift of £100 – a hangover from the patrician days of family control – had been scrapped. Yet far from leading from the front and suffering with them, their boss appeared to be cleaning up.

Having hailed him as a returning hero on his arrival in the spring of 2000, City investors, who had piled into the shares during the first two years and were now nursing bruising losses, turned against him. They ridiculed the idea that someone who had been in charge while the share price had fallen so precipitously, who had spent so much company money to so little purpose, should be rewarded with a bonus of any kind. They called upon directors to renegotiate his contract. Davis had become part of the 'paid to fail' brigade. When sales and profits were still struggling and costs were being squeezed out of the business at every level, the sight of the man who had led the company to the edge of the abyss walking off with £2.4m on top of his chairman's salary of £500,000 and other contractual entitlements was too much for those inside Sainsbury and out.

Davis had not endured what he described as the 'hard grind' of the previous four years to relinquish his shares easily but he found himself increasingly isolated on his own board. His ally Bull had gone and most of the other directors, even the head of the remuneration committee, Keith Butler-Wheelhouse, sided with Levene. Among Sainsbury's advisers, Robert Gillespie of UBS Warburg and Simon Robertson at Goldman Sachs tried to prepare him for the worst.

Those were busy times round at John Sainsbury's discreet offices in Queen Anne's Gate, so convenient for a lunchtime stroll in St James's Park. John, Tim and Simon Sainsbury, their cousin David and all their children, between them holders of more than a third of the shares, decided enough was enough and reluctantly agreed to Davis's removal. As the share price sank still further to 264p, underperforming the FTSE All Share index by more than 15 percentage points over the previous year, JD, who still retained the title of life president, convened a family meeting. For the first time in Sainsbury's history as a public company, the dividend looked in danger of being cut. If that happened it would be a severe blow to those in the younger generation who relied on the money for country-house purchases, school fees, foreign travel and donations to their pet charities. The unthinkable had happened – the Sainsbury family, although still far, far from being broke – was having to contemplate reining-in their spending.

Some visitors to JD's office pleaded with him to take the helm once more. But at 76 he knew his limitations. 'I am too old and it is too late. Our only hope of survival is to be taken over,' he confided to one friend. And despite press speculation, everyone knew that even if his cousin David were to return, he had not the talent to turn the group round. If the family's wealth was to be preserved, the Sainsburys regretfully decided that an approach from a private equity house with supermarket experience such as Kohlberg Kravis Roberts, or the Canadian Weston food empire, might be the only answer. But first they let it be known that they would give King six to eight months – to the spring of 2005 – to show what he could do.

On Wednesday, 30 June, Davis attended a lunch at Whitehead Mann along with William Lewis, the editor of the *Sunday Times* business section, who had known the Sainsbury boss for many years. Anna Mann had left the headhunting company and the woman billed as her replacement, Carol Leonard, a former journalist whose own firm, Leonard Hull, had recently been acquired by Whitehead Mann, hosted the lunch. Davis gave little sign of the turmoil he must have been feeling. The following Sunday Lewis wrote: 'An old City hand, Davis may have been distracted but he was giving nothing away to his lunch companions.' The talk was mainly of Philip Green's attempt to take over Marks & Spencer.

That same afternoon Davis attended his last Sainsbury board meeting. Peter Levene told him that not only did the directors feel he had to go, but that they wished to renegotiate his settlement. Once it was clear he had lost the support of all the non-executive directors – who had realised that their own jobs would soon be on the line – he agreed to resign. But true to his reputation for fighting his corner, he refused to accept a settlement of less than the terms of his contract.

The meeting was icily polite and Levene made sure his thanks to Davis for his services were minuted. Davis subsequently told friends that he would have been prepared to work through the night so that the Sainsbury board could have presented a united front, but no compromise was possible.

The next day, Thursday, 1 July, Sainsbury fired Davis – with immediate effect. To emphasise the reason, the company issued the second profit warning in six months, saying that its full-year profits would fall 'well below previous market forecasts'. Sales were barely stable and margins were under pressure because of price cuts while Taylor Nelson Sofres reported that Sainsbury's market share had edged lower to 15.6 per cent.

Overnight, relations between the board members and Davis became openly hostile. 'Suddenly it was war,' recalled one director. They took the embarrassing decision to withdraw their approval of a bonus they had agreed only months before. Davis refused to back down and Levene and his fellow directors felt they had little option but to call in the lawyers.

Philip Hampton, the former finance director of Lloyds TSB, had been persuaded to replace Davis as chairman. Egon Zhender had put him forward and he had been waiting in the wings, but when the crisis broke Levene needed to use all his persuasive powers to get him on board in a hurry. Hampton had a solid track record and a reputation for toughness. He had been finance director of four FTSE companies and had fallen out with Lloyds TSB because he believed it should cut the dividend and the board had disagreed.

For the second time in his career Davis left Sainsbury in unhappy circumstances. But on this occasion he also suffered the ignominy of failure at the end of a distinguished career. It was a horrible finale and he found little sympathy among the press or his peer group.

Speculation as to whether he would actually receive his bonus mounted ahead of the Sainsbury annual general meeting on 12 July, when his and the other directors' remuneration packages were due to be approved. What would the family with their crucial stake do? Judith Portrait, acting for David Sainsbury's trusts holding 24 per cent, had decided to abstain but last-minute negotiations that led to the exclusion of Sir Peter's bonus from the resolution changed her mind. Although John Sainsbury had replaced her as his adviser a few months before, employing NM Rothschild instead, they both feared the company would be damaged if the resolution was defeated and all the non-executive directors were forced to resign.

On the morning of the Sainsbury meeting the veteran columnist John Plender wrote a pointed piece in the *Financial Times* about shareholder activists in America who had highlighted the absence of the 'shame gene' and the 'tendency to think that if something is not prohibited by law it constitutes acceptable business behaviour'. Plender wrote: 'The honourable course for Sir Peter would be to forgo his right to the shares and to negotiate a severance package that visibly falls short of pushing things to the limit.' He held out little hope that this would happen. 'I have a funny feeling the shame gene will prove elusive.' He was right.

There is nothing like bad news to bring a good turnout of shareholders to an annual meeting, even on a Monday morning. The start had to be delayed to allow everyone to get through the security at the Queen Elizabeth Hall, the other side of Parliament Square from the Palace of Westminster. Levene had the tricky task of chairing the meeting as the board had decided it would be unfair to ask Philip Hampton, who was still on holiday. Levene explained to shareholders that although they were voting on the whole remuneration package, which still technically included Davis's pay-off, whether he received it or not was actually dependent on the lawyers, and would not be influenced by the vote. Levene also explained that as the matter was with lawyers the board could not answer any questions about Davis's bonus. In the event the family voted for the resolution. But some of the big insurance companies had already voted against by proxy, leaving only 70 per cent of shareholders in favour.

Once Levene threw open the meeting for questions, indignant shareholders had their say. One called for the resignation of the whole board, another for the resignation of the hatchet-faced Keith Butler-Wheelhouse for his role in agreeing to the bonus. One wanted the resignation of all five non-executive directors – all of whom they deemed culpable for allowing such a mess to develop.

Private shareholders who attend annual meetings are a breed apart and there was much ranting – not all of it about Davis. Levene dealt with all comers masterfully – allowing his irritation to show but remaining calmly in control – and displaying occasional glimpses of wry humour.

To those calling for resignations he replied that the new chairman, when he arrived, might not appreciate a completely empty boardroom and it would be up to him what changes he made. To those who insisted on asking about Davis's bonus, he repeatedly told them the matter was with the lawyers and he had no wish to prejudice that process.

'Why,' asked one aggrieved man, 'was Peter Davis paid so much when Tony Blair, the prime minister of England, who has to run the entire country, gets paid less than £150,000 a year?' 'Ah,' replied Levene sagely, 'but Tony Blair does not have to run Sainsbury.'

The most pertinent question came from a woman shareholder, who asked quite simply how it was that members of the board had been unaware of the depth of the problems at Sainsbury. 'If Justin King can come in and in a very short time ascertain that profits are going to be much lower than previously thought, do we then wonder if Sir Peter Davis has been economical with his reporting?' she asked. 'And why, if Mr King could come to his conclusions so quickly, did the rest of the board not know what was going on?'

The question received no clear answer but many shareholders pondered the same thing – how could the numbers have changed so dramatically within a few months? If Roger Matthews, the finance director, knew the answer, he was not telling. His resignation had been announced shortly before the meeting although he agreed to stay until March 2005.

The full story was buried and neither Davis nor the rest of the board appeared to want to dig beneath the surface to find it. Their heads had for much of the time been stuck in the sand.

Justin King may have felt nervous, but he looked confident as he moved to the lectern to outline his new strategy, aided by a slide show. Sainsbury would focus on the UK – hence the sale of Shaws in the US, which enabled the company to give 35p a share back to shareholders in a special dividend. He would concentrate on value – a combination of price, quality and service – rather than on price alone. He intended to cut back on capital spending and tackle the supply-chain problems. King then lurched into Asdaspeak, promising to 'put customers at the heart of what we do'. He would motivate all 'colleagues', stressing 'it is our colleagues who can make the business a little better every day'.

To many in the audience who had recently heard Stuart Rose outline his plans for Marks & Spencer, it sounded remarkably familiar. So much so that the *Guardian* carried a cartoon the next day showing King addressing the meeting but with a name-tag that read Justin Rose.

A few minutes before the end of the meeting, fearing the press would lay siege to them, John Sainsbury and Judith Portrait made their escape through a side exit, security men barring the way to journalists who tried to follow. As for Peter Davis, he had wisely gone to ground.

CHAPTER TWELVE

TESCO TRIUMPHANT

'To the victor belong the spoils of the enemy.'

William Learned Marcy, 1786–1857

Sainsbury was not the only supermarket group having a tough time in the summer of 2004. The day after Davis was shown the door Morrison issued its first profit warning in thirty-seven years, confirming what some, especially the old Safeway hands, had already suspected. Sales in the unconverted Safeway stores were plummeting, down by 8 per cent July to July. Even to casual shoppers this was no surprise. Along with all Safeway's computer systems, Morrison had abandoned Criado-Perez's high/low Gonzalez strategy, abruptly stopping the distribution of flyers bringing news of the forthcoming week's cut-price deals. Other than location, the only compelling reason to go to Safeway, rather than Tesco or Sainsbury, vanished. Less than three months after he had won the battle, Ken Morrison began to discover that victory could be a bitter pill.

On the weekend of 4 July, six months after it had billed him as businessman of the year, the *Sunday Times* ran a huge cartoon portraying Morrison as Mr Arrogant alongside Davis as Mr Greedy, their faces enclosed in Mister Men style drawings. The accompanying feature detailed their woes.

The four Safeway stores that had so far been fully converted to Morrison had piled on the sales, although analysts warned that it was unsafe to assume that similar gains would accrue at every converted store, but the unconverted Safeway stores, struggling to merge two cultures, found the going very tough. Persuading soft southern Safeway customers 'to change the way they shop, and shop the whole shop' was proving more difficult than Morrison had thought. Simply cutting prices across the board was not working.

Regular customers in the south resented many of Morrison's ways, such as packaging most fruit and vegetables in large quantities. Quality on the fresh produce side failed to match what they had been used to and goods shipped from the north of England sometimes suffered in transit: one customer reported buying mouldy strawberries that still had two days to run before their sell-by date. The across-the-board price cuts at Safeway came just as King instigated Sainsbury's own price-cutting campaign. This meant that few Safeway stores benefited from 'joining the Morrison's family'. Morrison's share price dropped by 11 per cent following the July statement.

Former Safeway staff had been muttering that things were not going well. 'They describe an arrogant Morrison management that would rather use Morrison's archaic distribution system than admit Safeway's was better,' according to the *Sunday Times*. Neither did they like what did arrive in store. 'We don't like Ken Morrison's products,' declared one store assistant in the early days. And the top Morrison managers antagonised staff with their superior attitude and talk of imposing discipline and culture.

The divisions between north and south became apparent. Forced out of his normal privacy by the bad news, Ken Morrison gave a rare interview to the BBC in which he appeared to say that southerners were not as hard-working as those from his native Yorkshire: 'We have the unique northern character where we're very cost conscious and we work very hard. I think once this culture is throughout the Safeway business, we'll see a big change in the results.'

A flurry of indignant complaints forced him into a 'clarification' the following week, but he must have pondered the wisdom of so quickly squeezing out Jack Sinclair and Lawrence Christensen, the only two former Safeway directors to join him. Morrison was discovering that not only were the staff different in the south, so were the customers. Perhaps they were not going to take to the trademark yellow and black labelling and the ersatz 'market street' store format with quite the zeal he had envisaged.

Those close to the Morrison management remained confident the bad trading was 'a blip' that could be put down to teething problems. Others were not so sure. As Sainsbury had discovered, troubles rarely come singly.

If Terry Leahy exulted in his competitor's troubles he did not show it. On 13 July, the day after Sainsbury's stormy annual meeting, the new Tesco chairman, David Reid, threw a summer party in the elegant rooms of the Orangery in Kensington Gardens. While Reid, who had put in place the international strategy and was the most relaxed of the Tesco directors, mingled amiably with his guests, laughing and joking, Leahy was his normal tense, earnest self. Standing without a drink, arms crossed, he chatted to the circle of guests hovering round him, repeating at any opportunity in the conversation the mantra that it was customers who mattered most at Tesco.

He gave the impression of a man with a lot on his mind and one who would rather be almost anywhere but at a party. A week later came the move the analysts had been waiting for: Tesco announced its entry into the People's Republic of China, the most populous country in the world, a step Leahy had been evaluating for several years. Tesco would form a £140m joint venture with a local hypermarket chain called Hymall, owned by the Chinese Ting Hsin Corporation. It was a first for any UK supermarket group and a way of learning about Chinese retailing with a partner. It was something of a culture shock.

Visitors to one of the largest stores in Shanghai enjoyed the lively atmosphere and the emphasis on in-store theatre. Dumplings and noodles bubbled in big pots in the centre of the store and smiling staff handed out free samples to eager shoppers. The cooked-food counter offered duck prepared in more ways than you could shake a stick at. But what caught squeamish Western eyes was the wide range of captive live animals destined for the cooking pot – from fish and crabs to plump, green toads. The Chinese, said a Tesco executive, liked their food very fresh.

Until July 2004, only Wal-Mart, the world leader, and Europe's biggest supermarket group, the French giant Carrefour, had set up operations in China. Although Tesco's move into the region involved only twenty-five stores and looked relatively modest, it signalled to the business community that Tesco had joined the global big boys in earnest.

By the end of 2004 Tesco had grabbed market leadership in six out of the twelve countries where it operated and it employed 80,000 people overseas. It had become the biggest retailer in Europe after Carrefour and the third largest in the world. Insiders put the success down to Leahy and the cast-iron culture. 'Terry is exceptional and he has a tough board,' said one insider. 'But there are reams of smart, aggressive people throughout the company who are encouraged to take their own decisions.' The contrast with paternalistic Sainsbury could not be more stark.

Not to be outdone, Asda's public relations machine went into overdrive during the quiet summer, when it claimed the company had overtaken Marks & Spencer to be the country's biggest clothing retailer – a claim that rapidly lost credibility as analysts realised Asda was talking about the volume of garments sold rather than their value.

As summer faded into autumn Peter Davis attempted to negotiate a severance-pay deal as his lawyers thrashed it out with the Sainsbury legal team. He reckoned that King would want the matter sorted out as soon as possible and would shy away from a lengthy courtroom battle. Levene meanwhile sounded out the institutions as to what they felt was an acceptable amount.

In September Sainsbury announced an agreement whereby Davis would receive £2.6m in cash – the value of his shares and options – and he would receive his £500,000 salary plus pension contributions until July 2005. Sainsbury said it was £1m less than his full contractual entitlement. Davis, who had by then extracted almost £5m in pay-offs from FTSE 100 companies, told friends he had offered the company a better deal back in July.

Levene resigned, furious that the company was not prepared to take the matter to court even though the legal advice had been clear that Davis would win. 'I felt unable to support the proposed way forward,' he told the *Financial Times*. He believed it was utter capitulation simply to draw a line under the matter and write a fat cheque. He had been present at all the board meetings where Davis's package was approved, but like the other directors he felt he had not received adequate information. The chairman of the remuneration committee who had agreed Davis's package, Keith Butler-Wheelhouse, was close behind him on his way out of the boardroom.

By the time Justin King gave his first business review to the City in October 2004, he and his new chairman, Philip Hampton, were the only permanent executive main board directors left, along with three surviving non-executives: Bridget Macaskill, Jamie Dundas and June de Moller. A stream of operational directors also departed and King began building a new team. First he employed his old boss at Asda, Mike Coupe, to be trading director. Next he bought in Lawrence Christensen, the former Safeway expert on distribution who had been shown the door by Morrison, and in October he announced that Ken McMeikan from Tesco would be joining as retail director. After fourteen years with the enemy, it was hoped he would bring a bracing blast of a different culture into the stores. Tesco fans said he would not be much missed.

At 9.15 a.m. on Tuesday, 19 October, investment analysts from stock-brokers, fund managers, insurance companies and banks began to arrive at Sainsbury's reception in Holborn Circus. Half an hour later King was scheduled to take the stage in the presentation theatre in the basement.

The review had been much leaked and he was widely expected to get all the bad news out in one go, a technique known as 'kitchen sinking'. The aim was to establish a new base from which to rebuild Sainsbury's reputation with customers and investors. It was what Archie Norman and Allan Leighton had done at Asda. He had seen it work then and, having spent many hours talking to his former mentors as well as to the McKinsey team, he believed it was the right thing to do now.

Three hundred or so analysts were kept waiting outside the presentation theatre until 9.50, placated with coffee, orange juice, blintzes and mince pies. When they finally filed into the auditorium with its ochre and red seating and wooden ceiling, Philip Hampton, making his first public appearance as chairman, opened the proceedings with a brief introduction followed by confirmation of their fears. The full-year dividend would be halved.

Then Justin King took the stage to deliver the worst news investors in Sainsbury had ever heard. The company had plunged into loss. Sainsbury might just make operating profits of £200m for the full year but the company would also suffer £550m of exceptional one-off losses from IT and distribution systems that would be abandoned. As kitchen sinks go, it was a big one. He might have added that, since he had arrived, Sainsbury's market share had slid even further to 15.3 per cent and availability of many everyday items had worsened.

Having dispensed with the bad news, King, dressed in shirtsleeves to highlight his hands-on attitude, outlined his three-year recovery plan entitled 'Making Sainsbury Great Again'. The company must stop focusing so hard on profit margins', sales were the thing to go for. 'Sales are the purest form of measuring customer satisfaction,' he declared, promising that they would grow by £2.5bn in the next three years.

He also promised inclusivity. Sara Weller's complicated segmented models of which customers shopped where – mothers and babies here, dinkies there, and so on – was consigned to dust.

Of the 721 UK stores only 461 were full-size supermarkets – and the product range was too complicated. King wanted all the ranges targeting all customers to be on sale in all big stores. He had discovered that Sainsbury's own-label low-priced orange juice was available at only 200 stores. But, as a father of young children, he believed that all Sainsbury customers should be given the chance to buy it. 'It is great value and it is great for kids because it has no bits,' he said to a ripple of appreciative laughter.

Time and again he emphasised the push for sales and of having an 'offer' that had something for everybody. 'We need to go back to having three clear ranges – good, better and best,' he said.

To Leahy and his merry men at Tesco, it must have sounded eerily familiar. In just the same way that Ian MacLaurin had 'benchmarked' Sainsbury in the 1980s and eventually ended up beating it; now twenty years later the story had come full circle and King was reaching for Tesco's winning formula with both hands. Asda's influence was also evident. Sainsbury staff had become 'colleagues' and many were to be incentivised with pay related to the share price. He had already introduced 'tell Justin' suggestion boxes in a shameless imitation of the 'tell Archie' boxes Norman had brought in at Asda and he set up awards schemes in stores in just the same way his old firm had done in 1991.

In Bradford, meanwhile, the Morrison management grappled with digesting Safeway. Sales in the unconverted Safeway stores continued to fall and Ken Morrison decided to speed up the rate of conversion and to sell off 120 smaller stores. Upbeat news accompanied the half-year profits of £121.6m on 21 October. Sales in the forty-one fully converted Safeway stores had risen by 13 per cent and in the core Morrison stores like-for-like sales had risen by 9 per cent. The shares recovered sharply, rising by 14 per cent following the results to 220p, although they were still a long way from their all-time high of 256p the previous March, just before Morrison took control of Safeway.

In a surprise move, Robert Tchenguiz, an Iranian property tycoon, backed Somerfield to buy 114 of the old Safeway Compact stores for £115m. Somerfield's sales growth had slowed down in the half year to November, partly due to lower consumer spending but also dragged down by Kwik Save, which it had bought several years before. But as conversions of Kwik Save into Somerfield gathered pace under the new chief executive, Steve Back, confidence within the group picked up as the number of fully revamped stores hit the halfway mark.

That autumn, Asda was also grappling with a slowdown in growth – a development that must have been music to Ken Morrison's ears. Wal-Mart revealed that Asda sales had risen by only 4 per cent in the three months to the end of October – a level that Sainsbury would have been delighted to achieve – compared with an 8 per cent rise in the previous three months. Profits, the company said tantalisingly, had risen faster than sales. But it was clear that the benefits of Wal-Martisation, particularly in the George clothing range and electrical items – Asda sells one in four DVD players in the UK – were slowing down. And analysts said that Asda sales had also been hit by the conversion of Safeway stores into Morrison.

Wal-Mart directors still found the planning rules for supermarket sites on the British side of the pond bemusing and were increasingly frustrated as they watched Tesco romp ahead. Asda's chief executive, Tony de Nunzio, also had to cope with an unrelentingly anti-Wal-Mart press. One of the most thoughtful comments came from John Plender of the *Financial Times*, who had dug out the 2003 accounts of Wal-Mart Stores (UK), owner of Asda, from Companies House. He noted that sales had risen from £12.2bn to £13.3bn and profits had jumped by £49m to £258m, but he homed in on the working-capital figure: '... trade creditors rose a whopping £314m to £1.6bn. As a percentage of trading stocks, that is a jump from 209 per cent to 262 per cent. In other words, the poor old suppliers, all 14,000 of them, are doubling up as bankers to Wal-Mart in an ever bigger way,' he wrote. 'This helps explain the stock-market underperformance of consumer groups such as Unilever and Nestlé.' He concluded that 'The folk from Bentonville, Arkansas, drive a very big steamroller.'

At Tesco, which had its own steamroller, a small army of contractors was busy turning the forty-five Europa, Harts and Cullens stores they had bought in London into Tesco Express, a move that met with mixed reviews in the capital. In one corner of Chelsea, where all three names had traded, well-heeled residents complained that having three Tesco Express shops in their stead deprived them of choice and variety. In Marylebone, where the standards of freshness and variety at the former Europa had been dismal, local office workers rejoiced at the sparkling new Express. But in Hampstead, some shoppers were outraged at the higher prices charged in the Express stores compared with the superstore at Brent Cross, two miles away. Flexi-pricing – charging more in some shops than others – had been criticised though not forbidden by the Competition Commissioners in 2003. Residents also complained that the garish red, white and blue Tesco Express fascias stood out like sore thumbs in their select London enclaves. The stigma of shopping in Tesco had obviously not been banished so completely as the directors liked to think, especially in the capital's posher suburbs, the heartland of 'opinion formers'.

The conversions sparked a welter of hostile articles. But when it came to overall trading, Tesco surged onwards and upwards to the delight of its shareholders. When the half-year results were announced in September, Tesco confounded sceptics with a 24 per cent jump in underlying pre-tax profits to £822m for the twenty-four weeks to 14 August, well above analysts' forecasts of between £761m and £799m.

In the UK, like-for-like sales, stripping out the effects of new selling space, accelerated, with home sales rising from 7.8 per cent in the first quarter to 8.8 per cent in the second. Even excluding petrol sales, which had been inflated by high oil prices, underlying sales were up 7 per cent, beating the 6.5 per cent rise analysts had been expecting.

The analysts did their sums and forecast that for the first time ever a British retailer was set to make £2bn of profit in a full year, more than all the other supermarket groups combined. The speed of progress had left competitors gasping and surprised even Tesco's keenest fans. The company had, after all, only broken through the £1bn barrier five years earlier. Concerned that forecasters would become too optimistic, Leahy cautioned that the second half-year would see slower growth.

In the City, though, Leahy could do no wrong. On 14 November the *Sunday Telegraph* made him its Business Person of the Year. 'Leahy has just got it all together,' declared one of the judges. 'He has kept Tesco focused and true to definite retail values. He has not been tempted to take the business into places where big elephant traps lie.' An interview with Leahy stressed how little he did apart from focusing on Tesco. His only outside interest, apart from Everton football club, was his chancellorship of the University of Manchester Institute of Science and Technology, where he had taken his degree in management sciences. 'Tesco is a very big job and I have to be able to focus 100 per cent on that,' he told the reporter, James Hall. 'I have a young family so the decision I made was that I would just do Tesco and any spare time would be with the family.'

After the accolades, however, came the brickbats. In the wider world Tesco's dominance began to tell against it and the groundswell of criticism that had been building up over the previous few years became more vociferous. Snipers were everywhere, whether at public planning meetings for new stores or on fat-content patrol. When Tesco was fined £25,000 after Health and Safety inspectors found an infestation of mice and mouldy food on sale at the New Malden store in London, the news hit the headlines. Commentators struggled to come up with new words to define this biggest of beasts. 'Juggernaut' and 'behemoth' became the new words of choice.

However ordinary Leahy might appear, however workaday the Cheshunt headquarters and however unglossy the annual report and review, the British public had woken up to the dominance of Tesco in their lives. Not only could you buy food, shampoo and toys in Tesco, you could buy DVDs, mobile phones and branded jeans. Before leaving you could insure your car and fill it with Tesco petrol. You could buy your house with a mortgage from the Tesco bank. From the cradle to the grave, Tesco had you covered and it made people uneasy.

Tesco might strive for a politically correct image – the cover of the 2004 annual review bore a photo of a middle-aged Caucasian woman at a Tesco fish counter being served by an Oriental man with an Afro-Caribbean in the background – but in the boardroom the top brass remained relentlessly white, male and long serving. Taken together, the executive directors had worked for Tesco a total of 177 years. With the exception of Leahy, all were golfers. The Tesco pro-am golf trip for suppliers and advisers in 2004 had been switched from Portugal to Les Bordes golf course, set among rolling countryside and historic castles in the Loire valley. Billed as the best and toughest course in France and surrounded by luxury hotels, it provided the perfect venue for bonding and a welcome break from the utilitarian offices in Cheshunt.

Of the six non-executive directors there was only one woman, Veronique Morali, the chief operating officer of Fimalac, a French industrial conglomerate that makes everything from hand tools to designer furniture. The other five were men in their fifties, some with high-powered full-time jobs such as Ken Hydon, the financial director of Vodafone, and Mervyn Davies, the chief executive of Standard Chartered Bank. Others had retired, including the deputy chairman, Rodney Chase, who had earned a heavyweight reputation during his career at BP.

Leahy and his team had always believed in thinking small, of keeping the mindset of a company coming from behind. That had worked well in the 1980s when Tesco, the plucky underdog, had taken on the establishment Sainsbury and won, but such an attitude was becoming increasingly difficult to maintain from a position so far ahead of the pack. Tesco had joined the ranks of the biggest companies in the world alongside Microsoft and Wal-Mart – and had become equally reviled. In the words of Richard Tomkins, writing in the *Financial Times*, such giants 'come to be seen as rapacious, arrogant and callous, as ugly monopolists, as swaggering corporate bullies'.

Tomkins made the point that for companies reaching that position, nothing in their history has prepared them for it: 'Executives who have spent their working lives learning how to manage successful businesses are suddenly required to become politicians, a role requiring a completely different set of skills and for which they tend to be completely ill-suited.' Hence non-executive directors at Tesco found that their concerns over public hostility fell on deaf ears.

The mainstream press had long been critical, taking up the cudgels on behalf of indepdent shopkeepers and farmers and voicing concern over the destruction of small communities. But Tesco's incursions into non-food, where it now claimed 6.5 per cent of the market, had seriously begun to frighten companies such as Boots, WHSmith, Dixons and even some clothing discounters such as Matalan.

That concern was apparent when *Retail Week* magazine held a conference in the autumn at the Café Royal entitled 'Competing with Tesco and Asda/Wal-Mart' aimed at non-supermarket retailers. The room was packed. Citigroup's Dave McCarthy was the second speaker, making the chilling point that in the areas of America where Wal-Mart dominated, shops with the format of Boots and WHSmith had ceased to exist.

The *Observer* newspaper carried a full-page feature about Tesco in early December 2004 headlined 'The Only Game in Town'. The accompanying line drawing was of a typical Tesco store with the words TESCOPOLY emblazoned on the frontage and other retailers' logos in the arches underneath.

The article by Sarah Ryle highlighted the same fears as the conference: 'The relatively new sectors it is moving into show almost vertical growth lines. Clothing sales have risen 39 per cent and home entertainment by 26 per cent in the first six months of the year [to end August 2004].'

At an industry conference Leahy had made it plain he was well aware of the issues. 'We all know that supermarkets come in for a fair amount of stick. Here are some of the things that are said about us,' he said. 'We destroy corner shops. We tear the heart out of local communities. We concrete over fields and cause millions of people to sit in traffic jams. We squeeze our suppliers and are bad for British farming. We encourage people to eat unhealthily. We are responsible for the epidemic of obesity. And that's just the more polite things.'

The speech also showed him as unrepentant and totally focused on the job in hand. 'I struggle with the notion that we should only want supermarkets to be half-good, so that they don't do too well,' he told Ryle. 'If you try to be half-good, you soon end up being all bad. And then you aren't in a position to do anything for anyone.' For Leahy, easing back the growth throttle at Tesco was not an option. To stop growing was to start dying.

As the big four squared up to each other for Christmas 2004 against a background of weak consumer spending, pundits predicted a tougher festive season than 2003. In the event retailers fell sharply into 'winners' and 'losers', with Waitrose and Tesco heading the pack, then a gap to Asda with Sainsbury and Morrison trailing badly. The biggest surprise was Waitrose, which revealed sales up by 50 per cent on the previous year in the seven weeks, albeit boosted by the nineteen new stores from Morrison. Sainsbury, although showing Christmas like-for-like sales down 1.2 per cent in the three months to January but only 0.4 per cent lower over the four-week festive period, was judged to have performed less badly than feared. Morrison, still struggling with integration, managed a rise of just 0.1 per cent overall and revealed that sales growth at the converted Safeway stores had slowed dramatically and that sales in stores still operating under the Safeway brand were down by 8.4 per cent. By contrast, Asda had recovered from the lacklustre autumn and reported record sales, 'thanks to the hard work of its colleagues' and proudly claimed that, of the top twenty performing Wal-Mart stores, eighteen of them were Asda.

And then came Tesco on 18 January with all guns blazing. Christmas trading had shown spectacular underlying sales growth of 7.6 per cent excluding petrol, while overall sales had risen by a stonking 13 per cent, helped by one-stop-shopping at the bigger stores. Shoppers piled their trolleys high with DVDs and T-shirts for Christmas presents along with mince pies and turkeys in one swoop. But for once, Tesco seemed almost embarrassed by its success.

The non-verbal communication said it all. Leahy was touring his Asian empire and Tim Mason, the silver-tongued marketing director, was nowhere to be seen. Instead it fell to the finance director, Andrew Higginson, to pour tepid water over his own figures to the analysts and press. In a masterful understatement he said: 'They are good. We don't want to use a word like "brilliant". We're thankful. It was a good team effort.'

Tesco had been helped by the problems at Sainsbury and Morrison, he said, but that situation could not be expected to continue. Analysts should not get too enthusiastic about the full-year profits due out in April; they would be merely in line with the consensus of just over £2bn. Underlying sales growth of 7.6 per cent was expected to slow to a more pedestrian 3–4 per cent.

In other words, those analysts who had been drooling over profits of £2.1 or £2.2bn for the full year were getting over-excited.

Tesco shares duly fell by 3.3 per cent to 313p, making it the worst performing FTSE 100 company of the day. Even so, that still left its stockmarket value at £24.2bn, more than double the £11.9bn value put on the rest of the FTSE food retail sector including Sainsbury, Morrison, Somerfield and the Big Food Group, owner of Iceland and Thorntons.

But the company that takes more than one pound in every eight spent in the UK was back-pedalling hard. Striving to play down its size, Higginson also suggested that instead of focusing on the Taylor Nelson Sofres definition of market share that showed Tesco with 28.1 per cent for the previous twelve months, analysts should focus on the Institute of Grocery Distribution figures, which showed Tesco with only 18 per cent of the market. The IGD is the trade association for the grocery trade and its calculations take in every single item of food bought by the public, including sandwiches bought at Boots, vegetables from a farmers market and sweets from a village shop. The IGD takes as broad a sweep as possible, although its detractors maintain that it does so only in order to show its bigger members in a less threatening light.

In the City, however, analysts preferred to stick with the Taylor Nelson Sofres analysis of grocery retailing over the twelve weeks to January in which its director Ed Garner commented on the 'dramatic contrast' between the performances of the big chains. Any hopes among competitors and critics that Tesco's march might have slowed were dashed as the TNS figures showed a new record monthly market share of 29 per cent, up from 26.6 per cent twelve months before. Tesco also had 6 per cent of the non-food market and more than 5 per cent of the convenience sector and according to Verdict Research was poised to leapfrog the Co-op, Spar, Budgens and Londis to become market leader in the fragmented world of 'neighbourhood stores'.

After Tesco, Asda had edged up to 17.1 per cent while Sainsbury's market share had recovered slightly to 15.9 per cent, helped by the bad times at

Safeway. Morrison had 12.4 per cent compared with 14.5 per cent a year before, although part of the decline was due to the enforced sale of fifty-two stores. New store openings boosted Waitrose to 3.6 per cent while Somerfield's share increased marginally to 3.7 per cent, mainly due to the conversion of Kwik Save stores to the new Somerfield format.

So enticing were Somerfield's revitalised stores, they attracted the attentions of Baugur, the predatory Icelandic group that owns Big Food Group, Hamleys and the Karen Millen fashion chain. In February 2005 Baugur made a bid approach to Somerfield which initially spurned the advance and refused to part with any confidential information. But Baugur, spurred on by tales that the Tchenguiz brothers were also potential bidders, continued to put plans in place for a £1bn plus hostile takeover of Somerfield.

On the other side of the Atlantic the consumer goods giant Procter & Gamble had put together a somewhat larger deal with Gillette. Procter & Gamble, which sells almost a fifth of its Pampers to Pringle crisps range of goods to Wal–Mart announced the £30bn acquisition of Gillette to form a global branded-goods titan with a combined turnover of £32bn. Observers saw the merger as a defensive move against the growing might of the retailers and pondered the next step for P&G's European rival, Unilever which was in the throes of merging its Dutch and British boards.

Indeed, the pace of change in the early months of the year highlighted both the competitive pressures in food retailing and the intense public and media scrutiny under which it operated.

The Sudan 1 food scare over the carcinogenic dye that had travelled a tortuous route from India into Premier Food's Worcester sauce and in turn into hundreds of supermarket ready-meals as well as some branded dishes sent a shiver of fear through consumers that was promptly whipped up into a frenzy by the media. Sudan 1 handed the anti-globalisation and anti-super-market lobbies the public relations equivalent of a lorry load of explosives.

For those who had long decried the British love of ready-meals it initially seemed like a gift but for the big chains the mitigating factor was that Sudan 1 hit them all. Tesco, Asda, Sainsbury and Morrison had to recall hundreds of thousands of pounds worth of goods from the shelves. More surprising was that Waitrose was just as badly hit with even some of its Food Explorers range, marketed as extra pure and healthy for children, affected. Even the normally squeaky-clean Marks & Spencer had to recall several of its recipe dishes leading old M&S hands to reflect that Nathan Goldberg, the punctilious father of Marks & Spencer's food business, must have been spinning in his grave. Intriguingly, although Sudan 1 originated in India, none of the supermarkets' Indian meals contained the dye. As evidence emerged that Sudan 1 had been used in catering for several years and that the likelihood of anyone actually developing cancer as a result of eating any of the products was remote, the scare lost impetus.

As this war diary ends 2005 promises to be a hard grind for all the trolley warriors. The challenges are many: for Morrison to make the breakthrough in south of England and for the plain speaking Ken Morrison to face his own mortality as he approaches his seventy-fourth birthday in October and map out a credible succession plan; for Sainsbury to begin to recover its lost reputation in the teeth of share sales by David Sainsbury and regular rumours of prowling predators; for Asda to stay ahead of Morrison, and for Tesco to resist complacency and to avoid accusations of abusing its power.

The managements of its three main rivals will be intent on stopping Tesco from growing any bigger in the UK – it opened eighty-one new outlets in 2004. The bigger it grows, the more keenly it can buy and the cheaper will be the goods in the stores. That leaves the competition with the unpleasant dilemma of whether to cut their own profit margins in order to match prices, or to pass on their higher costs to the customers and hope to lure them into the stores with innovative products or clever marketing.

While pressure groups continued to vilify Tesco, shareholders had no complaints. The total return on Tesco shares invested over five years was up by 95 per cent, way ahead of the second best performer Safeway, with 67.4 per cent, and Morrison up 66 per cent. The 45,000 Tesco staff who had joined the save as you earn schemes also benefited from the strong share price, sharing £106 million as two schemes matured in February.

As Tesco's market share crept towards 30 per cent the government came under increasing pressure from various lobby groups to take some regulatory action to curb it. Tesco has nurtured its political relations with great skill, but there may come a point when pressure groups start to make an impact. There is no precedent for restrictive legislation to curtail organic growth in the presence of strong competition, but Tesco's fevered expansion overseas and plans to open trial non-food standalone stores are evidence of Leahy's nervousness. The Office of Fair Trading's compliance audit intended to ensure that supermarkets treat their suppliers fairly is another concern.

At Sainsbury, all eyes are on Justin King. If he fails to revive the group and a predator does not emerge from the gathering gloom, the government might have to reconsider the Competition Commission's verdict that the four big groups should not be allowed to merge into three. The Sainsbury family would then have to suffer the ignominy of seeing their family firm carved up between Asda and Morrison like a prime Sunday roast.

Only one thing is certain – wherever it is waged, be it at the checkout, the farm gate or the chill cabinet – the war will go on.

LOGISTICS

Group sales £m*

	2000	2001	2002	2003	2004
Tesco	20,189	22,585	25,401	28,280	33,557
Sainsbury	17,414	18,441	18,206	18,144	18,239
Asda	n/a	11,591	13,207	14,433	
Safeway	8,328	8,937	9,396	9,517	
Morrison	2,969	3,496	3,915	4,290	4,944

Profit before tax £m*

	2000	2001	2002	2003	2004
Tesco	933	1,054	1,201	1,361	1,600
Sainsbury	580	549	627	695	675
Asda	n/a	495	608	671	n/a
Safeway	236	314	355	270	
Morrison	189	219	243	283	320

Number of stores*

	2000	2001	2002	2003	2004
Tesco UK	659	692	729	1,982	1,878
International	186	215	250	309	440
Sainsbury	432	453	463	498	583
Asda	241	250	258	265	271
Safeway	482	477	477	481	
Morrison	101	110	113	119	125

Retail space 'ooo square foot*

	2000	2001	2002	2003	2004
Tesco UK	16,895	17,965	18,822	21,829	23,291
International	7,144	10,397	13,669	18,115	22,111
Sainsbury	13,055	13,746	14,349	15,199	15,570
Asda	11,597	12,013	12,356	12,709	12,965
Safeway	10,233	10,195	10,296	10,296	
Morrison	3,482	3,729	3,964	4,113	4,399

Annual total return from shares (%)

	2000	2001	2002	2003	2004	2000–04
Tesco	48.3	−6.2	−19.9	37.5	28.2	95.5
Sainsbury	19.2	−4.2	−20.1	19.4	−8.3	−0.1
Wal–Mart†	−22.8	8.9	−11.8	5.7	0.5	−21.1
Safeway	46.25	10.2	−30.8	38.4	8.5‡	67.4‡
Morrison	38.56	12.0	8.3	6.3	−7.1	66.0
FTSE All–Share	−5.9	−13.3	−22.7	20.9	12.8	−14.0
FTSE 100	−8.2	−14.1	−22.2	17.9	11.3	−19.5
FTSE food retailing sector	36.7	−3.8	−18.1	30.8	15.2	62.3

Market value at year end (£bn)

	2000	2001	2002	2003	2004
Tesco	18.9	17.3	13.7	18.9	24.8
Sainsbury	7.6	7.1	5.4	6.1	4.6
Wal-Mart§	159.8	176.2	138.5	128.2	116.5
Safeway	3.1	3.4	2.2	3.0	n/a
William Morrison	2.8	3.1	3.4	3.6	5.5

* Financial year end figures

† US dollar returns

‡ Until shares delisted in March 2004 after William Morrison takeover

§ Converted into sterling from dollars

Grocery sector: market shares

	1965	1971	1974	1976	1980	1982	1984	1986	1988	1990	1992	1994	1995	1996	1997	1998	1999	2000	2001	2002
Grocer's sales																				
£bn ex–VAT	2.7	4.0	6.0	8.7	16.5	20.0	23.1	27.0	31.5	37.8	42.6	51.5	56.4	59.4	62.5	67.6	70.0	72.8	77.9	82.2
Shares (%)																				
Tesco	5	7	8	9	10	10.7	12.5	14.2	14.7	16.8	17.6	18.1	20.4	21.7	22.7	23.5	24.2	25.3	25.7	26.3
Sainsbury	5	6	7	7	8	9.5	11.0	14.6	15.3	17.2	18.8	18.4	18.3	18.3	18.7	19.3	18.5	18.0	17.9	17.6
Asda	–	2	3	4	6	6.5	7.0	7.4	7.8	10.4	10.2	9.9	10.4	11.2	12.0	12.7	13.0	13.3	13.7	14.5
Safeway	–	1	2	2	2	2.5	3.2	4.2	10.6	11.3	11.9	11.2	10.9	10.9	11.1	11.1	10.9	11.2	11.0	10.6
Somerfield	–	0.5	0.5	Neg	4	2.3	8.2	12.9	12.0	8.6	6.8	6.1	5.6	5.4	5.2	8.7	7.7	6.3	6.0	5.7
Kwik Save	–	Neg	1	1	2	2.5	2.8	3.0	3.0	4.1	5.6	5.6	5.7	5.4	4.8					
Co–Op	37	29	27	23	21	19.0	17.5	15.8	13.7	13.1	12.1	10.1	10.0	9.8	9.4	9.0	8.2	7.3	7.0	6.8
Morrison	Neg	0.4	0.6	0.7	1.0	1.1	1.5	1.6	1.9	2.2	3.1	3.5	3.7	3.7	3.7	3.7	4.2	4.7	5.0	5.2
Waitrose	Neg	1.0	1.4	1.4	1.8	2.0	2.3	2.6	2.7	2.6	2.6	2.3	23	2.5	2.5	2.4	2.5	2.7	2.8	2.8
Iceland	–	Neg	Neg	Neg	Neg	0.1	0.3	0.4	0.7	2.0	2.3	2.5	2.4	2.5	2.5	2.5	2.7	2.6	2.0	1.8

Sources: Based on official statistics and company results, prepared by Robert Clark, Retail Market Consultant

Long-term share of till-roll grocers

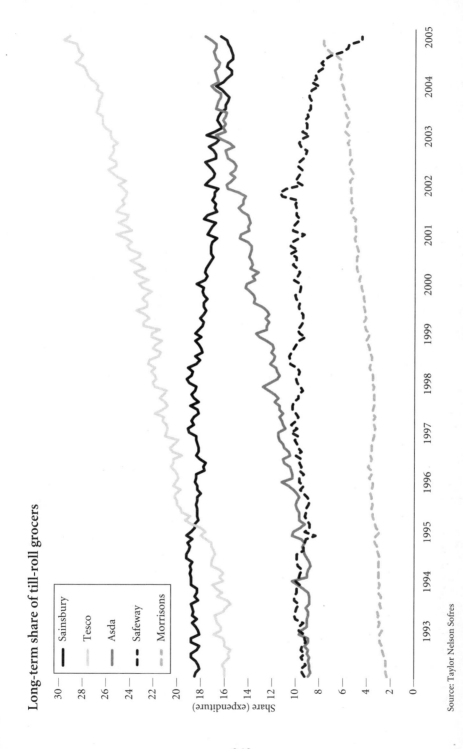

Source: Taylor Nelson Sofres

243

THE SAINSBURY DYNASTY

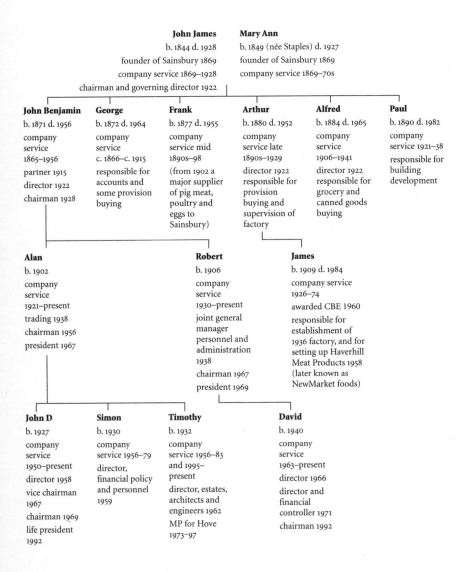

John James
b. 1844 d. 1928
founder of Sainsbury 1869
company service 1869–1928
chairman and governing director 1922

Mary Ann
b. 1849 (née Staples) d. 1927
founder of Sainsbury 1869
company service 1869–70s

John Benjamin
b. 1871 d. 1956
company service 1865–1956
partner 1915
director 1922
chairman 1928

George
b. 1872 d. 1964
company service c. 1866–c. 1915
responsible for accounts and some provision buying

Frank
b. 1877 d. 1955
company service mid 1890s–98
(from 1902 a major supplier of pig meat, poultry and eggs to Sainsbury)

Arthur
b. 1880 d. 1952
company service late 1890s–1929
director 1922
responsible for provision buying and supervision of factory

Alfred
b. 1884 d. 1965
company service 1906–1941
director 1922
responsible for grocery and canned goods buying

Paul
b. 1890 d. 1982
company service 1921–38
responsible for building development

Alan
b. 1902
company service 1921–present
trading 1938
chairman 1956
president 1967

Robert
b. 1906
company service 1930–present
joint general manager personnel and administration 1938
chairman 1967
president 1969

James
b. 1909 d. 1984
company service 1926–74
awarded CBE 1960
responsible for establishment of 1936 factory, and for setting up Haverhill Meat Products 1958 (later known as NewMarket foods)

John D
b. 1927
company service 1950–present
director 1958
vice chairman 1967
chairman 1969
life president 1992

Simon
b. 1930
company service 1956–79
director, financial policy and personnel 1959

Timothy
b. 1932
company service 1956–83 and 1995–present
director, estates, architects and engineers 1962
MP for Hove 1973–97

David
b. 1940
company service 1963–present
director 1966
director and financial controller 1971
chairman 1992

BIBLIOGRAPHY

Blythman, Joanna, *The Shocking Power of British Supermarkets*, Fourth Estate, London, 2004

Bootle, Roger, *Money for Nothing*, Nicholas Brealey Publishing, London, 2003

Boswell, J. S. *100: The Story of Sainsbury's*, J. Sainsbury, London, 1969

Competition Commission, *Supermarkets: A Report on the Supply of Groceries from Multiple Stores in the United Kingdom*, The Stationery Office, London, 2000

——*A Report on the Mergers in Contemplation*, The Stationery Office, London, 2003

Corina, Maurice, *Pile It High, Sell It Cheap*, Weidenfeld and Nicolson, London, 1971

Harvard Business School, *Asda*, Cambridge, Mass., 1998

Humby, Clive, Hunt, Terry and Phillips, Tim, *Scoring Points*, Kogan Page, London, 2003

Lawrence, Felicity, *Not on the Label*, Penguin, London, 2004

MacLaurin, Ian, *Tiger by the Tail*, Pan, London, 2000

McCarthy, David, *Pan-European Food Retail*, Citigroup Smith Barney, London, 2003

—— *Tesco*, Citigroup Smith Barney, London, 2004

Owen, Sir Geoffrey, A Paper on Supermarkets, London School of Economics Centre for the Analysis of Risk and Regulation, London 2003

Porter, Sir Leslie, *Life According to Leslie*, DocoStory Publishers, Ra'anana (Israel), 2003

Quinn, Bill, *How Wal-Mart is Destroying America (and the World)*, Ten Speed Press, Berkeley, CA., 2000

Seth, Andrew, Randall, Geoffrey, *The Grocers*, Kogan Page, London, 2001

Walton, Sam, with Huey, John, *Made in America – My Story*, Bantam Books, New York, 1993

Williams, Bridget, *The Best Butter in the World*, Ebury Press, London, 1994

INDEX